Ancient Sisterhood

Ancient Sisterhood

THE LOST TRADITIONS OF HAGAR AND SARAH

Savina J. Teubal

Swallow Press/Ohio University Press/*Athens*

Swallow Press/Ohio University Press, Athens, Ohio 45701
© 1990 Savina J. Teubal
Printed in the United States of America
All rights reserved. Published 1997

Swallow Press/Ohio University Press books are printed
on acid-free paper ⊚ ™

01 00 99 98 97   5 4 3 2 1

Library of Congress Cataloging-in-Publication Data
Teubal, Savina J., 1926–
      [Hagar the Egyptian]
      Ancient sisterhood : the lost traditions of Hagar and Sarah /
   Savina J. Teubal.
         p.   cm.
      Originally published: Hagar the Egyptian. 1st ed. San Francisco :
   Harper & Row, c1990.
      Includes bibliographical references and index.
      ISBN 0-8040-1001-3 (pbk. : alk. paper)
      1. Hagar (Biblical character) 2. Sarah (Biblical matriarch)
   3. Bible. O.T. Genesis—Feminist criticism. I. Title.
   [BS580.H24T48 1997]
   222'.11092—dc21   97-22592
                                                                   CIP

To the "Mikvah Ladies"
and all spiritual companions

Contents

List of Illustrations

TABLES

MAPS

PLATES

Preface

Mythology, legend, and sacred history have a common denominator: They present cultural truths as sanctioned by a supernatural being. A "truth," however, depends on the nature of the culture that views it. For example, one culture needed a doctrine that saw—in the story of Eve—an original transgression deserving of punishment that would be inherited by humankind for all of eternity. But this belief was not vital to an earlier epoch, in which sexual activity was approved of by deities as well as humans. The story of Adam and Eve may very well have served to establish the sanctity of monogamy and heterosexuality in a culture lacking these features. Thus the drift of interpretation determines a cultural "truth." In some cases, however, as in Exodus, the force of symbolism defies interpretation: The morality of liberation from slavery remains constant.

We must not forget that the biblical authors were not writing history—they were creating religion. The Bible was not written by historians but by priests; and what they wrote was a statement of faith—not a statement of fact.

However, I am more concerned about the contemporary attitude exacerbating the status quo in its translations and interpretations of the biblical texts.

Biblical scholarship worldwide has for many years regarded the stories of each patriarch in the Genesis narratives as independent in origin. The filial relationship in the generations from Terah to Joseph (see appendix B), for instance, is acknowledged to be more a literary development than a historical fact. But biblical scholarship is largely embedded in academia and has little influence on religious precepts of the general public. Jewish liturgy, for example, still calls on the blessings of the forefathers—Abraham, Isaac, and Jacob in patrilineal descent—despite the results of scholarly investigation. Furthermore, only slight recognition is given to the many women who played critical roles in the ancestry of the Hebrew people. Consequently, there is a wide discrepancy between the results of scholarly research in the field and public awareness of this information.

This problem is exacerbated in the field of women's studies and the women's movement in general. Although women's research in religion strives to address discrepancies, mainstream religious leaders are reluctant to disclose academic achievements to society. They prefer instead to perpetrate a status quo biased toward the male segment of the population.

Biblical scholarship depends largely on the interpretation of the texts as understood by the researcher. A researcher's interpretation also depends, to a considerable extent, on contemporaneous societal values.

When society places a woman's highest value on conjugal relations and motherhood, investigation tends to ascribe to all women who are neither wives nor mothers the roles of concubines or whores—or, at best, treat them as if they were invisible. The women in the Genesis narratives have not escaped this destiny.

The matriarch Hagar, like her biblical counterpart Sarah, played a significant role in the genesis of Hebrew culture. Yet she has been doomed to remain in contemporary consciousness as simply an adjunct to the patriarch Abraham. According to the biblical text Hagar was Sarah's handmaid, but most references describe her as Abraham's concubine.

In Muslim tradition, Hagar is the mother of the Arabs, yet the matriarch Hagar is never mentioned by name in the Qur'an, the Holy Book of Islam. She is represented simply as the wife of the patriarch Abraham and the mother of Ishmael, from whom the Arab peoples trace their descent.

In her biblical role as concubine, which is tantamount to slave, Hagar's *raison d'être* is the same as Sarah's: to give sexual service and provide offspring to Abraham. Both women were presumably capable of the former, but Sarah was incapable of the latter. In effect then, and for a period of time, both women enjoy comparable status—Sarah as the honored first wife, Hagar as the future provider of a son and heir. The story of the ensuing relationship between the two women is meant to reflect the powerlessness of a childless woman, the ascent in rank of a pregnant one, and both women's need for male approval of their status. The stories also portray the two women as dependent on the male (god or man) to resolve their conflicts.

In *Hagar the Egyptian* I compare the life of Hagar as presented in the Genesis narratives with the life of Sarah. Surprisingly, the two women share more similarities than they do differences. We shall see that the matriarch Hagar was no more a slave or concubine than Sarah was a conventional wife. Both these women have the elevated status of being regarded as the ancestress of a people: Hagar as the mother of Islam, Sarah as mother of the Hebrews. Was this distinction due solely to their role as receptacle of the husband's seed, or did they merit prestige in their own right?[1]

I suggested in a previous book *Sarah the Priestess* that Sarah held a position similar to that of a priestess.[2] The inquiry is also based on that assumption. However, I would like to reiterate the statement that while Sarah enjoyed a position *comparable* to that of the Mesopotamian *entu/naditu* priestesses, she herself was not actually associated with the religious institution represented by these women. There is no statement in the biblical texts that any of the matriarchs were priestesses: Only by inference drawn from the biblical stories do the matriarchs' activities appear to relate to the religious activities of women similar to those of the *entu/naditu* of Mesopotamia. Nevertheless, I have come to realize that Sarah's story is incomplete without an in-depth look at the role played by Hagar and the consequent relationship that existed between her and Sarah.

Traditionally, as the story is presented in the Hebrew Bible, antagonism and hostility were the overriding aspects in the relationship between Sarah, ancestress of the Jews, and Hagar, ancestress of the Arabs. I hope to present some evidence in this study to show that Hagar, like Sarah, was a woman struggling for religious and sociopolitical rights, in a social environment in which both women enjoyed a certain degree of stature and authority given to them or acknowledged by a deity.

It seems indispensable that we unearth, from the foundations of our beliefs, the possibility of cooperation among peoples as they may have existed in our traditions. We must also make every effort to override the traditional image of hostility that isolates women from each other, a segregation which has effectively though adversely helped to shape our unreasonably violent society. To this end the Hagar material must be recognized, together with the Sarah material, as an important document in the reconstruction of an understanding between the two closely related peoples: the Arabs and the Jews.

NOTES

1. A. E. Speiser, *Genesis: Introduction, Translation and Notes. The Anchor Bible* (Garden City, NY: Doubleday, 1964), 94.
2. Savina J. Teubal, *Sarah the Priestess: The First Matriarch of Genesis* (Athens, OH: Swallow Press, 1984), xv.

Acknowledgments

It is all but impossible to give due recognition of friendship, effort, and interest to the very special people who helped me with this book. I can only thank, in unison, all the recipients of sudden phone calls with obscure questions, brainstorming sessions, obsessive "Hagar talk," and the like.

To Lois Banner, Amalia Bergman, Alice Bloch, Raphael Patai, Drorah Setel, Nurit Shein, and Phyllis Sherman, who read drafts of my manuscript or helped me in other significant ways, my heartfelt thanks for your expert advice and comments.

I thank Mary McArthur for her patience and guidance in designing maps.

I am truly indebted to Jane Litman for her wise comments and help on the final draft.

I give special thanks to the Study of Women and Men in Society [SWMS] Program of the University of Southern California for facilitating my research during the years this investigation was in process. In particular, I thank Gloria Orenstein, whose encouragement and enthusiasm for my work never wavered.

No amount of acknowledgment and appreciation can convey my gratefulness to Miriyam Glazer for the last months of editing, brainstorming, criticism, and commentary, given both patiently and enthusiastically, as my work slowly progressed.

Last but not least I wish to acknowledge the people at Harper & Row for their input and support. Jan Johnson, John Loudon, Yvonne Keller, Arla Ertz, and Georgia Hughes each contributed significantly to the successful accomplishment of this endeavor.

PLATE 2. ". . . no more than a substitute womb for the barren Sarah."
Ivory statuette "Beer-sheva Venus" (Beer Safad fifth to fourth millennium BCE).
Courtesy of the Israel Department of Antiquities and Museums. Photo David Harris.

Women need a reorganization of knowledge, perspectives, and analytical tools that can help us know our foremothers, evaluate our present historical, political, and personal situation, and take ourselves seriously as agents in the creation of a more balanced culture.

To think like a woman in a man's world means thinking critically, refusing to accept the givens, making connections between facts and ideas which men have left unconnected.

[It means] listening and watching in art and literature, in the social sciences, in all the descriptions we are given of the world, for the silences, the absences, the nameless, the unspoken, the encoded, for there we will find the true knowledge of women.

We need access to the female past.

Adrienne Rich, from *On Lies, Secrets, and Silence*

Introduction

WHY HAGAR?

This book is about visionaries: ancient and contemporary visionaries. The ancient visionaries are women whose mystic experiences, though clearly described in the biblical texts, have been undermined by cultures that sought to usurp their vision. Contemporary scholarship, mostly by women, is offering a new vision of women in ancient cultures. It is on the basis of this scholarship that I have been able to retell the story of Hagar the Egyptian.

The figure of Hagar, as portrayed in the biblical texts and interpreted by sages and scholars alike, contains all the elements necessary for a doctrine of the subordination of women. Hagar, more than any other of the biblical matriarchs, is the prototype of the "objectivated" human being: the "other" whose lack of human qualities permits use and abuse by superiors. No male figure in the Bible plays a parallel role. This image of Hagar in the sacred writings has sanctioned the inferiority of women and the endorsement of slavery.

The most striking fact about Hagar is that she never utters a word. The only personal characteristics attributed to her are that she is Egyptian rather than Hebrew (black rather than white?), and is insolent toward her superior mistress. She is the woman who, with no apparent reservations, accepts her portion as provider of an heir to the patriarch. Hagar is presumed to be used in the sexual service of the patriarch as concubine and no more than a substitute womb for the barren Sarah (Plate 2). This woman can be harshly punished for insubordination and banished when her service is deemed superfluous.

Hagar is depicted as having no authority over her destiny. When she runs away from her mistress, Sarah, an angel demands that she return. She is promised a child, but that child is the patriarch's (that is, under his authority). After she is exiled her child almost dies of thirst, implying that a woman with offspring is not able to survive alone. God, however, comes to the rescue, and the boy lives to become the progenitor of a tribe.

The relationship of Hagar and Sarah depicts both hierarchy and hostility between women. Not only is Hagar the subordinate of Abraham, she is also subservient to Sarah. This is most apparent in Sarah's behavior toward Hagar. Although Hagar is to resolve the problem of Sarah's barrenness, Sarah seemingly has no feeling for her *shifhah,* her handmaid.* Her only actions toward Hagar are hostile and cruel. She treats Hagar harshly and banishes mother and child after she has her own son. It could therefore be argued that the presence of Hagar also serves to vilify Sarah.

A very clear impression of Hagar has been perpetrated over centuries. M. Newmann gives us a concise description of the typical portrayal of this woman: "The maid whom Sarah gave as concubine to Abraham and who became the mother of Ishmael."[1] In this description Hagar is (a) the inferior of Sarah, (b) the chattel of Abraham, and (c) the vehicle for the pregnancy of Ishmael, Abraham's seed. Phyllis Trible comments succinctly, "As one of the first females in scripture to experience use, abuse, and rejection, Hagar the Egyptian slave claims our attention."[2]

Hagar has indeed claimed our attention as the archetypal figure of the subordinate, abused, and rejected "other." Her very designation—"the Egyptian"—identifies her as of a culture and religion different from the dominant one of her master and mistress.

Two thousand years ago Paul of Tarsus explained the rationale for this attitude:

* See Glossary, page 199, for definition of unfamiliar terms.

For it is written, that Abraham had two sons, the one by a slave and the other by a free woman.

But the son of the slave was born according to the flesh; the son of the free woman through promise.

Now this is an allegory; these women are two covenants. One is from Mount Sinai, bearing children for slavery; she is Hagar.

Now Hagar is Mount Sinai in Arabia; she corresponds to the present Jerusalem, for she is in slavery with her children.

Now we, brethren, like Isaac was, are children of promise. But as at that time he who was born according to the flesh persecuted him who was born according to the Spirit, so it is now.

But what does the scripture say? "Cast out the slave and her son; for the son of the slave shall not inherit with the son of the free woman."

So, then, brethren, we are not children of the slave but of the free woman. (Gal. 4:22–31, RSV)

Paul (albeit in a different context) has clearly defined the slave (Hagar) as "of the flesh," and therefore inferior to the free woman (Sarah) who, though not "of the Spirit" herself, is of superior stature for having received "the promise." Paul has also delineated the hierarchical structure: Abraham the father, the free nameless woman, and the nameless slave. Interestingly, for Paul and the "brethren" he is addressing, the offspring acquire the status of their mother, not their father, implying matrilineality. Yet the underlying androcentric message in Paul's words is beyond doubt.

This atmosphere laid the foundation for the rejection of all things "other"—whether female divinity, priestess, or woman of any standing. And this transition is evidenced in the ancient Near Eastern laws and sacred lore, which culminated in the spirit/flesh dichotomy of Paul of Tarsus as described in his perception of the Hagar story: patriarch/unnamed matriarchs, free-woman/slave-woman, and child-of-spirit/child-of-flesh.

The stereotype of the alien "flesh" versus the dominant "spirit," as expressed by Paul, carried over into the religious sphere. Its fanaticism dubbed anything other than its own vision as "pagan" and "barbarous," to be identified with the inferiority of the "other"—the bondwoman without spirit (soul) and without station, to be used, abused, and driven out. Clearly, Paul's rationalization of Hagar and Sarah was not of divine provenance but an end result of a kernel buried in his remote past in the ancient Near East. A hierarchal social structure had developed on the basis of gender, in which the female was slowly but consistently relegated to a subordinate position in relation to males.

Many implications result from this rendering of Hagar's story. Most important, it ignores the religious experience of this woman, suggesting that mystic encounters with deity are the prerogative of males. Nevertheless, according to the narratives, Hagar experiences both an epiphany (manifestation) and a theophany (revelation). Her spiritual experiences in the desert have far-reaching implications for her story.

In *Hagar the Egyptian* we turn to the traditionally subordinate women in the Genesis narratives—the handmaids, concubines, or slaves—in an effort to recreate their experience. Concubinage is usually understood as being a characteristic of the female slave. Thus the terms "female slave" and "concubine" are used interchangeably in English parlance. The Hebrew expressions used for Hagar are *shifḥah* and *amah.*

Similarly, the conventional concept of "female slave" must be correlated with the function of the "handmaids" described in the Genesis narratives, and with Hagar in particular. Admittedly, there is precious little information to work with in the biblical material. Of sixty-one verses concerning Sarah, only nine include material on Hagar, and barely fourteen deal exclusively with the matriarch—Genesis 16:7–14 and Genesis 21:14–21.

But why has the story of Hagar been interpreted in this fashion? Sacred writings serve to indoctrinate people into a particular belief. So we must ask ourselves in whose interest would sanctioning the subordination of women and their enslavement be most advantageous? To find the answer we must follow two paths: We need to know who wrote the stories and whose interests the writers were serving. We also need to know what historical climate would benefit from these convictions.

In Mesopotamia evidence for the repression of females can be found in civic law and religious disposition. These attitudes toward women emerged about the time of the Eshnunna laws (twentieth century BCE), and became harsher during the time of the Babylonian ruler Hammurapi (eighteenth century BCE). They reached their zenith with the Assyrian laws about four centuries later. The most obvious deterioration took place within the milieu of religious officiants.[3]

The majority of the biblical stories and most of the law were produced by priests.[4] Women have always been excluded from Israelite clergy, therefore it is natural to presuppose a male priesthood's disinterest in female experience. The same can be said of the military. Israelite armies were predominantly male, guided by a male god; it is no surprise to find military leaders interested in the birth of male children to replenish those lost in battle. Under these circumstances doctrinaire material would be useful to a particular group at a particular time in history. The biblical narratives are no exception.

THE RISE OF PATRIARCHAL SOCIETIES

Similar chronological developments ushering in what we term "civilization" seem to have taken place in three major regions of the ancient Near East (see Map I): Mesopotamia, Egypt, and Israel. In all three cases a pioneer of Semitic ancestry imposed his leadership on the indigenous population: Sargon over the Sumerians, Narmer over the Egyptians, and Moses over the Hebrews (see Chronology, page 198).[5] In each case the leader's activities was sanctioned by a male deity.

In the ancient Near East historical records describing military exploits begin to appear in the form of a stela, a stone re-

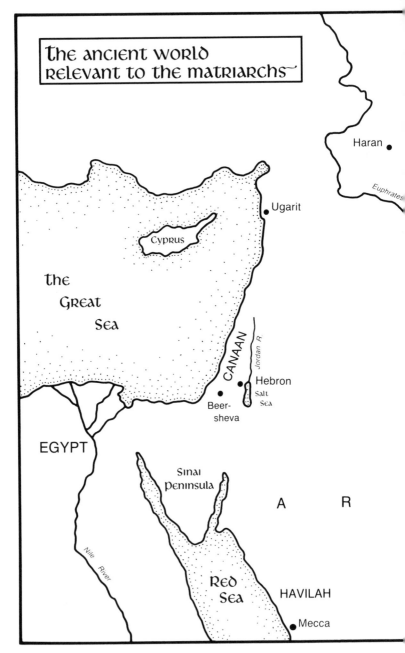

Mary McArthur, Cartographer.

Caspian
Sea

OPOTAMIA

AKKAD

Babylon

SUMER

Tigris River

Uruk

Ur

B I A

Persian
Gulf

0   80
miles

map 1

lief set up to mark the defeat of an enemy. The oldest, known as the "Palette of Narmer," depicts the first king of the First Dynasty of Upper Egypt defeating his enemies in the Delta (ca. fourth millennium BCE). The earliest inscription in Mesopotamia is known as the "Stela of the Vultures," which records the defeat of the city of Umma by Eanatum. But it was Sargon of Agade who left a permanent imprint on Mesopotamian history, gaining control not only of all of Sumer and Akkad but of much of the Near East as well.[6] Here were the beginnings of a fundamental change in human society: a takeover by an elite military group whose aim was the central control of vast regions of territory, which hitherto had consisted of small indigenous groups of settlers in villages or towns.[7] The leadership of Moses, though not military, maintained the same intent; for the founder and leader of all of Israel the aim is the control of the land promised to him by the deity who chose him.

In each region—in Egypt, Mesopotamia, and Canaan—a unification program eventually took place, consolidating northern and southern regions under one government and one god. In each case this was accomplished by a ruling elite whose interests had little in common with those of their subjects. Consequently, the culture and interests of the select governing group—which consisted of the aristocracy, the official clergy, and the military—had different ambitions from those of the rural group of farmers, artisans, healers, seers, and so on—women and men—who survived as best they could in their everyday lives with the help of their local sanctuaries and deities. It took many generations of "reformers" to change the attitudes of the rural population so that it served the interests of the elite.

These rulers aspired to unify and rule over broad regions. Culturally, unification was a slow process. It took generations of reformer kings like Amenemhet III of Egypt, Hammurapi of Babylon, and David of Israel to enforce patristic elements into the societal values of their subjects. In each case they achieved it by endowing the male priesthood with enormous power.

In every instance "the inception of the monarchy meant the beginning of urban development and a ruling elite."[8] But the ideology of a ruling elite does not necessarily transform the long-held cultural traditions of rural, nonurban settings. Carol Meyers observes that "the Bible as a source presents problems of omission in its treatment of women as individuals or as a group. Its androcentric bias and also its urban, elite orientation mean that even the information it contains may be a distortion or misrepresentation of the lives of women removed from urban centers and bureaucratic families."[9] Meyers's statement applies equally to Egypt and Mesopotamia. The actions, legislation, and edicts of Hammurapi and David were all in the interests of a relatively small portion of the subjects they governed—mostly military men and the male gods they served.

In the ancient polytheistic world, female and male divinities were regional and personal. They encompassed the spectrum of human activities, indifferent to gender. For example, the "maiden" (that is, childless) goddesses Ishtar (or Inanna) and Anath, of Babylonia and Ugarit (Syria-Canaan, see Map I) respectively, governed war as well as love (before war became the prerogative of males). Goddesses and gods were often envisioned as extensions of each other. This was evidenced in their close unions—the Canaanite Anath to her brother-husband Baal, the Egyptian Isis to her brother-husband Osiris, and so on—whose concerns for each other's welfare was paramount.

One of the most significant aspects of polytheism was the respect accorded divinities by other than their devotees. Travelers, for example, paid respect to local divinities whose regional protection they sought. Abraham did so at the sacred Canaanite terebinth tree of Moreh ("teacher" or "diviner"), when he was in the vicinity of Shechem.

One by one, however, within the polytheistic pantheon, a young male upstart eventually reigns supreme. In Babylon the young Marduk defeats Tiamat, mother of all the gods, and is venerated by the military general Hammurapi. In Ugarit the young Baal gains ascendancy with the help of his mother, Asherah. In Egypt Ptah becomes the powerful god of the elite, supplanting the rural deities.[10] In Jerusalem Yahweh is made to reign supreme. *In each case* the success of the male god was due to the overthrow of goddesses. Not only Tiamat, but the powerful Inanna, together with many other goddesses, were supplanted by Marduk. Baal, who boasts that he "alone will rule over the gods," has his sister/wife Anath support his claim.[11]

In Egypt the Heliopolitan priests attempted to unseat the goddess Neith of Sais (see Plate 14a) and the goddess Hat-Hor at Dendara (see Plate 9). But the worship of these goddesses was "extremely ancient and very important."[12] So the priests associated them with Tem, sun god of the Heliopolitan pantheon. They gave each goddess "suitable titles and ascribed to her proper attributes, in accordance with her sex, which would make her the feminine counterpart to the god Tem."[13] The venerated Canaanite goddess Asherah was worshiped by the Israelites throughout the monarchy. In Raphael Patai's opinion,

of the 370 years during which the Solomonic Temple stood in Jerusalem, for no less than 236 years (almost two-thirds of the time) the statue of Asherah was present in the Temple and her worship was part of the legitimate religion approved and led by the king, the court and the priesthood, and opposed by only a few prophetic voices crying out against it at relatively long intervals.[14]

However, as Patai himself describes in previous pages, the religion of Asherah was violently opposed by kings and priests as well as prophets. That Yahweh now reigns supreme is proof enough.

The concept of supreme ruler of a pantheon paved the way for the supreme ruler of the universe, the only *true* divinity. The perception of an absolute, unique, and authentic god permitted its antithesis, the false or "pagan" deities, and their subsequent dismissal. This in turn permitted dichotomies of the spirit/flesh, the self/other, and so on.

Clearly, in solving the mystery of Hagar, we must first distinguish the social milieu of the narratives concerned with events in women's lives from the male-centered structure that later encompassed them.

UNDERSTANDING THE URBAN SETTING IN GENESIS

First we must establish portions of the so-called patriarchal narratives in a matrilineal social setting (see Table 1). This I achieved to a certain extent in *Sarah the Priestess*.[15] There I showed that components such as ultimogeniture (precedence of the youngest child) and matrilocal marriages (residence of the husband with his wife's kin) were the norm in the Genesis narratives. The matristic nature of the social order in some of the biblical narratives is an essential foundation on which to reconstruct a core narrative devoid of patristic overtones.

Sarah the Priestess additionally establishes a precedent for a vision of the biblical matriarchs as equals in standing to the patriarchs, as closely associated with religion and religious observance, and as struggling in an increasingly patriarchal milieu to preserve their nonpatriarchal social system. However, I still understood the handmaids in the conventional patriarchal manner: as "concubines."[16] My research for this book showed me a very different picture.

Hagar is described as the *shifḥah* of Sarah. Much of our story hinges on the correct interpretation of this term. In ancient Mesopotamia as well as in Genesis, some women are found to be in the exclusive service of a wife but not of the woman's husband. The term *shifḥah,* then, *should only be employed for a woman in the service of another woman.* Whether characterized as *shifḥah* or *amah* (slave), Hagar thus was *not* the concubine of Abraham.

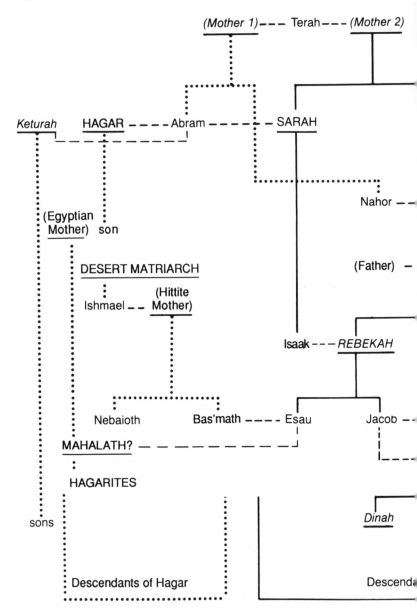

Table 1. Genealogy According to the Mothers

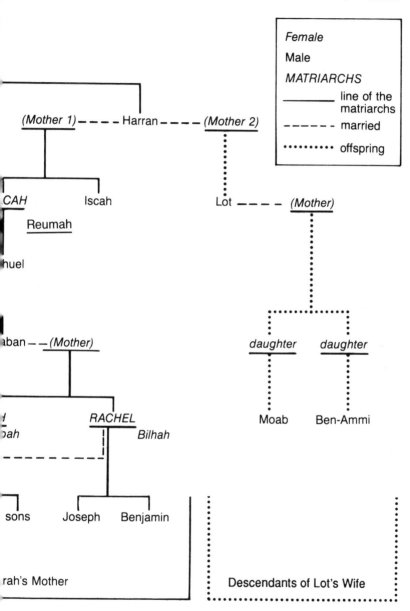

Female
Male
MATRIARCHS
———— line of the matriarchs
– – – – – married
·········· offspring

(Mother 1) – – – – Harran – – – – (Mother 2)

CAH   Iscah
Reumah
huel

Lot – – – (Mother)

aban – –(Mother)

d
ah   RACHEL
              Bilhah

sons   Joseph   Benjamin

rah's Mother

daughter   daughter

Moab   Ben-Ammi

Descendants of Lot's Wife

Similarly, we must correlate the conventional concept of "female slave" with the function of the "handmaid" or *shifhah* described in the Genesis narratives, and with Hagar in particular. Admittedly, there is precious little information to work with in the biblical material.

We must also consider Hagar's designation as "the Egyptian." Women enjoyed remarkable legal equality with men throughout much of Egypt's history. Although there was a distinct separation between men and women in terms of the public functions these performed, "that official functions were relegated to men seems more a matter of accepted custom than a conscious desire to keep women out of politics and government."[17] It is important to realize that ancient Egyptian society was originally matrilineal. Even in dynastic times the female line was of equal account with the male in certain respects—notably in tracing descent, inheritance, and drawing up a will.[18]

Does *Egyptian* refer to Hagar's race, her religious affiliation, her place of origin? Or was it meant to identify the time frame in which a historical association existed between Egypt and Canaan? Egypt and Canaan-Syria were linked both historically and religiously. From as early as the Old Kingdom (ca. 2778 BCE), an Egyptian colony had been established at Byblos; Snofru, founder of the Fourth Egyptian Dynasty (2723–2563 BCE), imported wood for his buildings from Phoenicia; Pepi I, ruler of the Sixth Dynasty (2423–2300 BCE), also infiltrated Palestinian territory on various occasions.[19] In religious mythology the dark-skinned goddess Isis enlisted the help of the Canaanite goddess Astarte at Byblos in her search for the body of her dead husband-brother Osiris.[20] Is any of this relevant to the identity of Hagar as Egyptian? None of these issues are addressed in the biblical texts, but the narratives do record that the protagonists in the stories, except for Hagar, originate in Mesopotamia and live in Canaan. Nevertheless, Egypt is prominent in both the opening and closing narratives (Gen. 12:10 and 50:22).

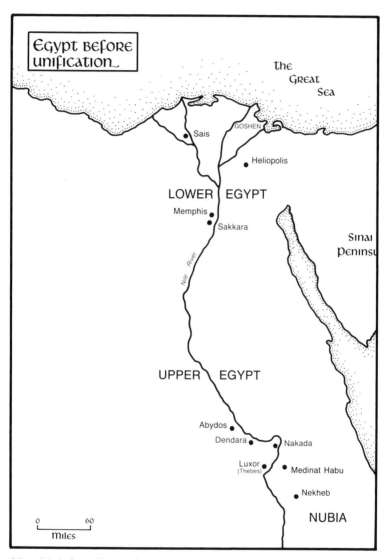

Egypt before unification

the Great Sea

Sais

GOSHEN

Heliopolis

LOWER EGYPT

Memphis

Sakkara

Nile River

Sinai Peninsu

UPPER EGYPT

Abydos

Dendara

Nakada

Luxor
(Thebes)

Medinat Habu

Nekheb

NUBIA

0   60
miles

Mary McArthur, Cartographer.

Map II

It is impossible to understand the identity of Hagar or comprehend her function as *shifḥah* without a perspective on the historical climate of the times in which the events may have taken place, as well as that of the period in which her story was recorded. The events in Hagar's story, contemporaneous with Sarah's, would also have taken place at an early period in historical times.[21]

Hagar's story must be told in the context of her own culture and religious experience, separate from that of Abraham's.[22] Nothing in the biblical record describes Hagar's service as other than becoming the mother of an heir of Sarah's. This was a service rendered by women in similar situations to Mesopotamian "priestesses," who were destined to remain childless on account of their profession.[23] The need to describe Hagar as slave is more political than factual.

Notwithstanding, the Hagar episodes record *the only time in the bible that a god is given a name, and the name is given by a woman.* Hagar's god is a god who knows her, who addresses her in familiar terms: "What troubles you, Hagar?" he asks with the tender concern of a loving relative. Hagar may be lost in the desert, but she is not alone, her divine protector is close at hand. The characteristics of slave or concubine have no bearing on the theophanies experienced by the matriarch in the desert—religious episodes that served to explain the naming of a sacred well and the origins of a people just as they served Abraham's naming of the well of Beer-sheva (Gen. 21:31) and Mt. Moriah (Gen. 22:14).[24] The parallels of Abraham's naming of a well to Hagar's naming of a well, Abraham's naming of the site on Mt. Moriah *YHWH Yireh* (YHWH sees), and the naming of the well in Hagar's story *Beer-lahai-ro'i* (Well of the Living One Who Sees), is notable.

Perhaps the most profound disservice perpetrated on humanity has been the disassociation of woman from her own female religious experience. We shall see that the biblical matriarchs themselves enjoyed ritual practices and spiritual experiences separate from those of men. Personal religious experience is different for men and women because males and females are biologically different. This is, of course, a difficult and perhaps dangerous statement to make in an era seeking "gender equality," precisely because difference has been understood in terms of hierarchy. Power has been assigned to one gender, the male, over the other, the female, in terms of its supposed closer association to "spirit" rather than "flesh." As I see it, however, in the religious sphere the biblical matriarchs had equal but different input from that of men. Power is not contingent on sex, and the nature of mystic experience cannot be severed from its source. Furthermore, consideration must be given to Hagar's ethnic background. If her experience was different from Abraham's on account of gender difference, it may also have been different from Sarah's due to their ethnic and cultural diversity.

We must also address the issue of power between Sarah and Hagar, and the *shifḥah's* situation in the "family of Abraham." Are Sarah's dominant position and her antagonism toward her *shifḥah* accurately depicted? Or is the difference in station the understanding of the hierarchically minded author? Does the Hebrew term *shifḥah* truly represent Hagar as handmaid, concubine, or slave? Or is this a concept acquired over time? Finally, was the social structure of the early biblical family akin to the nuclear family, or are we imposing a late development on an early structure?

It seems that the query of (the angel of) Elohim, "What troubles you, Hagar?" was prophetic. The spirit of the matriarch must surely be troubled—not because she was lost in the desert of Beer-sheva, but because her essence has been lost in her depiction as downtrodden slave, rival of Sarah.

Hagar's destiny was closely entwined with that of the awesome *naditu* priestess. That she represented the priestess in conception and childbirth was no small matter. That she too is the recipient of a promise that elevates her from ordinary mother to a mother of nations is no small matter either.

It is my hope that this study will contribute a positive light to the image of all of the matriarchs: Sarah, Hagar, Rachel, Bilhah, Leah, and Zilpah.

NOTES

1. M. Newmann, "Hagar," in the *Interpreter's Dictionary of the Bible,* Vol. 2 (Nashville: Abingdon, 1962), 508.

2. Phyllis Trible, *Texts of Terror: Literary-Feminist Readings of Biblical Narratives* (Philadelphia: Fortress Press, 1984), 9.

3. Savina J. Teubal, "Women, the Law, and the Ancient Near East," in *Fields of Offerings: Studies in Honor of Raphael Patai,* edited by Victor D. Sanua (London and Toronto: Associated University Presses, A Herzl Press Publication, 1983), 305.

4. Carol Meyers, *Discovering Eve: Ancient Israelite Women in Context* (Oxford University Press, 1988), 221.

5. I include Moses here because he was presumably brought up as an Egyptian (he was brought up by the elite, he was not a slave) and therefore not culturally akin to the Hebrews he led. Theoretically, then, the situation is comparable to that of Egypt and Mesopotamia.

6. H. W. F. Saggs, *The Greatness That Was Babylon: A Sketch of the Ancient Civilization of the Tigris-Euphrates Valley* (New York and Toronto: New American Library, 1962), 66–68.

7. Jill Kamil, *Sakkara and Memphis: A Guide to the Necropolis and the Ancient Capital,* 2d.ed. (London: Longman, 1985), 16–17.

8. Meyers, *Discovering Eve,* 16.

9. *Ibid.,* 13.

10. W. B. Emery, *Archaic Egypt: Culture and Civilization in Egypt Five Thousand Years Ago* (London: Penguin, 1961), 122.

11. Cyrus H. Gordon, *Ugaritic Literature: A Comprehensive Translation of the Poetic and Prose Texts* (Rome: Pontificum Institutum Biblicum, 1949), 51:III:20–25.

12. E. A. Wallis Budge, *The Gods of the Egyptians: Studies in Egyptian Mythology,* Vol. 1 (New York: Dover, 1969), 92–93.

13. *Ibid.*

14. Raphael Patai, *The Hebrew Goddess* (New York: KTAV, 1967), 50.

15. Savina J. Teubal, *Sarah the Priestess: The First Matriarch of Genesis,* Part I (Athens, OH: Swallow Press, 1984).

16. *Ibid.,* 66, 94–95, for example.

17. William A. Ward, *Essays on Feminine Titles in the Middle Kingdom and Related Subjects* (Beirut, Lebanon: American University of Beirut, 1986), 61.

18. J. E. Manchip White, *Ancient Egypt: Its Culture and History* (New York: Dover, 1970), 15.

19. *Ibid.,* 148, 150.

20. Budge, *Gods of the Egyptians,* 189–90.

21. Teubal, *Sarah the Priestess,* 73–75.

22. Hagar is denied her own experience. For example, in her dealings with supernatural events: "Hagar was used to seeing angels in Abraham's house, so she was not phased when one appeared to her." Rabbis Nosson Scherman and Meir Zlotowitz, eds., *Bereshis: A New Translation with Commentary Anthologized from Talmudic, Midrashic, and Rabbinic Sources* (Brooklyn, N.Y.: Mesorah Publications, 1978), 549.

23. See Teubal, *Sarah the Priestess,* 31 ff.

The Genesis Narratives Relative to the Hagar Story, According to the Masoretic Text*

12 1 The Lord said to Abram, "Go forth from your native land and from your father's house to a land that I will show you.
2 I will make of you a great nation,
And I will bless you;
I will make your name great,
And you shall be a blessing:
3 I will bless those who bless you,
And curse him that curses you;
All the families of the earth
Shall bless themselves by you."
4 Abram went forth as the Lord had spoken to him, and Lot went with him. Abram was seventy-five years old when he left Haran. 5 Abram took his wife Sarai and his brother's son Lot, and all the wealth that they had amassed, and the persons that they had acquired in Haran; and they set out for the land of Canaan. 9 Then Abram journeyed by stages towards the Negeb.
10 There was famine in the land, and Abram went down to Egypt to sojourn there, for the famine was severe in the land. 11 As he was about to enter Egypt, he said to his wife Sarai, "I am well aware that you are a beautiful woman. 12 When the Egyptians see you, they will say, 'She is his wife,' and they will kill me, but let you live. 13 Say then that you are my sister, that it may go well with me because of you, that I may remain alive thanks to you."
14 When Abram entered Egypt, the Egyptians saw how very beautiful the woman was. 15 Pharaoh's courtiers saw her and praised her to Pharaoh, and the woman was taken to Pharaoh's palace. 16 And because of her it went well with Abram; he acquired sheep, oxen, asses, male and female slaves, she-asses and camels.
17 But the Lord afflicted Pharaoh and his household with mighty plagues on account of Sarai, the wife of Abram.

---

* Used by permission of the Jewish Publication Society, Philadelphia, Pennsylvania, 1962.

18 Pharaoh sent for Abram and said, "What is this you have done to me! Why did you not tell me that she was your wife? 19 Why did you say, 'She is my sister,' so that I took her as my wife? Now, here is your wife; take her and be gone!" 20 And Pharaoh put men in charge of him, and they sent him away with his wife and all that he possessed.

13 1 From Egypt, Abram went up into the Negeb, with his wife and all that he possessed, together with Lot. 2 Now Abram was very rich in cattle, silver, and gold. 3 And he proceeded by stages from the Negeb as far as Bethel, to the place where his tent had been formerly, between Bethel and Ai, 4 the site of the altar he had built there at first; and there Abram invoked the Lord by name. 18 And Abram moved his tent, and came to dwell at the terebinths of Mamre which are in Hebron; and he built an altar there to the Lord.

16 1 Sarai, Abram's wife, had borne him no children. She had an Egyptian maidservant whose name was Hagar.

2 And Sarai said to Abram, "See, the Lord has kept me from bearing. Consort with my maid; perhaps I shall have a son through her." And Abram heeded Sarai's request.

3 So Sarai, Abram's wife, took her maid, Hagar the Egyptian—after Abram had dwelt in the land of Canaan ten year's—and gave her to her husband as concubine.

4 And he cohabited with Hagar and she conceived; and when she saw that she had conceived, her mistress was lowered in her esteem.

5 And Sarai said to Abram, "The wrong done me is your fault! I myself gave my maid into your bosom; now that she sees that she is pregnant, I am lowered in her esteem. The Lord decide between you and me!" 6 And Abram said to Sarai, "Your maid is in your hands. Deal with her as you think right." Then Sarai treated her harshly, and she ran away from her.

7 An angel of the Lord found her by a spring of water in the wilderness, the spring on the road to Shur, 8 and said, "Hagar, slave of Sarah, where have you come from, and where are you going?" And she said, "I am running away from my mistress Sarai."

9 And the angel of the Lord said to her, "Go back to your mistress, and submit to her harsh treatment." 10 And the angel of

the Lord said to her,

"I will greatly increase your offspring,

And they shall be too many to count."

11 And the angel of the Lord said to her further,

"Behold, you are with child

And shall bear a son;

You shall call him Ishmael,

For the Lord has paid heed to your suffering.

12 He shall be a wild ass of a man;

His hand against everyone,

And everyone's hand against him;

In defiance of all his kinsmen he shall camp."

13 And she called the Lord who spoke to her, "You Are El-r'oi," by which she meant, "Have I not gone on seeing after he saw me!"

14 Therefore the well is called Beer-lahai-r'oi; it is between Kadesh and Bered.

15 And Hagar bore a son to Abram, and Abram was eighty-six years old when Hagar bore Ishmael to Abram.

18 1 The Lord appeared to him by the terebinths of Mamre; he was sitting at the entrance of the tent as the day grew hot.

2 Looking up, he saw three men standing near him. As soon as he saw them, he ran from the entrance of the tent to greet them and, bowing to the ground, 3 he said, "My Lords, if it please you, do not go on past your servant. 4 Let a little water be brought; bathe your feet and recline under the tree. 5 And let me fetch a morsel of bread that you may refresh yourselves; then go on—seeing that you have come your servant's way." They replied, "Do as you have said."

6 Abraham hastened to the tent to Sarah, and said, "Quick, three measures of choice flour! Knead and make cakes!" 7 Then Abraham ran to the herd, took a calf, tender and choice, and gave it to the servant-boy, who hastened to prepare it. 8 He took curds and milk and the calf that had been prepared, and set them before them; and he waited on them by the tree as they ate.

9 They said to him, "Where is your wife Sarah?" And he replied, "In the tent." 10 Then one said, "I will return to you when life is due, and your wife Sarah shall have a son!" Sarah

was listening at the entrance of the tent, which was behind him. 11 Now Abraham and Sarah were old, advanced in years; Sarah had stopped having the periods of women. 12 And Sarah laughed to herself, saying, "Now that I am withered, am I to have enjoyment—with my husband so old?" 13 Then the Lord said to Abraham, "Why did Sarah laugh, saying, 'Shall I in truth bear a child, old as I am?' 14 Is anything too wondrous for the Lord? I will return to you at the time that life is due, and Sarah shall have a son." 15 Sarah dissembled, saying, "I did not laugh," for she was frightened. He replied, "But you did laugh." 16 The men set out from there and looked toward Sodom.

20 1 Abraham journeyed from there to the region of the Negeb and settled between Kadesh and Shur. While he was sojourning in Gerar, 2 Abraham said of his wife, "She is my sister." So Abimelech king of Gerar had Sarah brought to him. 3 But God came to Abimelech in a dream by night and said to him, "You are to die because of the woman you have taken, for she is a married woman." 4 Now Abimelech had not approached her. He said, "O Lord, will you slay people even though innocent? 5 He himself said to me, 'She is my sister!' Moreover she said, 'He is my brother.' When I did this, my heart was blameless and my hands were clean." 6 And God said to him in the dream, "I knew you did this with a blameless heart, so I kept you from sinning against me. That is why I did not let you touch her. 7 But you must restore the man's wife—since he is a prophet, he will intercede for you—to save your life. If you fail to restore her, know that you shall surely die, you and all that are yours."

8 Early next morning, Abimelech called all his servants and told them what had happened; and the men were greatly frightened. 9 Then Abimelech summoned Abraham and said to him, "What have you done to us? What have I done that you should bring so great a guilt upon me and my kingdom? You have done to me things that ought not to be done. 10 What then," Abimelech demanded of Abraham, "was your purpose in doing this thing?" 11 "I thought," said Abraham, "surely there was no fear of God in this place, and they will kill me because of my wife. 12 And besides, she is in truth my sister, my father's daughter though not my mother's; and she became my wife.

13 So when God made me wander from my father's house, I said to her, 'Let this be a kindness that you shall do me: whatever place we come to, say there of me: He is my brother.' "

14 Abimelech took sheep and oxen, and male and female slaves, and gave them to Abraham; and he restored his wife Sarah to him. 15 And Abimelech said, "Here, my land is before you; settle wherever you please." 16 And to Sarah he said, "I herewith give your brother a thousand pieces of silver; this will serve you as vindication before all who are with you, and you are cleared before everyone."

17 Abraham then prayed to God, and God healed Abimelech, his wife and his slave girls, so that they bore children; 18 for the Lord had closed fast every womb of the household of Abimelech because of Sarah, the wife of Abraham.

21 1 The Lord took note of Sarah as He had promised, and the Lord did for Sarah as He had spoken. 2 Sarah conceived and bore a son to Abraham in his old age, at the set time that God had spoken. 3 Abraham gave his newborn son, whom Sarah had borne to him, the name Isaac. 4 And when his son Isaac was eight days old, Abraham circumcised him, as God had commanded him. 5 Now Abraham was a hundred years old when his son Isaac was born to him.

6 Sarah said, "God has brought me laughter; everyone who hears will laugh with me." 7 And she added,

"Who would have said to Abraham

That Sarah would suckle children!

Yet I have borne a son in his old age!"

8 The child grew up and was weaned, and Abraham held a great feast on the day that Isaac was weaned.

9 Sarah saw the son, whom Hagar the Egyptian had borne to Abraham, playing. 10 She said to Abraham, "Cast out that slave-woman and her son, for the son of that slave-woman shall not share in the inheritance with my son Isaac." 11 The matter distressed Abraham greatly, for it concerned a son of his. 12 But God said to Abraham, "Do not be distressed over the boy or your slave; whatever Sarah tells you, do as she says, for it is through Isaac that offspring shall be continued for you. 13 As for the son of the slave-woman, I will make a nation of him too, for he is your seed."

14 Early next morning Abraham took some bread and a skin of water, and gave them to Hagar. He placed them on her shoulder, together with the child, and sent her away. And she wandered about in the wilderness of Beer-sheva. 15 When the water was gone from the skin, she left her child under one of the bushes, 16 and went and sat down at a distance, a bowshot away; for she thought, "Let me not look on as the child dies." And sitting thus afar, she burst into tears.

17 God heard the cry of the boy, and an angel of God called to Hagar from heaven and said to her, "What troubles you, Hagar? Fear not, for God has heeded the cry of the boy where he is. Come, lift up the boy and hold him by the hand, for I will make a great nation of him." 19 Then God opened her eyes and she saw a well of water. She went and filled the skin with water, and let the boy drink.

20 God was with the boy and he grew up; he dwelt in the wilderness and became a bowman. 21 He lived in the wilderness of Paran; and his mother got a wife for him from the land of Egypt.

23 1 Sarah's lifetime—the span of Sarah's life—came to one hundred and twenty-seven years. 2 Sarah died in Kiraith-arba— now Hebron—in the land of Canaan; and Abraham proceeded to mourn for her and bewail her.

19 And then Abraham buried his wife Sarah in the cave of the field of Machpelah, facing Mamre—now Hebron—in the land of Canaan.

PART I. DISCOVERING THE SOURCES

To many people the Hebrew Bible is the word of God. This means that God chose certain people to reveal his will, people we call prophets, and they or others who heard them were inspired to record the revelations. The first five books, known as the Pentateuch or Torah, were accredited to Moses.

In the past two hundred years, however, clergy and scholars began to realize that these five books could not have originated from a sole source because they contained too many variations in style and context. It was initially with Genesis, the first of the five books, that the hypothesis of the existence of more than one source evolved.

Genesis consists of two sections: stories that deal with prehistory (creation, the flood, and so on) and narratives of the settlement in Canaan (Palestine) of the first Hebrew families. My investigation focuses on the narratives of the first of those families: Sarah, Abraham, Sarah's handmaid Hagar, and their children.

The discovery that the text of Genesis may have originated with more than one source, or "author," opened biblical scholarship to many new disciplines. Critical scholarship produced commentaries and interpretations of the biblical material that were now supported by other fields, such as archaeology and anthropology. Archaeological finds have been particularly exciting to scholars because they produced not only artifacts but also written records. (As we shall see, one of those documents, the Code of Hammurapi, is helpful in shedding light on the story of Hagar.)

However, it is a scholar's viewpoint and emphasis that leads to the *interpretation* of biblical material. Most scholarly exegesis is focused on the male role in the Genesis narratives to the detriment of the female role. This bias has deprived women of female spiritual experience.

An understanding of how the narratives came about, why they were written, and how they were edited is essential to their interpretation. Let us now begin these explorations.

1. The Importance of Interpretation

The biblical texts known as the Genesis narratives are the only ancient account available to us of the origins and history of the Arab and Hebrew peoples.[1] Genesis 12 through 23 concentrate both on Abraham, the progenitor, and on Hagar and Sarah, each the mother of a people. Archaeologists have intensely searched the regions mentioned in the narratives for evidence of the historicity of these accounts.[2] Despite their efforts no text or artifact has ever come to light that directly relates to any of the narrative's protagonists. Furthermore, it has been "beyond the ability of any critical scholarship to establish a link between tradition and originating event" regarding the historical origins of ancient Israel.[3]

In all probability the Genesis narratives interweave history *and* legend. Since the biblical intent was to focus on males, the authors of the narratives chose to emphasize certain events and perhaps to forget others, according to the needs of the times in which they wrote. However, the surprisingly detailed accounts of females that remain suggest that the editors felt compelled to include at least fragmentary recollections of actual events. Conclusive proof of the historical existence of these women is unavailable. Nonetheless the Book of Genesis can be seen as offering us elaborations on stories originally told about women who had special significance to the people in the area in which they lived. The sacred character of some of the stories about women must have been too entrenched in the culture for the authors to eliminate those stories completely.

Did Hagar actually exist? Perhaps not in the way she is presented in Genesis. But I believe that an Egyptian woman lived who came to be regarded as exceptional by the people of Canaan, and whose memory they held in awe. It is notable that representations of Egyptian women are not uncommon in the region (see Plate 1). Without such a kernel of truth in the underlying account, it would be unlikely that a *woman's* story would survive throughout the ages in the literature of an androcentric society.

DATING THE EVENTS

It is important to attempt to date the events because they were not recorded at the time that they happened. If centuries transpired between the time of an event and the time it was written down, a great deal of variation can and will occur.

A good illustration of this transformation is evident in the different approaches to the same stories as told in the Qur'an, the sacred Book of Islam, as compared to the Hebrew Bible. The Prophet Muḥammed, understood to be the author of the Qur'an, "did not himself read the Old Testament, but merely built upon what he had been told" Charles Cutler Torrey informs us.[4] The inference here is that Muḥammed misquoted the Hebrew Bible because he had not read it himself. But Mohammed was creating religion, not writing history. His audience inhabited the Arabian Peninsula. To him, quite naturally, Abraham is the ancestor of the Arabs, the first Muslim.[5] He was married to the woman the biblical writers identify as Hagar. The prophet wisely (as will become apparent) did not name Abraham's wife.

The biblical texts endured a similar process. "During the past fifty years, in books seeking to relate the Bible to archeology, the 'Patriarchal period' has most often been dated either to some part of the Middle Bronze Age (circa 2000–1500 BCE) . . . or to an advanced date in the Late Bronze Age (circa 1550–1150 BCE)."[6] However, "it is important in this connec-

tion to remember that there are no extra-Biblical texts of sufficient direct relevance to test the Old Testament's value as a re-
liable historical source in the period before about 900 BC, the
opening of the Davidic Monarchy."[7] One of the confusing elements in the dating of the biblical texts is that they are composed of many interwoven episodes that originate in different
regions at different times. To compound the confusion, the
episodes were composed by a variety of authors and editors.

Kathleen Kenyon concludes

It was their concepts and purposes that combined older documents of
various dates into the amalgam that we now read. In other words, the
surviving text of the Old Testament, for all save ultra-conservative or
fundamentalist school of historians, is as 'stratified' as any of the
mounds excavated by archaeologists. Analyzing specific Biblical passages through form, source or tradition criticism is, then, no more, or
less, subjective than interpreting a small area in a tell (mound)
excavation.[8]

In my opinion, the Sarah-Hagar episodes belong to the Early
Bronze Age (3200–2000 BCE). Genesis 11:31 records that
"Terah took his son Abram, his grandson Lot, the son of Harran, and his daughter-in-law Sarai, wife of Abram, and they
set out together from Ur of the Chaldeans for the land of Canaan." Ur, an influential city-state, is first mentioned in the
Sumerian King List at a period corresponding to Early Dynastic III (ca. 2600 BCE). Theoretically, then, one could regard
2600 BCE as the earliest period in which the protagonists
lived. There are two other reasons why an early period is per-
suasive: One, woman's position began to deteriorate at the beginning of recorded history, and history was recorded by cultures bent on military expansionism in the third millennium
BCE. Although accounts of women of note may have survived
for generations, it is unlikely that women-centered cultures
existed to any extent after the advent of what we now term
"civilization."

Two, early human settlements were primarily made up of a
network of small open villages, and it was not until the begin-

ning of the third millennium that village populations sought protection behind walls. The biblical principals appear to live in small open villages. There are two allusions to a town gate in the narratives, but in these passages the texts suggest that all the people of the town were present in one place (Gen. 19:1–4; 23:10, 18), an indication of a very small population. In other words, the description in the narratives is one of small pastoral settlements remote from the cultural climate of a warrior society.[9]

We can date the events, then, in a period from 2600–2000 BCE, a span of at least six hundred years.

IN SEARCH OF THE BIBLICAL AUTHORS

Speculation abounds as to how the biblical text was conceived—from the tradition that supposed Moses to have been the author of the Pentateuch, to various critical approaches (such as literary criticism and form criticism) developed by scholars for analyzing the texts.[10] Biblical scholars today generally agree that the Pentateuch is based on several independent traditions, which in the course of time became fused.[11]

Some of these traditions are separate units that have no bearing on the narrative to which they have been appended. The most obvious of these is the story of Abraham's militaristic expedition and his meeting with the high priest Melchizedek in Genesis 14. This episode is different from any other in the Pentateuch: The setting is international, the approach impersonal, and the narration is notable for its unusual style and vocabulary.[12]

Some episodes are repeated, but with a change of characters and locale. For example, the story of Sarah's encounter with the Pharaoh of Egypt, in which Abraham asks her to present herself as his sister rather than his wife (Gen. 12), is first retold substituting King Abimelech of Gerar for Pharaoh (Gen. 20), and then again with Rebekah and Isaac as the deceitful couple (Gen. 26). Two episodes of Hagar in the desert also seem repetitious (Gen. 16:7–14 and 21:14–21). We will explore these in depth during the course of this book. For now, let's take a brief overview.

Robert Alter comments, "Different repeated episodes have elicited different explanations, but the most common strategy among scholars is to attribute all ostensible duplication in the narratives to a duplication of the sources, to a kind of recurrent stammer in the process of transmission, whether written or oral."[13] This view does not seem to do justice to the two desert stories, recorded by different authors, which seem to me quite distinct and selectively drawn from an original cycle that initially had nothing in common with the Sarah or Abraham cycles to which they are appended. I suggest that the desert episodes were appended at different times and to different portions of the Sarah/Abraham traditions. In the course of this book it will become apparent that the Sarah/Hagar episodes and the Hagar/desert sequences record events that took place at different periods and with different participants. Internal evidence suggests that the events were not necessarily sequential, as the biblical texts imply.

Some traditions form cycles in which stories are told of the same individuals in specific geographic regions. These, however, are broken up and interspersed with other narratives. There are cycles of Abraham and Lot (Gen. 13) in which they separate their herds, with Lot going to the area of Sodom and Abraham settling in Hebron. The following Abraham/Lot episode, however, occurs in the middle of the story of the conception and birth of Isaac (Gen. 18).

Traditions that pertain to certain regions are also regarded as forming cycles. Martin Noth, for example, places Jacob in central Palestine.[14] He assumes that only later was the tradition of the "Rachel" tribes (also from central Palestine) added to the Jacob material. Noth suggests that the southern traditions of Abraham-Isaac were subsequently appended, thus building up the genealogical relationship of the patriarchs backwards. He adds, "But it is clear that *Isaac first of all* was added as the father of Jacob"; and "elements of the tradition that appear in duplicate belong originally to Abraham since demonstrably Abraham, as the later popular figure of tradition, attracted narrative elements originally foreign to him."[15]

I think the valuable analyses done by scholars such as Noth would have been even better served had they taken into consideration the possibility of a legacy of the matriarchs, rather than solely of the patriarchs. Noth, for instance, suggests that cycles from the same geographical region—the Jacob tradition and the "Rachel" *tribes* tradition of central Palestine— were fused with the southern traditions of Abraham-Isaac. In my view these cycles must include the traditions of women. Rachel is the wife of Jacob, but Noth fails to investigate a Rachel tradition before including that of her tribes—that is, sons.

I have proposed a Sarah tradition different from the Abraham tradition in part because there are Abraham-in-Hebron episodes as well as Abraham-in-Beer-sheva episodes in the south. Furthermore, the characters of the two "Abrahams" are not alike.[16] I agree with Noth, for instance, that the narratives attached to the region of Hebron, and specifically to the famous sanctuary of the terebinths of Mamre, do not belong to the original material of the [southern] "Abraham tradition" such as those of Abraham and Lot (Gen. 13, 18:22–33) or Abraham and Abimelech at the well (Gen. 21:22–34).[17] This determined "southern" Abraham is quite different in character from the Abram of the Sarah tradition: Sarah's brother-husband is a compliant (Gen. 16:1–6) and passive (Gen. 12; 13; 18; 21:11–12) participant in the Sarah episodes, quite unlike his southern counterpart. To these I would now add a *Desert tradition* or cycle.

THE DOCUMENTARY THEORY: J, E, P, AND R

The concept of cycles is derived from perhaps the most widely accepted theory of separate narrative roots, the *documentary hypothesis*.[18] This theory traces the Genesis narratives to various authors and suggests that one or more authors worked on the same traditions or cycles.

The proponents of this theory consider variations of language and style, contradictions and divergences of view, and duplications and repetition of texts, as arguments for diverse origins. The result of this painstaking analysis will help us to discover what each original source may have looked like before it was fused with other material to form the received text.

The documentary hypothesis identifies different narratives by the use of the divine names used in them: "J" for YHWH (Jehovah), "E" for Elohim, "P" for a priestly school of authors and editors, and "R" for the redactors (those who later reworked oral or literary material, editing and rewriting it).[19] All the authors and the redactors were priests who had access to documents and the religious authority to promulgate the documents.[20]

J and E are considered to be the oldest of the sources; author J came from Judah and author E from Israel (Map III). It is not surprising, then, to find that all the stories that take place in Hebron are written by J of Judah, whose ancient capital was Hebron.[21]

J is considered to be the author of the main block of narratives, those with particularly moving stories and vivid characters. The story of Cain and Abel (Gen. 4) or that of Joseph and his coat of many colors (Gen. 37) are, for example, attributed to him. While J and E often relate many parallel stories, the stylistic differences between them help make their contributions individually recognizable in form and content.

The first Hagar desert sequence (Gen. 16) is accredited to J, whose materials, Robert Friedman tells us, "are, on the whole, much more concerned with women and much more sensitive to women than are the E stories."[22] J's story of Hagar and Sarah in Genesis 16 is told from the women's point of view, not the patriarch's. In the parallel stories of Sarah and the kings, J has Sarah taken to the court because she is beautiful. Then the courtiers praise her to Pharaoh and on account of her it went well with Abraham. And it was because of Sarah that God afflicted Pharaoh with plagues (Gen. 12). E's

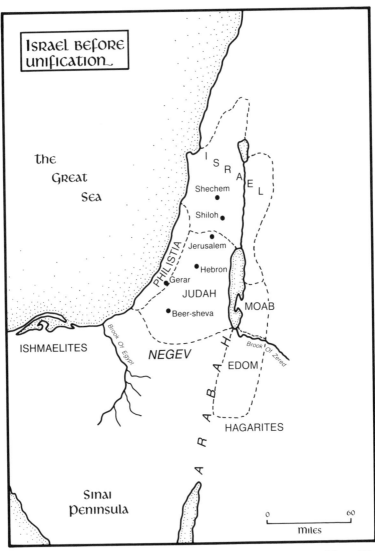

Israel Before Unification

the
Great
Sea

I
S
R
A
E
L

Shechem

Shiloh

Jerusalem

PHILISTIA

Hebron

Gerar

JUDAH

MOAB

Beer-sheva

Brook Of Egypt

ISHMAELITES

NEGEV

A R A B A H

Brook Of Zered

EDOM

HAGARITES

Sinai
Peninsula

0   60
miles

Mary McArthur, Cartographer.

Map III

account, on the other hand, says nothing personal about Sarah. The whole story revolves around Abimelech, Abraham, and God (Gen. 20).

Moreover, the deity J describes is often anthropomorphic; whereas E replaces the manifestation of deity on earth with a dream or a messenger's voice from heaven. Thus J has YHWH "pause in front of Abraham" and speak to him (Gen. 18:22), while in E's account "God came to Abimelech in a dream" (Gen. 20:3). Likewise J tells the story of Jacob stopping at sunset on his journey between Beer-sheva and Haran and there was "YHWH standing beside him and saying . . . " (Gen. 28:10, 13). But such an encounter suggested too anthropomorphic a deity for E. He thus interposed a passage between verses 10 and 13, turning Jacob's meeting with YHWH into a dream. In the stories that directly concern us J's YHWH stands on earth and speaks to Hagar (Gen. 16:7), while E's Elohim calls to her from heaven (Gen. 21:17).

The material of the Priestly school, P, differs from that of both J and E. Dry and to the point, the biblical texts edited or narrated by P offer us statements of fact. P, for example, is responsible for establishing descent in the male line, repeatedly using such phrases as "And Hagar bore a son to Abram, and Abram gave the son that Hagar bore him the name Ishmael. Abram was eighty-six years old when Hagar bore Ishmael to Abram" (Gen. 16:15–16).

As scholars developed this documentary theory they came, therefore, to specify each editor of the texts. To avoid confusion, then, I will assign all post-J and post-E editing to P, since most of these editors were priests in the Temple of Jerusalem.

WHO TOLD THE STORY?

Just as we have no conclusive evidence for the dates of the original events—nor, indeed, unambiguous evidence that the characters of the biblical narratives actually existed—neither do we have documented knowledge of the original sources for the stories told in the received text. We do not know how the narratives were handed down. Were they originally legends evolved from actual events and transmitted from one generation to another by word of mouth? Were they available to the first editors in written form but then destroyed or lost? However the stories were transmitted and whatever their fidelity to history, given the androcentric bias of the received text the sheer survival of a woman-centered story strongly argues for the power of the legend and for the possibility of its being rooted in an actual experience.

The question now arises: Who first told Hagar's story?

The tale of Hagar's flight to the desert, like most biblical stories, is told in the third person. But no one witnessed Hagar's experience. She was alone, or with her son. If the event actually occurred, therefore, the first telling of it would have had to have been in the first person: Hagar would have had to be the first "author" of her story. There are certainly precedents for first-person literature in ancient times. A paramount example is perhaps the oldest recorded narrative, the magnificent soliloquy to the goddess Inanna: the *nin-me-sar-ra,* composed by En-hedu-anna, priestess of Ur (Sarah's birthplace) in 2400 BCE.[24]

Could Hagar have written her own story? Rivkah Harris finds evidence that women were scribes in Mesopotamia. Harris draws on third-millennium material in which there is "at least one reference to a female scribe receiving rations in an Ur III text which suggests that she was perhaps a slave-girl belonging to the temple force."[25] Harris also mentions a list from Mari in which nine women received rations as scribes but who were "slaves or at least of low status."[26] It seems too that *naditu* women served as scribes for other *naditu* in the cloisters of Sippar, and that *naditu* scribes "acted as recorders of and witnesses to the transactions of *naditu* women only." Harris also points out, "At times, a Mari princess leaving her natal home to marry a ruler of another town might be given a slave-girl trained as a scribe as part of her dowry."[27] This would be more relevant to Hagar if we knew the origin of her relationship to Sarah (which in Hebrew means princess). Significantly, female scribes "are attested only for the earlier part of the Old Babylonian period and then disappeared from the scene some time in the reign of [the son of Hammurapi] Samsuiluna," (1749–1712 BCE) indicating a change in the status of these women.[28] It is plausible, then, that a woman in Hagar's position could write, particularly if she lived in the Early Bronze Age.

That the narrative of Hagar originated with its protagonist, of course, presupposes her historical reality. There must be a kernel of truth in the stories where the women are concerned, because their experience has been so radically excised in the sacred writings generally; but specific traditions must have been too entrenched in the culture to eradicate completely.

If the narrative characters are based even slightly on historic personages, then it is more likely that some sequences—particularly those in which there were no witnesses—were originally transmitted, whether in oral or written tradition, by the protagonists themselves. This suggestion leaves us with three possibilities: (1) that women, as well as men, were originators of the texts; (2) that both J and E could have used a source that generated from Hagar as the author, at least of that part that deals with her experience in the desert; and (3) that portions of the J source may very well have been female but were subsequently edited by an androcentric hand.

To be effective and for the accounts to create some semblance of authenticity, they needed to maintain a kernel of truth. But for the stories also to be believable to those who heard them, they must reflect the social values of the times. In other words, I think that the narratives about women describe events that actually happened to real people but were adjusted, by stages, to suit contemporary ideology.

THE PURPOSE OF THE NARRATIVES

Much of the tenor of the Bible as it now stands, including the roles portrayed of women, was influenced by the political ambitions of King David and his successors. It is vital to recognize the vast historical and ideological interval between the time of the early Hebrews, whom the stories concern, and their later compilation by various editors of the Genesis narratives. The events involving the early Hebrews occurred between 2600–2400 BCE. The authors J and E are believed to have written their material in the tenth and ninth centuries, respectively, in the early years of the monarchy. Not only, then, was there a gap of at least five hundred years between the events themselves and the recording of those events, but there were also major changes in the political organization of the region.

A common feature of a new social organization is the assumption of the name of an originally important lineage or tribal segment within the whole.[29] David as conqueror of greater Israel would certainly have benefited from a tradition that posited "this land, from the River of Egypt to the great River Euphrates" (Map I) as a combined unit conferred by a deity on offspring to come (Gen. 15:18). To become an inheritor of this bequest David had to connect his own genealogy to that of the early Hebrew ancestors and to legitimate himself as the object of the divine promise.

David's new political organization influenced the way in which the stories were recast. As George Mendenhall observes, "There can be little doubt that the major function of the narrative was to indicate that David as king represented the legitimate successor to the old pre-Israelite dynastic tradition."[30]

The following sequence of events set the process in motion: David was crowned king after the oracle at the cultic center at Hebron was consulted, uniting all of Judah under his rule. Once kingship at Hebron was established, "The old political legends became valuable as a means of ideological unification of a diverse population."[31] In the northern kingdom of Israel, a series of intrigues that brought on the deaths of King Saul, his son Jonathan, and Saul's successor, Ish-bosheth, opened the way for David to be anointed king over Israel also. This potential was strengthened by David's earlier marriage to Michal, daughter of Saul. David's first step after becoming king of Israel was to move his residence from Hebron, the capital of Judah, to the neutral ground of Jerusalem, which until that time had been the home of the Jebusites.[32]

David's next political move was in the religious sphere: He brought to Jerusalem the ark of the covenant of YHWH, the sacred symbol of the northern kingdom, and filled the ministerial posts with priests (2 Sam. 8:15–18). A minor but thought-provoking passage in 2 Samuel chronicles the effect David's establishment of YHWH in Jerusalem had on Queen Michal: "As the ark entered the City of David, Michal, daughter of Saul was watching through the window, and when she saw King David leaping and strumming before Yahweh, she felt contempt for him" (2 Sam. 6:20–23). Later, Michal derides the king for his behavior in front of the maidservants (*amahot*). Clearly, Michal does not approve of the religious innovations David introduces by bringing the ark of the deity YHWH into Jerusalem. Several elements in the story suggest that David's action is an affront to a religious position of authority held by Michal.[33]

Earlier in the narrative David had fled from Saul in northern Gibeah, leaving his wife Michal behind (1 Sam. 19:12). He then married Abigail of Carmel and Ahinoam of Jezreel. But in the meantime, 25:44 tells us, "Saul had given David's wife [his daughter] Michal, to Palti, the son of Laish, who was from Gallim" (1 Sam. 25:44). P. Kyle McCarter, Jr., explains the politics of these events as follows:

David has lost his newly acquired base of power in consequence not only of his exile from Gibeah, where he had become a popular hero, but also, as we learn in v. 44, the loss of his royal-blooded wife, Michal. He has been required to return to his [southern] homeland [Judah]. Now we find him marrying [Abigail] the widow of a high-ranking member of the clan that controlled Hebron as well as another woman from nearby Jezreel. He is becoming a prominent figure in the heartland of Judah.[34]

Queen Michal bears a close resemblance to the matriarchs of Genesis: "Michal, daughter of Saul was childless to the day of her death" (6:23). The motif of 2 Samuel 4:20–23 may indicate that, like Sarah, she experienced a "sacred wedding."[35] Michal is also associated with handmaids, (*amahot*) a term used of Hagar (*amah*). Like Rachel, Michal was a youngest daughter and owned *teraphim,* sacred images, and indeed had descended from Rachel via Benjamin. Michal therefore may have been a priestess, with an influential religious position in her father's court.[36]

By taking Michal away Saul must have hoped to weaken David's claims to the throne of Israel. By insisting on her return as his wife, David reinforced his claim to the northern kingdom of Israel. But once established in his new capital, Jerusalem, David turned to YHWH.

David was probably able to depose Michal from her hallowed position because of the demise of her father, just as Enhedu-anna, the poet-daughter of Sargon of Akkad, was banished from her post as *en* (the equivalent of high-priestess) when Ur and Uruk were wrested from her father by the usurper Lugalanne.[37]

This episode concerning Michal is also symbolic of a struggle within the amphyctiony (the twelve tribes) between primogeniture and ultimogeniture—that is, as to whether the older or the younger took precedence. In the Genesis narratives precedence was given to the youngest: Isaak, the son of Sarah, is chosen instead of Abraham's firstborn, Ishmael; Bethuel, Milkah's youngest, is chosen instead of Nahor's firstborn, Uz; Jacob, the son of Rebekah, is chosen instead of Isaak's firstborn and favorite, Esau. Of Jacob's descendants Leah's youngest, Judah (according to J) became more prominent than the oldest, Reuben.[38]

Michal (the youngest daughter) belonged to the tribe of Rachel (also youngest daughter) via Benjamin, Rachel's youngest son; while David, a youngest son himself, was establishing his ancestry, the tribe of Judah, the fourth of the Leah tribes, as priests.[39] David's "sin," in Michal's eyes, was that the tribe of Judah was taking over the priestly functions of her tribe, the Benjaminites.[40] That Michal too was a youngest child implies that she was indeed a religious representative of her people, a priestess like her foremother Rachel.

Clearly, in that capacity she would have serious misgivings about David transporting the cult of YHWH to Jerusalem and presenting himself as Israel's new cult founder.[41] The disgust shown by the daughter of the first king of a unified Israel at this religious turn of events certainly represents the sentiments of a portion of the population. J's material would sanction the preeminent position of YHWH, and the prominent position of Judah as the deity's representatives—all in disaccord with the tradition represented by Michal.

The significance to the Judean David of Judah's preeminence is evident in the genealogy. Robert R. Wilson explains:

The twelve-tribe genealogy seems to have been frozen sometime near the end of the period of the judges. We may therefore suggest that revised versions of the genealogy were no longer created after the rise of the monarchy because those genealogies would have no political function. Rather, the twelve-tribe genealogy was taken into the religious sphere, where it became the standard expression of the ideal Israel, even in the post biblical period when the tribes themselves had ceased to exist. Israel did not abandon the use of political genealogies entirely, however, but after the rise of the monarchy, linear genealogies were used in the normal way to support the political claims of kings.[42]

Like that of Hor-aha of Memphis and Hammurapi of Babylon before him, David's genius for telescoping political and religious power into one controllable center at Jerusalem must have required a similar vision with which to legitimize the unification of the kingdoms of Israel and Judah in the eyes of all the people—people with different ancestry and different traditions.[43] One method, used by successive pharaohs, was to consolidate the union of Egypt by "combining the different traditions of Upper and Lower Egypt in an attempt to create a single common culture."[44] David's attempt to fuse the ancestry and the religious traditions into one controllable unit would have generated an unprecedented search for information from one end of the kingdom to another.

The paragraph describing the ministerial posts mentioned above includes the statement "Shausha was scribe," indicating that David's court contained an official scribe.[45] Was Shausha an editor of the J material? Gathering, recording, and editing information was surely a project of enormous dimensions and must have involved the cooperation of many people: storytellers, scribes, and perhaps even some descendants of the principals who kept the stories of their ancestors alive within the extended family or clan. These latter would have been matristic descendants' stories, stories in which religious experience, betrothal, marriage, and offspring would have been prominent.[46] It may also explain why the genesis of Jewish history is not of war but of nurture, regeneration, and spirituality.

The stories associated with Hagar, like those relating to Sarah, Abraham, and the other protagonists of the Genesis narratives, were collected and revised to suit the needs of the young monarchy's political unification program. The repercussions of this vital task are still with us today.

The cyclical predominance of a different social system requires its values to be legitimized with aspects of mythology and tradition. The foundations established by the monarchy served a religious community (in antiquity there was no such thing as a secular community) whose interests lay in territorial expansion and military exploits. "The inception of the monarchy meant the beginning of urban development and a ruling elite."[47] This vision did not include the participation of most women or their religious or societal associations.

One of the social values that suffered most in the new militaristic vision of the monarchy was that of cooperation between individuals—women and men, and women and women. The effect of androcentric writing and editing of the biblical narratives resulted mainly in conflicts between women: Hagar/Sarah, Rachel/Leah, who vie for the attention of their husbands or sons.

Hagar's conflict traditionally arose from the "barren" matriarch's jealousy toward her fertile handmaid (somewhat reminiscent of the controversy between Horus, ancestral deity of fertile Lower Egypt and Set of the almost barren Upper Egypt). A closer look at the story that pits Hagar and Sarah against each other reveals a deeper cause of conflict than mere jealousy.

2. Androcentrism: Texts Out of Context

Genesis 16 and 21

The stories from Genesis are known to scholars as the *Patriarchal Narratives*. The intent of this designation is to draw the reader's attention exclusively to the activities of the male. It conceals the importance of women and the plurality of divinity and gender, leaving the archetypal figure of the father as predominant: the *"patriarchal"* prototype.[1]

The theme of the Genesis narratives is spelled out in the first sentence YHWH addressed to Abraham while he is still in Mesopotamia: "Go, and leave your country and your people and [go] from the house of your father to the land that I will show you, and I will make you into a great nation, and I will bless you and you will be a blessing" (Gen. 12:1–3a). For most interpreters *this command and promise sums up the entire theme of the Genesis narratives.* By making "YHWH's promise to the patriarch" central to the theme, a plot is created in which all other elements become subordinate to an androcentric motif.

But there is evidence in the biblical texts of an underlying strain different from the original theme of the promise to Abraham. That strain is manifest, in part, in the spiritual experiences of Hagar. To reveal it we must first peel off some of the material incorporated by the biblical writers.

The biblical editors—J, E, P, and R—were united on the patriarchal plotline; yet each had his own concern. J's interest lies in southern Judean cycles, and his vision of deity is anthropomorphic. E is a more shadowy figure. His work is fragmentary and his god more remote than J's. Both J and E may have utilized earlier written, as well as oral, sources. I would argue that E's use of Elohim, as opposed to J's use of YHWH, suggests that the E material originates from the northern region as yet opposed to the primacy of YHWH.

Elohim in Hebrew means "divinities." It is possible then that the original designation(s) was the name of one or more deities, which the R or P source was forced to modify to conform to the monotheistic norm of a later period. P is the theologian who structured the narratives to form a chronological sequence, imbuing them with patriliny and monotheism.

It is only with a knowledge of the sources and an understanding of the intent of the editors that the core material—the intent of the initial legend—can be revealed.

REVEALING THE ENIGMAS

During research on *Sarah the Priestess* I focused my attention entirely on that matriarch as I read the biblical material that dealt with her. I set aside YHWH's promise to Abraham that "None but your own issue shall be your heir" (Gen. 15:4), and concentrated instead on Sarah's appeal to her husband: "Go into my *shifḥah,* perhaps I can be built up through her." In so doing I came to recognize that this pivotal episode concerned Sarah's lineage, not Abraham's. Now, by giving attention exclusively to Hagar, we can recreate her story from a point of view distinct from that of Sarah or Abraham.

Hagar's story is limited to two segments of the Sarah and Abraham story: Genesis 16 (by J) and Genesis 21 (by E). Each segment is itself divided into two sections: one in the household of Sarah, the other in the desert.

Biblical scholars have understood these sections to be either a story of Ishmael, the tribal ancestor of the Ishmaelites, or a personal rather than tribal event, in which "The focal concentration is on the struggle between two women."[2] More importantly, however, John Skinner says, "In reality Ch. 16 (J) and 21:8–21 (E) are variants of one tradition."[3] That is, the two episodes in Genesis 16 and Genesis 21 are two different versions of one theme. But Skinner and other scholars have missed the point. The stories are consecutive, and there are *two* sets of stories, not one: The stories that belong to the Sarah household are distinct from the desert sequences, and the desert sequences belong to a sole source.

To understand why this is so we must visualize the world from our ancestors' point of view and focus our attention on the possible interests of the women, particularly in the realm of their beliefs. If YHWH was not the deity known to Sarah (as Exodus tells us), who was? Were YHWH and the deity Hagar named El-ro'i one and the same? If the answers to both these questions are negative, what significance does it have to the retrieval of the core material?

To comprehend the significance of Hagar's biblical role, it is vital that we seek to visualize the world in which she lived so as to ascertain the motivation for her actions. Yet it is almost impossible, from the standpoint of Western culture, to recreate the emotional and spiritual forces that directed the actions of our ancestors. Our fundamental concepts, our moral values, are radically changed from those of the biblical period. We must be aware that our assumptions of nationalism, race, individualism, relationship to environment, and our very concept of religion differ considerably from theirs.

ANCIENT RELIGIOUS EXPERIENCE

In ancient times people did not experience spirituality as separate from everyday life but as an integral part of it. There are at least two reasons for this: One, our concept of religion—with its emphasis on a single abstract God—was foreign to ancient biblical thought. Two, we have internalized a philosophy we call "patriarchy," a concept that was quite unfamiliar to most rural societies of premonarchic times.

In prehistoric times groups of settlers chose ensigns from the natural phenomena of their districts or from birds, animals, or water creatures common to their area. In historic times, when provinces rose to power, local deities were promoted politically and accredited with diverse powers.[4]

Ancient divinities were usually associated with specific regions. Thus the goddess Neith of Sais is the protector of the Egyptian Delta; Ptah is the god of Memphis; Ningal is the goddess of Ur in Sumer; Marduk is the protector of Babylon; El Elyon is connected to Jerusalem (Gen. 14); El Olam is connected to the ancient Canaanite sanctuary at Beer-Sheva (Gen. 21:33); and so on. This means that each region had its own distinctive beliefs. It is thus not clear, for example, how the god YHWH, who later identifies himself as being the same as the El Shaddai (Exod. 6:2–3) who bade Abraham and Sarah leave their native land, can be the same god as El-ro'i, a desert divinity unfamiliar to the matriarch to whom he appears at the well of Beer-lahai-ro'i.

In ancient times gods, demons, and humans were believed to interact. The later focus on "one-man one-god" in the biblical texts helped dispel this spiritual climate.[5] In Canaan divinities were not restricted to centralized places of worship. They were assumed to appear at certain times in specific places, which then often became their sacred abode. For example Beer-lahai-ro'i became a sanctuary because it was there that a god, El-ro'i, appeared.

Biblical peoples believed that supernatural forces affected and controlled the destinies of human beings. Human beings, however, could direct the course of a destiny decreed by a divinity.[6] These supernatural forces could materialize as anthropomorphic or as natural elements, water, or vegetation; they could be earthly or astral. Communication with deities could be direct or indirect. One could actually come face to face—at great personal risk, of course—with an anthropomorphic deity.[7] One might also experience divinity in dreams or visions, or contact it through oracles or oracular devices, or divine its will by means of omens. The biblical world, then, was very different from our own.

We can envision the immanence of the spiritual in the mundane if we look more closely at the significant episodes in the narratives. A close look shows us that almost every chapter of the Genesis (J) narratives about Sarah, Hagar, or Abraham contains some form of ritual or oracular communication. Hagar, for example, is introduced performing a ritual service for Sarah in Genesis 16:1–3.[8] From the time that Sarah and Abraham set out from Mesopotamia, with the moving oracular admonition *lekh lekha,* "Go, take yourself" [to a land that I will show you], to Sarah's death, each episode involves a form of ritualistic communication with the supernatural: Sarah's ritual event with Pharaoh of Egypt and with Abimelech of Gerar; Abraham's vision; Sarah's ceremonial acquisition of an heir/ess; the two sections of a desert epiphany; the sequence of the three mysterious visitors to Mamre; the deity's fulfillment of the promise of a child to Sarah, and the ritual of the Akedah (the Binding of Isaak), all demonstrate the integral part played by the spiritual in the lives of the protagonists.

Rituals were deemed necessary to avert catastrophe: Certain rituals were devised with precise formulations needed to insure correct behavior and to avoid divine displeasure. Ancient peoples took this need for granted as an integral part of daily life. Because of this, the message in a story transmitted to our ancestors might have been radically different from our contemporary understanding of it.

Heterogeneous elements formed part of the conventional lives of our ancestors. Stories that contained patterns and symbols that were commonplace to them sufficed to incorporate a rich variety of detail we may never recover. As Robert Alter explains: "In some cases . . . the biblical authors, counting on their audience's familiarity with the features and function of the type-scene, could merely allude to the type-scene or present a transfigured version of it."[9]

Type-scenes contain similar basic elements and imply a corresponding symbolic meaning, but may differ in characters, locale and even time frame. Alter's list of type-scene elements include the birth of a hero to a barren mother, and the encounter of the future betrothed at a well.[10] Esther Fuchs, who treats the same theme as Alter in her paper, "Three times in the Hebrew Bible, a prospective wife and husband meet at a well," uses Genesis 24:1–58 (Rebekah and emissary of Isaac), Genesis 29:1–20 (Rachel and Jacob), Exodus 2:16–21 (Zipporah and Moses), as examples.[11]

I would suggest that Hagar's meeting with El-ro'i at the well, as it is described in the biblical text, also belongs to this type-scene. The archetypal plot, as expressed by Alter, includes: (a) the hero's emergence from the immediate family circle to discover a mate in a foreign land; (b) the well at an oasis, which he says is "obviously a symbol of fertility" and "in all likelihood, also a female symbol"; (c) drawing the water from the well and (d) gestures of hospitality, the actual betrothal. The plot of the type-scene, Alter continues, dramatically enacts the coming together of mutually unknown parties in marriage.[12] Except for the drawing of water, and the fact that the protagonist is a *heroine,* not a hero, the Hagar sequence fulfills all the characteristics of the betrothal type-scene: (a) The heroine leaves the immediate family circle, discovers a mate in an unknown desert, (b) at a well or oasis, symbol of fertility. (c) The statement "You are now pregnant," (Gen. 16:11) confirms the sexual union.

GENESIS AND THE GODDESS

Springs, fountains, ponds, and wells were female symbols in archaic religions, and were often considered water-passages to the underground womb.[13] Sacred wells especially are credited with the property of causing women to become pregnant.[14] In Genesis 16 the *god* is named El-ro'i, god of seeing or vision. But the *well* is called Beer-lahai-ro'i, "well of the living one that sees me," because of the woman's experience. It does not necessarily mean that the well is now the abode of El-ro'i. Most often it is a goddess or water spirit who governs the life-

giving force of water, and the springs of the goddess are credited with the power of facilitating delivery as well as conception. It is probable that the life-giving waters of the divine
earth mother were equated with the amniotic fluid of the human mother.

We need hardly be reminded that all androcentric religions
attempted to eradicate religious experience that did not conform to the cult of a male deity.[15] But there is ample evidence
in biblical literature that such eradication was not entirely
achieved until the reformations of King Josiah in the seventh
century BCE and of the priests Ezra and Nehemiah in the fifth
century BCE.

Peggie Reeves Sanday suggests that Hebrew women were
not attracted to the cult of YHWH because they held an inferior position in it.[16] Women's inferior position, however, is
not exclusive to the cult of YHWH; women of Babylonia,
Assyria, Canaan, Egypt, or anywhere else in the ancient Near
East were constantly being pressured into subordinate positions, whatever their religious affiliations.

We must also acknowledge that monotheism was not the
religious concept held by the ancient Hebrews and Israelites.
In his monograph *Asherah and the Cult of Yahweh in Israel,* Saul
M. Olyan concludes,

Asherah and her cult symbol were legitimate not only in popular
Yahwism, but in the official cult as well. The evidence in the Hebrew Bible alone suggests strongly that Asherah and the ashera [ter-
ebinth tree, tree-trunk, or pole, Plate 3] were considered legitimate
in the state cult, both of the north and the south, in Jerusalem, Sa-
maria, and Bethel, and probably in very conservative circles.[17]

It also seems reasonable to infer that no woman would wish
to relinquish the numen of a goddess, whose protection in
childbirth would seem vital, given the frequency of stillbirth,
death in infancy, and the death of women giving birth.

In this context it is interesting to note that El Shaddai, the
divinity who led our ancestors out of Ur, may have been perceived by them as a female divinity because of this deity's

strong imagery of fertility and procreation.[18] Since the biblical material does not give any particular connotation to the name *shaddai,* scholars use different roots to interpret the meaning.[19] *shad'i* or *shadu* (mountain) is the root most commonly used to interpret *shaddai* (that is, god of the mountain).

Drorah Setel points out that most current academic discussion of the linguistic history of the name, while acknowledging the connection, fails to consider the option of interpreting "shaddai" in relationship to "breast."[20] Nevertheless, as Setel indicates, the Hebrew word for "breast" may be derived from the root "*shadeh*" or "*shadad.*"

The earliest mention and the clearest evidence of a relationship between the term *shaddai* and "breast" is given in the language of Genesis 49:25, in Jacob's blessing of Joseph:

> From your father's God, who will help you
> And from *shaddai,* who will bless you
> Blessings of the heavens above,
> Blessings of the primeval waters (*tehom*), lying below;
> Blessings of breasts (*shadayim*) and womb (*rehem*).

Of the five times El Shaddai is mentioned in Genesis, four are directly concerned with procreation (Gen. 17:1; 28:3; 35:11; and 43:14). Three of these—Genesis 17, 28, and 35—are tied to the experience of the matriarchs, although the passages do not seem to have any specific or explicit connection to human female experience.

Both Hagar and Sarah, and in all probability Abraham also, would have acknowledged the presence of female deities in their lives. They not only knew the Canaanite-Hebrew goddess Asherah, but chose to live in her sacred grove at Mamre.[21] Scholarship suggests that the worship of this goddess was primarily the responsibility of women, although men also participated fully.[22] As Setel illustrates,

In the first reference [to *shaddai*] (Gen. 28) Isaak sends Jacob to Paddan-Aram to find a wife. The passage mentions three times in the course of four verses that he is to go to the home of his mother's brother, a kinship reference indicative of matrilineality. Genesis 35 makes explicit reference to "putting away foreign gods." It also mentions Shechem, where, in the previous chapter, Dinah met with great misfortune after attempting to make contact with the "daughters of the land," in other words, Canaanite women; (the term "Canaanite" is used here as a euphemism for the community of "uncircumcised males" the women are members of). In addition, Gen. 35:8 is the only reference to Deborah, Rebekah's nursemaid, who is buried under an oak tree, the *allon bakuth* [oak of weeping].[23] Finally, *El Shaddai* is again associated with Paddan-Aram, the home of Rachel and Leah.[24]

The name of Rebekah's wet-nurse, Deborah, (Hebrew "bee"), like those of Sarah (Hebrew "princess" or Akkadian "queen") and Milkah ("queen") may also have been titles. Priestesses of Demeter at Eleusis were called "bees," and the oracular priestess at Delphi was called Bee.[25] Erich Neumann suggests that bee-priestesses are "virgins"—that is, unmarried—because of their "independence of the male," as in bee society, "where only the queen is fecundated by the male, and she only once."[26]

It seems evident from all these examples that the beliefs and spiritual experiences of the biblical women were quite different from that portrayed in the received texts.

Two sons borne by Zilpah, the *shifḥah* of Leah, are also worthy of note. After her fourth son, Judah, Leah stopped bearing (Gen. 29:35).[27] Zilpah, Leah's *shifḥah,* then bears her two sons. It is these two sons whom Leah names with names of Arameo-Canaanite divinities. The naming of Zilpah's sons by Leah suggests a ritual in which she claims the sons of her *shifḥah.*

In the ancient world nothing exists unless it has a name. The power of naming is akin to creating (Gen. 1:9, for example). Zilpah bore the child and Leah brought him into existence through her naming of him; thus the child she names comes under her authority and protection.[28] When the first is born Leah exclaims, *"Ba-gad!"* "How fortunate!" and she named him Gad. Gad is the name of the god of fortune.[29] At the birth of the second son Leah exclaims, *"B'ashri!"* interpreted as: "How happy I am, now the daughters will call me happy," so Leah named him Asher. Asher is the Amorite god of fortune; however, *b'ashri* has also been understood to mean "with Asherah's help."[30] (Asher is the masculine form of Asherah.)[31] Was Asherah also known as the goddess of happiness at that time?

During their pregnancies and the births of their sons, it is not inconceivable that Hagar and Sarah sought the help or protection of a female deity. Images of pregnant women have been discovered in Israel from as far back as the middle of the fourth millennium BCE (see Plate 2 from the region of Beersheva). Since these figurines give no evidence of representing divinities, they may have been used as amulets to ensure safe pregnancies. One beautiful pottery figurine of a pregnant woman (Plate 1, from the vicinity of Phoenicia) is interesting on two counts: One, many similar figurines have been found on numerous sites in Israel, such as Tell Zippor, Makmish, Tell Abu Hawam, and Beth Shean.[32] Various identical models hundreds of years apart can be seen in the Collection of Israel, Department of Antiquities. Two, the woman wears an Egyptian-style wig. If these figurines were used as amulets, were they associated with the story of an Egyptian matriarch whose pregnancy was intended to benefit another woman? Or did they reflect a miraculous conception by a woman lost in the desert?

Significant to the matriarchs would be a goddess dubbed the *dea nutrix,* the nurturing goddess, often represented with her breasts cupped in her hands (Canaanite figurine, Plate 4). The narratives mention Sarah suckling her child, and legend elaborates on the theme: Sarah "uncovered her breasts and the milk gushed forth as from two fountains, and noble ladies came and had their children suckled by her, saying, 'We do not merit that our children should be suckled with the milk of that righteous woman.' "[33] The nurturing goddess would have been an important spiritual support in an environment in which infant mortality was so prevalent as a result of famine.

PLATE 3. "Asherah and her cult symbol were legitimate in the state cult of Israel." *Ashera (Lachish seventh century BCE). Courtesy of the Metropolitan Museum of Art. Gift of Harris D. Colt and H. Dunscombe.*

PLATE 4. "It is not inconceivable that Hagar and Sarah sought help or protection from a female deity." *Canaanite figurine (Deir el-Balah? 1500–1200 BCE). Courtesy of the Israel Department of Antiquities and Museums. Photo Zeev Radovan.*

PLATE 5. "Astarte in two distinct aspects of divinity."
a. Astarte (Late Canaanite 1500–1200 BCE). Israel Museum, Jerusalem. Reifberg Collection.

b. Astarte figurines with flowers (Canaan 1500–1000 BCE). Courtesy of the Israel Department of Antiquities and Museums. Photo Nachum Slapak.

As an Egyptian Hagar would have looked to the Egyptian Isis suckling Horus (Plate 16) or to Hat-Hor, the great cow-goddess who was claimed by pharaohs to have suckled them (Plate 10).

The distinction between conception, birth, and nurturing goddesses is lost when they are designated as "fertility" goddesses. Raphael Patai mentions a seventh-century Hebrew incantation text in which help for *delivery* was sought from the goddess Asherah. He suggests that, because of this, she may have been believed to "promote fertility."[34] But "fertile" means productive, prolific. The "fertility" label effectively obscures the true function sought from that goddess: safe delivery.

In fact skinny maiden goddesses with or without distinctively marked vulva or pubic triangle are also dubbed "fertility" goddesses, even though they do not bear children. A favorite term for the childless goddess is the Victorian euphemism "goddess of love"—this, despite our ancestors' proclivity for representations of sex and the sexual. Sexuality was most likely regarded as a gift of the goddess, together with her power of life-giving birth and life-sustaining milk.

Astarte-Ashtoret, goddess of the Canaanites and the Sidonians, and her Babylonian counterpart Ashtar (see appendix C) were often represented with arms upraised, holding flowers, lily stalks, or serpents and sometimes holding her breasts. The "Astartes" in Plate 5 are clear indications that this goddess personified at least two distinct aspects of divinity. Thousands of Astarte figurines made of clay have been found at most of the excavated areas of the Canaanite and Israelite periods, whose primary devotees were women.[35] In Egypt Astarte and Anath are described as "the great goddesses who conceive but do not bear."[36]

The association of women with a religion that afforded primary trust to women would reinforce the view that the Sarah/Hagar narratives were initially by and for women, and that the divinities they worshiped were neither primarily nor solely male, as the biblical narratives suggest.

It is in this context that I submit that the most significant modification established by the J source is the substitution of the god YHWH as the predominant deity throughout this author's narrative material. As professed by YHWH himself: "I appeared to Abraham, Isaac and Jacob as El Shaddai but I did not make myself known to them by my name Yahweh" (Exod. 6:2). Jo Ann Hackett has shown that in Priestly usage Shaddai is always paired with El in the patriarchal narratives (as opposed to the use of Shaddai found elsewhere in the Hebrew Bible).[37] He is presented by this source as a nurturing deity, who blesses Sarah and Ishmael (Gen. 17), and who uses the familiar formula of El Shaddai, "Be fruitful and multiply" (Gen. 17:16, 20). This view is particularly unlike El Shaddai the storm god/divine warrior image, occurring elsewhere.

My concern here is not to argue for El Shaddai as god of the "patriarchs" over YHWH. Rather I want to emphasize the certainty that the *deity* reflected in the core material was not the warrior god of later narratives, where a single all-powerful deity was substituted for a plurality of divinity. Our ancestors must indeed have experienced divine female presence.

Diverse images of deity, of course, could undermine an emerging androcentric monarchy; in particular, female deities or divinities associated with females, would have to be transformed to suit the contemporary ideology. A male god would become the god of creation (pregnancy) and nurturing and would be represented as having practically no association with females, human or divine. In this way, Asherah, El Shaddai, Elohim, and El-ro'i all came to be identified with "YHWH, the God of Abraham." Any striking event—such as the meeting of a woman with a divine being in the desert—would be downplayed, her theophany minimized, and her identity obscured.

Table 2. The **Gynocentric** and the <u>Androcentric</u> Categories

Gen. 12:10–20	**Sarah with Pharaoh (J)**
<u>Gen. 1–5</u>	<u>Abraham's vision and promise of progeny (J)</u>
Gen. 16:1–6	**Sarah's (attempt at) acquisition of offspring (J)**
Gen. 16:7–14	**The theophany in the desert**
	The conception and birth of Ishmael (J)
<u>Gen. 17</u>	<u>Covenant and circumcision</u> (P)
Gen. 18:1a,10–14	**The promise of an heir to Sarah (J)**
<u>Gen. 18:16–33</u>	<u>Abraham intercedes for Sodom</u> (J)
<u>Gen. 19:1–29</u>	<u>Lot flees Sodom</u> (J)
<u>Gen. 19:30–36</u>	<u>Lot's daughters</u> (J)
Gen. 20:1–17	**Sarah with Abimelech (E)**
Gen. 21:1–2a,6–8	**The conception and birth of Isaac (J)**
Gen. 21:6–12	**Sarah rejects the son of the <u>amah</u> (E)**
Gen. 21:14b–21	**The trial in the desert (E)**
<u>Gen. 22</u>	<u>The trial of Abraham</u> (J and E? or P?)
Gen. 23:1–2	**Record of the death of Sarah (J or P)**

DISTINGUISHING THE CYCLES

In our analysis of Hagar we will be dealing with only a portion of the Genesis narratives (see list below): (1) those that deal exclusively with the interests of two matriarchs; and (2) those of the patriarch that directly affect the destinies of the women and their offspring. We can distinguish two classifications: gynocentric (female centered) and androcentric (male centered). Some episodes in the narratives focus exclusively on the needs and aspirations of females (almost all from the J source); others on those of males.

John Van Seters divides the record in a similar way, but with a different purpose: "The Yahwist, usually regarded as the earliest source, was in fact preceded by an earlier J written level of tradition."[38] In light of my argument, the fact that Van Seters's list of what he believes to be the *earlier* tradition coincides almost exactly with my *gynocentric* list (see Table 2) is significant.[39]

Each of the segments listed in Table 2 can be understood as independent recollections of events that were compiled, recorded, and edited by a scribe (J or E) during the early monarchy, into a cycle that formed a more or less chronological sequence with an androcentric bias. A later hand (P and/or R), probably of the exile community residing in Babylon in the sixth century BCE, fused the cycles, giving form and framework to the narrative. The framework of P and some of the narrative P material—Genesis 17—was cleverly woven into the previously edited theme to give it its definitive androcentric focus.

Martin Noth points out that, were P to be eliminated, "the remainder of the Pentateuch . . . would be neither unified nor homogeneous."[40] I would add that the remaining material would not belong to an exclusively androcentric cycle.

The inclusion of texts in which the sole protagonists are men helps conceal some of the original gynocentric data. Other independent narratives from the Abrahamic cycle, episodes in which the patriarch has an active role—such as those of Abraham and the Invaders of the North (Gen. 14) and the cycles of Abraham and Lot (in chapters 13, 18, 19), as well as the Binding of Isaak (Gen. 22)—help to enforce the androcentric theme.

REMOVING THE STRUCTURE

The cycles we will attempt to unravel are complex. Characters as well as stories have been fused in an effort to achieve a later "monotheistic" unity: one god, one patriarch, one ethic. As the core stories come to life, however, we will be forced to acknowledge the pluralism of both deities and individuals.

The masterful interweaving of the separate traditions of males and females is accomplished by short phrases joining together fragments from various legends. The effect was to lose the original intent of the separate accounts, and to focus attention on the theme the editor considered essential. Because the primary purpose was to reinforce an androcentric persuasion, the original elements alien to that purpose were obscured or lost. As a rule the connecting phrases were from the hand of the P school, which sought to infuse the core material with a completely different message.

The connecting sentences inserted by P are often easy to recognize. Let us take an example from Genesis 16. Verses 1, 3, 15, and 16 are acknowledged as belonging to P.[41] If verse 1 ("Now Sarai, Abram's wife had borne him no children") is omitted, the episode would actually begin with "She had an Egyptian *shifḥah* named Hagar."

Then, by deleting P in verse 3—"So after Abram had been living in Canaan ten years, Sarai his wife took her Egyptian *shifḥah* and gave her to her husband to be his wife"—the original story would have commenced as follows (the **J** material is in bold type and E is underlined, for easy identification):

She had an Egyptian *shifḥah* named Hagar; so she said to Abram, 'See, now, YHWH has kept me from bearing, go now into my *shifḥah* perhaps I can be built up by her.' And Abram listened to the voice of Sarai and he went into Hagar and she conceived.

Because it commences with "She had" rather than "Sarai had" this paragraph must have formed part of another anecdote. The preceding portion presumably alluded to and named Sarai but was replaced by P's introductory phrase making Abraham the focus of the sequence.[42]

Similarly, Genesis 21 commences,

YHWH visited Sarah as he had spoken and YHWH did for Sarah as he had promised, and she became pregnant . . .

Then P inserts: "and Sarah bore a son to Abraham in his old age. And Abraham gave his son, the one being born to him, whom Sarah bore to him, the name Isaak. Now Abraham was a hundred years old when his son Isaak was born to him." The first sentence, in which the deity is called YHWH, belongs to the J strand (not E) and should not form part of the Elohist's narrative; it belongs at the end of J's account of the annunciation of Isaak's birth (Gen. 18). So this episode, if entirely by E, originally commenced with the matriarch: <u>"Sarah said, Elohim brought me laughter . . . "</u>[43]

It makes much more sense for the Hagar-Sarah episode in Genesis 16 that ends with Sarah's plea: "YHWH decide between me and between you," to be followed by YHWH's annunciation that Sarah would bear her own child, the resolution of the conflict. The thread of the story would then be as follows:

I [YHWH] will return to you at the time that life is due and Sarah shall have a son (Gen. 18:10, 13). **YHWH visited Sarah as he had spoken and YHWH did for Sarah as he had promised** (Gen. 21:1).

Episode with Abimelech: Sarah conceives (Gen. 20). <u>Sarah said, "Elohim has brought me laughter . . . I have borne a son . . . "</u> (Gen. 21:6).

The independent desert story in Genesis 16 and the covenant and circumcision of Genesis 17, which interrupt the continuity of the sequence, have no relevance to the progression of the story of Hagar or Sarah.

HAGAR AND THE DESERT MATRIARCH

How was the Sarah/Hagar episode (Gen. 16:2–6) coupled with the Hagar/desert story (Gen. 16:10–14)? In the former the childless Sarai has asked her husband Abram to *bo-na et shifhati* "go into my *shifhah*" Hagar, in order that she procure an heir/ess.[44] Hagar becomes disrespectful to her mistress Sarai, and Abram leaves it to Sarai to resolve the conflict. In the latter an *unnamed woman* lost in the desert conceives a child with the aid of the supernatural. So we are dealing with two traditions and three matriarchs: Hagar, Sarah, and an unnamed *Desert Matriarch*. The P phrases that connect the two J episodes are:

Then Sarai treated her harshly and she ran away (Gen. 16:6b).[45]

And he [the messenger of YHWH] said, "Hagar, handmaid of Sarai, from where have you come and where are you going?" She said, "I am fleeing from my mistress Sarai" (16:8). And the messenger of YHWH said to her, "Go back to your mistress, and submit to her harsh treatment" (16:9)[46]

P introduces Genesis 16:6b, 8–9 here to link the independent tradition of the protagonist of the desert theophany with the previous Sarah tradition.[47] It does this *by naming the desert woman Hagar,* thus identifying her as slave-concubine, and *by having Hagar leave and return to the harshness of Sarah.* This confuses the identity of two matriarchs and establishes the nasty personality of one matriarch and the subordinate status of the other, hence diminishing the importance of the female experience.

Furthermore, we must ask ourselves what kind of divinity would have subjected a devotee to the harsh treatment of her mistress? In fact, what kind of god would force a victim to return to her victimizer? And what would induce a woman to accept this injustice from a god she had just met? In one of the most beautiful—and theologically relevant—episodes Abraham confronts the injustice of his god over the destruction of Sodom. "Will you sweep along the innocent with the guilty?" the patriarch challenges (Gen. 18:23). Abraham won his case and the innocent were saved. Hagar, it seems, meekly accepts her god's injustice. What was to be her reward? The deity promises her a child and too many descendants to count. But these compensations are directed at the *males* in the story. P's statement reveals that these will be Abraham's heirs, not Hagar's. From a woman's point of view I find P's logic highly unconvincing, and his premise that women should silently accede to injustice particularly dangerous.

The last part of the paragraph is presumably a prophecy to the Desert Matriarch (16: 10):

And [the messenger of] YHWH said to her, "I will greatly increase your descendants so they will be too many to count because of their size."

This connects the child born in the desert to YHWH's previous promise to Abraham:[48]

"Look, now, at the heavens and count the stars if you can count them, and then he said to him, so shall your offspring be" (Gen. 15:5)[49]

which David later took into account:

"But David did not count those twenty years old or under because Yahweh had promised to make Israel as numerous as the stars in the heavens" (1 Chron. 26:23)[50]

Notwithstanding additions and interpretations, the prophecy in the desert is the promise of descendants to the matriarch, not to Abraham.[51] The Priestly version effectively discounts the circumstances of the unnamed Desert Matriarch's theophany (1) by identifying her with the subordinate Hagar, *shifḥah* of Sarah, and (2) by associating the son born in the desert to the promise of Abraham. However, the introduction to the promise of offspring "too many to count" to Abraham is then followed by a different introduction with the promise of a son to the Desert Matriarch: **"See, you are now pregnant and shall bear a son,"** and so on.

Westermann comments that "It is much more likely that the promise of descendants has been added to the promise of a son.[52] Westermann also gives evidence that "The promise [of a son] in vv. 11–12 has a defined structure, attested by a series of parallels, which points to a narrative form which has its base in the oral tradition stage," which he interprets as more authentic. Thus we may conclude that the promise of a son to the Desert Matriarch formed part of the original story and that the promise of descendants was included to attach the story to Abraham.

P concludes the section in his inimitable way, with classic references to the patriarch: "And Hagar bore a son to Abram, and Abram gave the son that Hagar bore him the name Ishmael. Abram was eighty-six years old when Hagar bore Ishmael to Abram" (Gen. 16:15–16). In this conclusion Hagar is established as mother; Abraham is confirmed as father; *he* names the son (even though the divine presence has the mother name the child); and mention of the patriarch's age confirms an event in Abraham's life. Thus gynocentric segments—accounts of Sarah, Hagar, and the Desert Matriarch—have been transformed into an androcentric account, which is now focused on the birth of Abraham's son Ishmael.

Recognizing the desert story as independent, this tradition should begin:

YHWH found her [no name] by the spring of water in the desert, by the spring of water in the Way to Shur. And YHWH said to her, "See, you are now pregnant and shall bear a son," and so on.

In the original story, then, this matriarch is impregnated by a deity who then foretells the future of her descendant. As Edgar Fripp observes, "There is nothing in the Iahvistic story to indicate that Ishmael ever was in Abram's house.[53]

The fact that Abraham is *not* the eponymous ancestor of the Ishmaelites seems to corroborate Fripp's statement.[54] Fripp also tends to confirm the independent nature of the Desert Matriarch episode.

The story of Hagar in Genesis 16, then, must be divided into two parts: the Hagar-Sarah episode, and the Desert Matriarch sequences. Once this is done it becomes evident that nothing in the desert story alludes to the previous episode. In fact, apart from Hagar being mentioned by name in the connecting sentences, the woman in the desert *has no name.*

THE HAGAR TEXTS

If it is not Hagar who fled into the desert, then what happened to the Hagar of the Sarah episode? Or, to put it differently, where does the Sarah/Hagar story of J continue after Sarah is harsh to her?

The answer is that it does not go *anywhere*. Strikingly absent, between Sarah's anger in Genesis 16 and the birth and weaning of the Isaak episode in Genesis 21, is a core note about the birth of Hagar's son. J's story proceeds with the birth of Isaak, without mention of the birth of Hagar's son. In J's version Hagar is left in Sarah's hands and is not heard of again. Presumably, Sarah awaits the decision of the deity, which evolves in Genesis 18. E's story, however, does continue with the destiny of Hagar, the *shifhah* of Sarah, who remained in Sarah's household (Gen. 21).

Whatever way we look at J's story, it is about the experience and destiny of three women and the birth of their sons, (Table 3) with the patriarch playing a minor and passive role in the events.

The truncated Sarah story in Genesis 16 must originally have told of the birth of the *shifhah's* son and it also must have clarified whether or not Hagar's son became Sarah's heir, as was initially intended. Only then must the story have continued with the annunciation, conception, and birth of Isaak in Genesis 18:1–15, 20, and 21:1–2. P's attempt to include Abram/Abraham into the story of the Matriarchs by inserting Genesis 17 confuses the issue of the sons' age and parentage.

The Priestly source (whose aim was to establish the authority of YHWH, male succession, and the sanctity of the law) introduces a segment (Gen. 17) in which YHWH promises Isaak to Abraham as part of the covenant. But Ishmael, as Abraham's son, who is now thirteen, is also blessed. The cov-

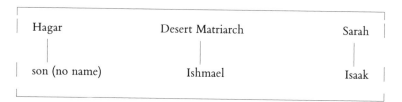

Hagar	Desert Matriarch	Sarah
son (no name)	Ishmael	Isaak

Table 3.   The Matriarchs' Sons

enant is ratified by both father and son with circumcision, the new mark of the covenant.

In E's story (which is a segment of the same core source story used by J) both Sarah and Hagar have children. Sarah's son Isaak is just being weaned, and Hagar's son is still young enough to be carried.[55] The motif of E's story is similar to J's in that a conflict arises, Hagar is made to leave Hebron, and goes to live in the desert with her son. She does not return to Sarah or Hebron.

It seems probable, then, that in the original source the first story of Hagar/Sarah (Gen. 16:1–5), which must have included an account of the birth of Hagar's son, was followed by the conception of Isaak (Gen. 18; 20). And the birth of Isaak (Gen. 21:2a) must have been followed by the second Hagar/Sarah story, which actually begins with Genesis 21:6: "Sarah said, Elohim has brought me laughter."[56]

The previous verses, Genesis 21:2–5, as noted above, are another classic P interpolation. They establish the fatherhood of Abraham, Abraham's naming of Isaak, the boy's circumcision, and Abraham's age at the time, all characteristic of the Priestly school's effort to make a patriarch the focus of the story.

THE RESULTS OF ANDROCENTRIC EDITING

Biblical androcentrism is not only detrimental to the female characters it portrays, but also misinterprets the nature of the society in which the women lived. Were concerns such as racism, hierarchy, or individualism included in the tenets of early Hebrew society?

The extant biblical texts have clouded the probable character of the events experienced by all of the protagonists—Hagar, Sarah, the Desert Matriarch, Abraham, Ishmael, and Isaak—obscuring our understanding of the discernible societal values of the times.

According to the biblical account neither Sarah nor Abraham was concerned with the racial background of Hagar, the mother of their would-be heir.[57] Hagar is characterized as

Egyptian, but what does this mean? The designation "Egyptian" is vague at best. Hagar's identity would depend on the historical time frame and the geographical setting within the account. Apart from that, it would be imperative to know whether she belonged to the Egyptian "aristocracy" as legend suggests, or whether she belonged to the rural class. W. B. Emery tells us,

Towards the close of the fourth millennium BC we find the people known traditionally as the "Followers of Horus" apparently forming a civilized aristocracy or master race ruling over the whole of Egypt . . . the existence of this master race is supported by the discovery that graves of the predynastic period in the northern part of Upper Egypt were found to contain the anatomical remains of a people whose skulls are of greater size and whose bodies were larger than those of the natives . . . throughout the whole of the archaic period the distinction between the civilized aristocracy and the mass of the natives is very marked.[58]

By the third millennium Egyptian influence had spread around the Mediterranean to Lybia, Crete, the Aegean Islands, Greece, Syria, and Palestine, and southward to Nubia and Sudan (see Map I).[59] Trade also existed in the archaic period between Egypt and Syria, Palestine and the Sinai, as well as south with Nubia.[60] So it would be of utmost importance to know whether Hagar came from Upper or Lower Egypt (see Map II) and what was the status of her family before we can understand her designation as "Egyptian." Whatever Hagar's ethnic background, it was presumably different from that of Sarah or Abraham.

In the Bible, especially concerning Israel, the concept of nationality usually has a religious connotation that distinguishes those who worship YHWH from those who served other gods. Nationality only took on a political sense with the rise of the monarchy.[61] I suggest that, in part, Hagar was described as an Egyptian to differentiate her race and religion and culture from that of Sarah and Abraham and their respective descendants.

In Hebrew lore Hagar is said to be the daughter of *Pharaoh.* Apart from his royal wife—who was his sister, half-sister, or cousin, or even perhaps his daughter—the king married many women, usually as part of political alliances. Hagar may have been the daughter of one of these affiliations. Since matriliny was the norm in Egypt we cannot know her ethnic circumstances or her religion without knowledge of her maternal background. If she were truly of royal descent, what would be the identity of Hagar's mother? Was she perhaps Queen Neith-hotep, whose political marriage to Narmer helped legitimize his position as ruler of the North? Or was she Meryet-Neith, a queen who probably succeeded to the throne herself as pharaoh, also in the First Dynasty of the fourth millennium? Was Hagar the daughter of any of the many monarchs buried in the Valley of the Queens on the west bank opposite Luxor, or at Abydos or Sakkara (see Map II), where rulers of the archaic period were buried?

Many names of the queens contained the element *neith.*[62] Neith was the protector-goddess of Sais, chief city of the North before and after the unification of Upper and Lower Egypt (see Map II).[63] Emblems of two crossed arrows (and sometimes a shield) became the symbols of the huntress-goddess Neith of Sais in the Delta.[64] A stela of Queen Meryet-Neith was found at Abydos bearing the insignia of crossed arrows (see Plate 14a). Could the queens whose name contained the element *neith* and whose symbol incorporated arrows have any relevance to the woman, lost in the desert, who measured distance by the length of a bow-shot (Gen. 21:15)?

Sarah's choice of Hagar as the mother of her heir, whatever her background, and Abraham's willingness to acknowledge her son as his heir, reveals the community's disinterest in ethnicity. This society also seems to have been cooperative, focusing on the interest of the community or unit rather than on the individual. The objective of the episode in Genesis 16 was for Sarah to acquire an heir. Both Hagar and Abraham collaborate to that end, knowing that their participation was for Sarah's benefit, not their own.

Abraham's role in the Hagar-Sarah passages is not as an active participant. The women take the action, the Patriarch reacts. This is not a submissive role, but one traditionally understood as the helpmeet of Genesis 4:18.

The social position of the *shifḥah* is a reflection of that of the matriarch to whom she is associated. Rachel is always named before her older sister Leah. Similarly, Bilhah, the *shifḥah* of Rachel, is named before Zilpah, the *shifḥah* of Leah.

"Familial" kinship ties seem to have sufficed to link the members of the *mishpaḥah* (family or clan) to each other. It was obviously not necessary that the mother of the child Sarah was to acquire belong to her bloodline. It may in fact be possible that the concept of *blood* as the medium to transmit the line of descent came at a much later date. The concept of a bloodline can only have served elitist groups who envisioned themselves as divinely endowed, as evidenced in the dynastic succession of warrior aristocracies. On the other hand, clan status was inherited directly from the mother: the sons of Hagar, Bilhah, and Zilpah (that is, Ishmael, Asher and Naphtali, Dan and Gad) maintained the status of their mothers and became less influential tribes in Hebrew lore than those of their "brothers" born to Sarah, Rachel, and Leah.

From the time of the monarchy (ca. 1000 BCE), during which these particular episodes were presumably collected and recorded, to the time of the reformer King Josiah (640 BCE) and the scribes Ezra and Nehemiah (ca. 430 BCE), a great program of indoctrination to an androcentric ideology took place. It seems apparent that the description of the social system in which Hagar, Sarah, and Abraham operated was edited in transmission to be centered around the patriarch and his god, by many stages of revision. Socially, a reordering of relationships within the kinship group was implemented by a code of ethics.

Leviticus 18 is this code of ethics. Generally, it covers laws regarding sexual relationships. Significantly, this work comes from the P source. Before the concept of descent through the bloodline was favored, circumcision was endorsed by the P school (Gen. 17) to identify a male unit as separate from the obvious connection to the mother.

Religious reform is, of course, the fundamental tenet of Judaism. The reformation is apparent at an early stage, when Jacob (Gen. 35:2–4)—like Joshua (Josh. 24:14–15) and others after them—demand that alien gods be "put away." This was a far cry from the intent of their ancestors.

3. Hagar the *Shifḥah:* Neither Slave nor Concubine

When I began my research on Hagar I still conceived of her as the concubine-slave of Abraham, as I had in my previous work.[1] I did this despite my recognition that Hagar was the handmaid of Sarah and that the child she was to bear was to be Sarah's heir/ess, not Abraham's. Conventional assumptions are deeply embedded in our consciousness and therefore difficult to alter.

As my research proceeded I came to realize that the slave/concubine characterization of Hagar in the Hebrew Bible steers the reader's interest away from centrality of the mother to what was considered a more relevant issue: the birth of her son. Those assumptions, moreover, were reinforced by traditional interpreters.

The objectives of the episode in Genesis 16:1-6 are twofold: to explain (1) the purpose of Hagar's sexual union with Abraham and (2) the basis for the conflict that developed as a result of that association.

The androcentric reorientation seems to have worked quite well. A. E. Speiser, for instance, in his commentary on Genesis 16, entitles the episode in which Hagar conceives a child for Sarah "The Birth of Ishmael."[2] Claus Westermann calls it "Sarah and Hagar: Flight and Promise of a Son," thus effectively directing attention from the women to the birth.[3] John Skinner circumvents the Sarah-Hagar issue completely: "The Flight of Hagar and the Birth of Ishmael" simply ignores the matriarchs.[4] From the Islamic point of view, regarding Hagar as slave is a necessary consequence of the theory on which the Hebrew myth is based, the notion that Ishmael was of inferior origin.[5] It is particularly easy to dismiss the presence of a matriarch if she is regarded as a slave-concubine, an inferior being.

Another difficulty in discovering the true position of Hagar comes from the dearth of roles assigned to biblical women. Biblical men are portrayed as active leaders—patriarchs, kings, princes, warriors, prophets—and in close relation to deity. Women, on the other hand, are portrayed as passive adjuncts to men or to superiors—wives and mothers, queens, princesses, harlots, hierodules (sacred prostitutes), concubines, and slaves. Since scholars assess women in relation to men, Hagar's identity is viewed in relation to Abraham: slave-concubine.[6] This despite many corollary assertions that she was exclusively the maidservant of Sarah.[7]

THE ROLE OF HAGAR AS SLAVE-CONCUBINE

The biblical narratives slowly lead up to Hagar's lowly position:

1. Hagar is the *shifḥah* (handmaid, maidservant) of Sarah.
2. She becomes Abraham's second wife.
3. Hagar's sexual services are controlled by her mistress.
4. Her progeny will belong to her mistress.
5. She is harshly punished because she does not conform to her mistress's wishes.
6. Hagar is seemingly not in control of her own destiny.
7. Hagar changes from being the *shifḥah* of Sarah to becoming the *amah* of Abraham.
8. Finally, Hagar is regarded solely as the mother of a son of Abraham's: Because of the Patriarch, this son of Hagar is blessed by God as ancestor of a people, who are albeit the enemies of the Israelites.

These eight particulars have been garnered from two episodes, Genesis 16 and 21, which comprise only eleven sentences. (I do not include the desert episodes, which belong to the cycle of the Desert Matriarch.)

In the first episode, Genesis 16, Sarah is childless. She has an Egyptian maid, Hagar, whom she offers to her husband Abraham so that she can build up a family. Phyllis Trible sums up the intent of the matter:

Beginning with Sarai and ending with Hagar, the narrated introduction opposes two women around the man Abram. Sarai the Hebrew is married, rich, and free; she is also old and barren. Hagar the Egyptian is single, poor, and bonded; she is also young [there is no evidence for this!] and fertile. Power belongs to Sarai, the subject of action; powerlessness marks Hagar, the object.[8]

Abraham "listened to the voice of Sarah," and Hagar conceived, the story continues. Moses ben Nahman elucidates:

Scripture does not state "And he did so." Rather it says that he harkened to the voice of Sarai, thus indicating that even though Abram was very desirous of having children, he did not do so without the permission of Sarai. Even now it was not his intention to build up a family from Hagar, and that his children be from her. His intent was merely to do Sarai's will so that she may build a family from Hagar for she will find satisfaction in her handmaid's children, or that by the merit of this act she will become worthy to have children, as our Rabbis have said.[9]

In Genesis 21 E depicts Hagar in the most disparaging terms. Her name is only mentioned once in verse 9, and her designation has been changed from *shifḥah* to *amah,* slave. The designation of her son is equally disdainful, *ben ha-amah,* son of the slave. Neither Sarah nor Abraham talks to Hagar directly, even though the subject of their dialogue is an exceptional occurrence in her life: She and her son are being banished. In fact, even though the episode reports Abraham's distress over the exile of his son, the eviction of Hagar does not seem to bother the patriarch, or even Sarah.

Only God seems to care: "Do not be distressed over the lad or your slave," he is reported to have said, "as for the son of the slave-woman I will make a nation of him too, for he is your seed." But even here, Trible claims, Hagar is humiliated: "To minimize Abraham's relationship to Ishmael, God calls him 'the lad' rather than 'your son.' Moreover, the deity describes Hagar not as 'your wife' but as 'your slave woman' a description that tellingly emulates the vocabulary of Sarah (21:10). If Abraham neglected Hagar, God belittles her."[10]

But before we can accept or reject the nature of Hagar's role as slave we need to dismiss contemporary notions and search the ancient records for evidence of the meanings of the term "slave" in ancient times. Only then can we decide whether the depiction of Hagar conforms to those meanings.

SLAVERY IN ANCIENT TIMES

The most important sources for the study of slavery in the ancient Near East between the third and the eighteenth centuries BCE come from Mesopotamia. The earliest extant regulations that deal with the issue of a slave in the position of Hagar is from Ur-Nammu, "mighty warrior, king of Ur, king of Sumer and Akkad," circa 2050 BCE. A relevant law (#22) reads: "If a man's slave-woman, comparing herself to her mistress, speaks insolently to her (or him) her mouth shall be scoured with one quart of salt."[11] Another possibly relevant regulation, this time from Hammurapi of Babylonia (ca. 1750 BCE), states that "If a man married a *naditu* (priestess who did not bear children) and she did not provide him with children and he has made up his mind to marry a *sugetu* (priestess who did bear children) that man may marry that *sugetu,* thus bringing her into his house but with the *sugetu* in no way ranking with the *naditu*." The laws (Sumerian, Akkadian, Babylonian, Assyrian, and Hebrew) deal primarily with female slaves of the master, not with those of the mistress. Hagar was affiliated with Sarah, not Abraham, so it is difficult to establish in what measure these regulations apply to them.

The conventional view of the female salve is that she was treated as a commodity:

She was leased for work, given as a pledge, or handed over as part of a dowry. In addition to her routine as maidservant, she was subject also to the burdens peculiar to her sex. Ownership of a female slave meant, not only the right to employ her physical strength, but also, and in many cases primarily, the exploitation of her charms by the male members of her master's household, and the utilization of her body for the breeding of slave children. The highest position a female slave could achieve was to become a child-bearing concubine to her master, and the lowest, to be used as a professional prostitute.[12]

The earliest use of the terms for male and female slaves, which indicate foreign persons, implies that human enslavement was the consequence of war.[13] However, Akkadian, Ugaritic, and Hebrew terms for "slave" are often employed to designate the lesser status of a freeborn person in relation to royalty or divinity, as in the case of Abraham, who is designated "slave of YHWH" (Gen. 26:24).[14]

A QUESTION OF TERMINOLOGY

Three different Hebrew terms presumably fit the description of slave: *shifḥah, 'avriyah,* and *amah.* These terms are translated into English interchangeably as: slave, handmaid, bondmaid, woman-servant, and maid-servant.[15] It nevertheless seems strange that so much terminology was required, in either language, to verbalize a single function. As Carol Meyers explains it: "[Biblical] language is theological; it describes human events in terms of God's action. Furthermore, the language itself was in many cases formalized only several centuries after the events that gave rise to the sacred texts, with the result that the writings reflect later concerns intertwined with original materials."[16] Thus Akkadian, Ugaritic, and Hebrew terms for "slave," which are often employed to denote the secondary status of a freeborn person in relation to royalty or divinity, may not always bear the connotation of laborer.

That this terminology was originally more precise seems evident. Specifically, there must have been a distinction made between the "slave" of a woman as compared to that of a man, since they would have had different primary functions: Women usually bore their own children, and concubinage is not customary between women.

Female slaves of men always became concubines at the whim of their masters. Hagar's case, however, is different. Skinner clarifies: "Hagar is not an ordinary household slave, but the peculiar property of Sarai, and therefore not at the free disposal of her master." He then notes, with a quote from Lane, that "Some wives have female slaves who are their own property, generally purchased for them, or presented to them, before their marriage. These cannot be the husband's concubines without their mistresses' permission, which is sometimes granted (as in the case of Hagar); but very seldom."[17]

Hagar had only one child even though she lived with Sarah and Abraham for about seventeen years. This means that Hagar's sexual association with Abraham occurred only once, and that was with the intent of providing Sarah with an heir/ess.[18] Did Hagar know that she had become "pregnant from the first act of sexual relations," as the sages put it?[19]

One would assume that she had sexual relations with Abraham until she was sure of having conceived. Since Hagar's sexual encounter with Abraham was proscribed, it would be interesting to know whether a ceremony was performed for the occasion. Since Hagar was given to Abraham l'ishah (as wife) but had only one pregnancy, it is feasible that a specific wedding ceremony took place sanctifying that particular occasion. This was not a marriage in the conventional sense of an alliance between families or clans. It would seem that Hagar was neither slave nor concubine nor conventional wife of Abraham. But she was the shifḥah of Sarah. Nevertheless, because there is no term to fit this particular function, there is no reason to relate it to concubinage.

The sons of supposed concubines like Bilhah and Zilpah became the heirs of Rachel and Leah, not of their own mothers.[20] This implies that the women had children for each other and that the function of these women was childbearing *for*

PLATE 6. "I see no reason to describe this woman as a concubine."
*"Concubine figurine" on bed (Canaan thirteenth to twelfth centuries BCE). Israel
Museum, Jerusalem. Photo Nachum Slapak.*

a mother, not concubinage for a master. In every instance the woman presents her *shifḥah* to her husband *l'ishah* (as wife), not as concubine, which in Hebrew is *pilegesh*.[21]

According to William A. Ward, the Egyptian term rendered "concubine" is also a misrepresentation. Ward argues that terms usually rendered "harem-women" or "concubine" in English are doubtful, since monogamous marriage and legal equality were facts of ancient Egyptian society.[22] In fact, Ward says, "Marriage, strangely enough, was not a legal but a social institution in which the wife's rights were as scrupulously maintained as those of husbands."[23] Textual misrepresentations are also transferred to plastic representations. The beautiful figure of a woman lying on a bed, for example, is entitled "Concubine Figurine" (Plate 6). It is a Canaanite object made of Egyptian-style stone in the thirteenth to twelfth centuries BCE. I see no reason to describe the woman as a concubine.

A single statement in Genesis 25:6 portrays Abraham as giving gifts to the sons of his *concubines.* These were presumed by scholars to be Hagar and Keturah.[24] This single misconception, perpetuated by scholars, has allowed these women to have been classified as mistresses in every available commentary. But Hagar, as we see, was not the patriarch's concubine, and Keturah was the patriarch's second wife!

It is also clear in the Leah/Rachel stories that Bilhah and Zilpah are presented to Jacob for the specific purpose of providing the matriarchs with offspring. Jacob has many children when Rachel presents Bilhah to him so that "through her I too may be built up" (Gen. 30:3b).Furthermore, the *sh'faḥot* have sexual relations with Jacob solely when requested by the matriarchs. The function of the *shifḥah,* then, is to have the honorable purpose of fulfilling the injunction to "be fertile and increase" (Gen. 1:28) the lineage of the matriarch. This directive, it will be remembered, was always associated with the nurturing deity, El Shaddai.[25]

Finally, Hagar is described both as *shifḥah* (by J) and *amah* (by E). Both terms are used by Ruth (Ruth 2:13, 3:9), by Abigail (1 Sam. 25:24–41), and by the wise woman from Tekoa (2 Sam. 14:6–19) to describe themselves. However, since J and E did not use them interchangeably in relation to Hagar, but each writer used his own terminology, this is evidence that the meanings of both words were initially different from each other. In Hagar's case E uses *amah* with a more derogatory denotation than J's use of *shifḥah*. Furthermore, J uses *shifḥah* in relation to women who conceive and become pregnant. E's section is solely about the banishment of Hagar and her son.

THE FUNCTION OF HAGAR

A slave would be expected to perform menial tasks. In no instance is Hagar depicted as servile to either Sarah or Abraham.

In the first episode in which Hagar appears, her function is exclusively to provide Sarah with an heir/ess; she is not depicted as engaged in any other responsibility. It is only on the basis of her sexual association with Abraham that scholars regard Hagar as associated with servility. When Sarah's own conception of Isaak is imminent (Gen. 18), Abraham offers a meal to his visitors. Abraham and a servant-boy prepare the meal (18:7–8). Abraham hastens to Sarah to tell her to knead and make cakes (18:6).

No mention is made of Hagar. (Though she had fled from Sarah, she had been commanded by the deity to return in Genesis 16:9.) The absence of the supposed slave in this episode is striking. Hagar next appears only when Abraham holds a great feast on the day that Isaak is weaned (Gen. 21:8). But Hagar is not helping to prepare the feast, nor does she seem to have anything to do with it. In fact, this episode is about the son of the *amah* (bond-woman), who—according to Sarah—has the same status of inheritance as her son Isaak (Gen. 21:10). And it is only with the sanction of the deity that the boy is banished (21:12). Hagar makes an appearance solely to escort her son away.

TOWARD AN INTERPRETATION OF *SHIFḤAH*

The etymology of *shifḥah* is obscure. It has been suggested that it is connected to the verb *sh-f-h,* meaning "to pour out, shed blood" and has been used in the sense of "commit fornication with her."[26] *Shifḥah* has also been interpreted to mean the maid or maidservant *of the mistress* even though she may be the concubine of the master.[27] Although conventionally synonymous with *amah, shifḥah* is sometimes erroneously described as "someone more servile."[28]

The more probable root, *s-f-h,* is Ugaritic. It denotes *famulus,* "being together," and *mishpaḥah* in the sense of the Latin *familia.*[29] C. Umhad Wolf does not see *sh-f-h* as semantically related to *mishpaḥah* and proposes a more probable affinity with *s-f-h-,* "to join," "attach oneself to."[30] This interpretation is feasible because there is a precedent for a group of women with a similar determinative in Ugarit, known as *insht,* meaning "female companions" or "intimate friends."[31] In other words, *shifḥah* could mean "someone who joins or is attached to" a person or a clan.

It seems obvious, then, that the term *shifḥah* must originally have described a woman whose particular function was to bear children when a priestess did not bear heirs of her own. Furthermore, the *shifḥah,* though beholden to the priestess, must have functioned in some religious capacity herself. Both Hagar and Bilhah remain childless for a number of years. Sarah (and presumably Hagar also) "dwelt in the land of Canaan ten years" (Gen. 16:3) before she decided that Hagar should have sexual relations with her husband, Abraham, in order to provide herself with an heir. Leah already had four sons (Gen. 29:33–35) before Bilhah (the *shifḥah* of Rachel) conceived (Gen. 30:3). Moreover, the *shifḥah* acquired the status of the priestess. Bilhah is mentioned before Zilpah (the *shifḥah* of Leah, Gen. 35:25–26), just as Rachel is named before Leah (Gen. 31:14). Furthermore, Bilhah conceives and bears children before Zilpah.

The childlessness of Hagar tends to confirm a status other than ordinary slave (with no rights) or even handmaid (with some), since voluntary childlessness at that time is usually associated with goddesses and priestesses. *Ishtaritu,* for instance, were priestess-devotees of the goddess Ishtar; and like her they remained childless.

The crucial issue for a better understanding of the Genesis narratives in general and the accounts of Hagar in particular lies in the sense of the term *shifḥah.* Biblical writers limited their descriptions of the characters they wrote about to their relationship to one another: Sarah is wife of Abraham, Hagar is *shifḥah* of Sarah, Rebekah's brother is Laban, and so on. Since we have no terminology to fit Hagar's status vis-à-vis Abraham, Hagar should be referred to as what she was: the *shifḥah* of Sarah.

THE *MISHPAḤAH* CONNECTION

A closer look at the biblical term *mishpaḥah* will give us a better understanding of the social climate expressed in the narratives.

Politically, the social units in the biblical narratives are neither national nor tribal, but are more accurately described in terms of a clan.[32] A clan is a group of households or extended families that usually claim a common ancestry or association through common occupation. (There may be traces of such a related origin reflected in the names of Rachel and Leah.)[33] Alliances were probably made within a similar language group. The clan was the link between the extended family and the larger unit, the tribe (Num. 2:34). In the Hebrew Bible the term used for family, *mishpaḥah,* is also used for household or clan (Josh. 6:23). Thus a *mishpaḥah,* is understood to be a composition of several "households." These, however, need not be blood-related; nor, in fact, do they necessarily contain husband and wife.

As the *mishpaḥah,* extended beyond pure kinship growing in wealth, size, and power, it came to include strong territorial ties as well.[34] For example, the kingdom of Saul, the first king of Israel, was a loosely organized confederacy, which David later unified. Hundreds of years earlier, however, various groups of Mesopotamians had set out for the land of Canaan and founded the "houses" or clans—established by the women—that later became the confederacy ruled by Saul.

These clans already existed in Mesopotamia. After Sarah's death Abraham sends his servant to bring a wife for Isaak from his *mishpaḥah,* in Haran (Gen. 24:38). This *mishpaḥah,* is the "house" of Rebekah's mother.[35] In the next generation Leah and Rachel very clearly run their own establishments, separate from each other, and separate too from their husband Jacob's. When Laban, father of the sisters, searched for "his" *teraphim* (sacred images), he went in to "Jacob's tent and Leah's tent and the tents of the two maidservants" (with "tent" having the same connotation as "household"), but he did not find the *teraphim.* Leaving Leah's tent, he entered Rachel's tent (Gen. 31:46). From these "households" stemmed the tribes of Rachel and Leah. It is significant—and it bears further investigation—that the territories encompassed by Rachel's youngest, Benjamin, and Leah's youngest, Judah, contained the most important religious sanctuaries of the time: Bethel and Jerusalem, and Hebron and Beer-sheva, respectively.[36]

That each woman administers her own separate household is even more evident when Rachel asks that *her* lineage be built up (*ibane,* Gen. 30:3). Rachel is referring to her own lineage, not that of the clan. Rachel's seemingly anguished plea to her husband Jacob, "Give me children or I will die," does not express envy of her sister's fertility (Gen. 30:1). To Rachel, "I will die" meant "my house will die out." This is borne out by the fact that Rachel is not anxious about having a child of the body to compete with Leah, her sister, because she presents her husband with Bilhah. The *shifḥah* was not "barren" and could presumably have given Rachel a child at any time, if competition for progeny were the issue, and if concubinage of the handmaid had been the norm. Instead,

Rachel's attitude reflects the same lengthy time requirement as Sarah's before acquiring an heir by means of her *shifḥah*.

Rachel is concerned because her lineage embodies survival of her religious station, of whom the "childless" Michal, Saul's daughter, may have been the last survivor. Significantly, Michal's father, Saul, was from the tribe of Rachel by way of her youngest son, Benjamin. I would suggest that the rivalry of Leah and Rachel for children is a later gloss and was not part of the original story, which initially must have portrayed Rachel as the ancestress of the priesthood concerned with its survival.

The biblical "family" unit was the *mishpaḥah* of the narratives.[37] It was composed of a matriarch-priestess;[38] their *sh'faḥot* and their children; and the woman's husband. Like *shifḥah*, *mishpaḥah* also has the connotation of being together—that is, family. This would support my contention that the *sh'faḥot* were regarded as clan members rather than slaves or concubines, because they bore the children whom the priestesses then claimed by naming them; and it was for this reason that their offspring held the status of sons of the matriarchs. In other words *it is the combined effort of the sh'faḥot-mothers and the matriarchs that is significant* in the *mishpaḥah,* and not the status of the offspring. The status of the offspring is due to their relationship with both mothers, and not the fathers, since matriliny was still observed.[39]

Each matriarch would become the ancestress of a clan, the *mishpaḥah.* The sons of the women in each unit became the legitimate heirs of the matriarchs but maintained the status of their mothers. This in itself implies that the matriarchs had a legacy to endow. (They presumably also had daughters, but these are not mentioned except for Leah's daughter Dinah; we lack information in the biblical record as to the status and function of daughters.)

Hagar is first mentioned in the Genesis narrative ten years after Sarah and Abraham have been in Canaan (Gen. 16:3). Since she was not named in the preliminary report of the immigration of Terah and his family from Ur to Haran (Gen. 11:31), Hagar was presumably not presented to Sarah by her father Terah at her marriage, as later Zilpah and Bilhah were granted to Leah and Rachel by their father Laban.

From the very start Hagar is characterized as "the Egyptian." Because of this portrayal legend concludes that "Hagar was Sarah's property, not her husband's. She had received her from Pharaoh, the father of Hagar," at the time of Sarah and Abraham's visit to Egypt shortly after they arrive in Canaan (Gen. 12:10).[40] On the basis of legend, then, we can surmise that the two women had been associated with one another for the better part of a decade (Gen. 16:3) before the biblical account mentions the handmaid's existence. Hagar, however, is the mother of Abraham's firstborn son; but for the priests, the child of a slave cannot be the son of a patriarch. There was obviously a necessity to elevate Hagar's status even though she continued to be regarded as a slave by them. A special place was devised for her by imagining her as the daughter of pharaoh.

It is imperative, then, that we view the accounts of Hagar in the climate in which she functioned, without our preconceived ideas of nuclear family and concubine/slave adjunct. Instead, we must now conceive of Hagar as what she most probably was: the companion of Sarah.

NOTES

1. The Importance of Interpretation

1. In the Hebrew Bible Hagar is the ancestress of the Arab peoples; in the Qur'an she is the ancestress of the Islamic nation. It is well to remember that not all Arabs are Muslim, and not all Muslims are Arab. The term "Arab" is a linguistic designation.

2. For example, Kathleen M. Kenyon, *The Bible and Recent Archaeology,* rev. ed. (Atlanta: John Knox Press, 1987), 19 ff; and Gaalya Cornfeld and David Noel Freedman, *Archaeology of the Bible: Book by Book* (San Francisco: Harper & Row, 1976), 17 ff. However, I do not know of any archaeologist who has specifically searched for any of the Matriarchs or objects and activities associated with them.

3. Quoted in Thomas L. Thompson, *The Origin Tradition of Ancient Israel* (Sheffield: JSOT Press, #55, 1987), 51. Thomas L. Thompson, *The Historicity of Patriarchal Narratives: A Quest for the Historical Abraham* (Berlin and New York: Walter de Gruyter, 1974), is a good example.

4. Charles Cutler Torrey, *The Jewish Foundation of Islam* (New York: Bloch, 1933), 64. However, there is no evidence for Torrey's statement.

5. From the root meaning "to surrender," that is, to Allah.

6. Kathleen M. Kenyon, *The Bible and Recent Archaeology* (Atlanta: John Knox Press, Revised Edition, 1987), 20.

7. Kenyon, 24.

8. Kenyon, 25–26.

9. See my section on the Jemdet Nasr period in Savina J. Teubal, *Sarah the Priestess: The First Matriarch of Genesis* (Athens, OH: Swallow Press, 1984), 73–76.

10. The Pentateuch comprises the first five books of the Hebrew Bible—Genesis, Exodus, Leviticus, Numbers, and Deuteronomy—called the Torah, in Hebrew. On literary criticism see Norman C. Habel, *Literary Criticism of the Old Testament* (Philadelphia: Fortress Press, 1973). On form criticism see Gene M. Tucker, *Form Criticism of the Old Testament* (Philadelphia: Fortress Press, 1971). For an excellent summary of narrative approaches to the Pentateuch, see Thompson, *Origin Tradition,* 42–59.

11. Douglas A. Knight, "The Pentateuch," in *The Hebrew Bible and Its Modern Interpreters,* edited by Douglas A. Knight and Gene M. Tucker (Philadelphia: Fortress Press, 1985), 267.

12. E. A. Speiser, *Genesis.* See his comment, 105 ff.

13. Robert Alter, *The Art of Biblical Narrative* (New York: Basic Books, 1981), 50.

14. Martin Noth, *A History of Pentateuchal Traditions,* translated by Bernhard W. Anderson (Englewood Cliffs, NJ: Prentice-Hall, 1972), 36.

15. *Ibid.,* 57–58, 103–104.

16. Compare Teubal, *Sarah the Priestess,* 137.

17. Noth, *History,* 109.

18. This subsection is a brief commentary on the considerable volume of material on the subject. Students may refer to the works of Noth, Gunkel, and van Seters (see Bibliography). Followers of the German school no longer use the Documentary

Hypothesis as a tool to clarify or analyze text. For an overview of this opposition see Thompson, *Origin Tradition,* chapter 2, and in particular, 49.

19. Tucker, *Form Criticism,* 19.

20. Richard Elliott Friedman, *Who Wrote the Bible?* (New York: Summit Books, 1987), 221.

21. *Ibid.,* 62.

22. *Ibid.,* 86.

23. *Ibid.,* 85.

24. William W. Hallo and J. J. A. van Dijk, *The Exaltation of Inanna* (New Haven and London: Yale University Press, 1968).

25. Rivkah Harris, "The Female 'Sage' in Ancient Near Eastern Literature," unpublished, 4–5. Dr. Harris was kind enough to send me a copy of her manuscript before publication.

26. *Ibid.,* 6.

27. *Ibid.,* 6.

28. *Ibid.,* 5.

29. George E. Mendenhall, *The Tenth Generation: The Origins of Biblical Tradition* (Baltimore and London: Johns Hopkins University Press, 1973), 182.

30. *Ibid.,* 182–83.

31. *Ibid.,* 182.

32. Judges 1:8 attributes the capture of Jerusalem to the tribe of Judah, long before David and Joab.

33. P. Kyle McCarter, Jr., does not see in this incident a religious connotation. Compare *II Samuel: A New Translation with Introduction and Commentary. The Anchor Bible,* Vol. 9 (Garden City, NY: Doubleday, 1984), 189.

34. *Ibid.,* 189.

35. *Ibid.,* 188.

36. *Ibid.,* 172 and 188.

37. Hallo and van Dijk, *Exaltation of Inanna,* chapter 2, "*nin-me-sar-ra:* Transliteration and Translation" (New Haven: Yale University Press, 1968), 25–27.

38. Teubal, *Sarah the Priestess,* 60.

39. It is feasible that Judah was Leah's youngest son. According to Genesis 29:35, after Judah, Leah stopped bearing; and, when Leah saw that she had stopped bearing, she took her *shifhah* Zilpah and gave her to Jacob as wife (Gen. 30:9). The story of the mandrakes (Gen. 14–21) is self-contained and does not seem to belong to the Leah lore, since she had no trouble conceiving. At any rate it is unique that Leah bore her children before her *shifhah,* as with the other Matriarchs and their handmaids. It is believed that verses 17–24 are the work of later editors. See *The Interpreter's Dictionary of the Bible,* Vol. 3 (Nashville: Abingdon, 1962), 256.

40. That is, Leah's (youngest) tribe was taking over the priestly functions of the Rachel('s youngest) tribe.

41. Simon J. De Vries, "Moses and David as Cult Founders," *Journal of Biblical Literature 107* No. 4 (1988). De Vries traces the Chronicler's promotion of David as cult founder, establishing the legitimacy of the Levites over the priests, the "sons of Aaron."

42. Robert R. Wilson, *Genealogy and History in the Biblical World* (New Haven and London: Yale University Press, 1977), 194.

43. W. B. Emery, *Archaic Egypt: Culture and Civilization in Egypt Five Thousand Years Ago* (Middlesex, England: Penguin, 1987), 51.

44. Jill Kamil, *Sakkara and Memphis: A Guide to the Necropolis and the Ancient Capital,* 2d ed. (London and New York: Longman, 1985), 23.

45. The name *Shausa* is uncertain. McCarter, Jr., *II Samuel,* 256, referring to pronunciation: Its origin is non-Semitic and is probably Egyptian.

46. Matriliny was still observed in family relationships at least till the time of Solomon. See my "Matrilineal Descent" in Teubal, *Sarah the Priestess,* 54–58.

47. Carol Meyers, *Discovering Eve: Ancient Israelite Women in Context* (Oxford: Oxford University Press, 1988), 16.

2. Androcentrism: Texts Out of Context

1. For some characteristics of biblical patriarchy see Raphael Patai, *The Seed of Abraham: Jews and Arabs in Contact and Conflict* (Salt Lake City: University of Utah Press, 1986), 233–34.

2. Claus Westermann, *Genesis 12–36, A Commentary,* translated by John J. Scullion S.J. (Minneapolis: Augsburgh, 1985), 234–35.

3. A misprint in the Skinner original has a reference to Genesis *22:8–21.* See John Skinner, *A Critical and Exegetical Commentary on Genesis* (Edinburgh: T. & T. Clark, 1969), 285.

4. Jill Kamil, *Sakkara and Memphis: A Guide to the Necropolis and the Ancient Capital,* 2d ed. (London and New York: Longman, 1985), 18. Kamil's comment, though consigned to Egypt, can be generalized to include the whole of the ancient Near East.

5. Hermann Gunkel's argument that "the manner in which the narratives speak of God is one of the surest means of determining whether they are historic or poetic" is unconvincing. Gunkel's statement does not consider religious experience other than his own. Belief in the interaction between people and the supernatural was no less sincere in ancient times than the contemporary certainty of Christians that Jesus was a deity among humans. Hermann Gunkel, *The Legends of Genesis: The Biblical Saga and History* (New York: Schocken Books, 1964), 8.

6. In Genesis 16:2 Sarah determines to procure a child even though she claims that "YHWH kept me from bearing." Also Abraham, who negotiates the destiny of Sodom with YHWH, in Genesis 18:24–25.

7. Hermann Gunkel views anthropomorphism as evidence that the narratives are poetic rather than historical. Gunkel, *Legends of Genesis,* 8.

8. Westermann acknowledges that Sarah may be using a "standard formula" but does not link the action to a religious ceremony (Westermann, *Genesis 12–36,* 299). However, I think it is a question of how religion is defined. See below.

9. Robert Alter, *The Art of Biblical Narrative* (New York: Basic Books, 1981), 58.

10. *Ibid.,* 51.

11. Esther Fuchs, "Structure and Patriarchal Functions in the Biblical Betrothal Type-Scene: Some Preliminary Notes," *Journal of Feminist Studies in Religion 3,* No. 1 (Spring 1987): 7.

12. Alter, *Biblical Narratives,* 52.

13. Barbara Walker, *The Woman's Encyclopedia of Myths and Symbols* (San Francisco: Harper & Row, 1983), 1067.

14. Robert Briffault, *The Mothers* (New York: Athenaeum, 1977), 316.

15. In antiquity the gods Marduk of Babylonia, Baal of Ugarit, Ptah, Amon-Re, and Aton of Egypt, were all instituted as supreme gods, overshadowing their female counterparts. Judaism, Christianity, and Islam eventually eradicated goddess worship and banned women from high religious office.

16. Peggie Reeves Sanday, *Female Power and Male Dominance: On the Origins of Sexual Inequality* (Cambridge University Press, 1981), 224.

17. Saul M. Olyan, *Asherah and the Cult of Yahweh in Israel* (Atlanta: Scholars Press, Society of Biblical Literature Monograph Series, #34, 1988), 74.

18. I owe the following analysis of my material on El Shaddai to the unpublished paper of Drorah Setel, "El Sadday and the Religion of the Matriarchs," 1986.

19. Semitic languages are written with consonants; vowels must be supplied. Thus meanings can be manipulated to suit an interpretation.

20. Setel's footnote: Frank Moore Cross, *Canaanite Myth and Hebrew Epic* (Cambridge: Harvard University Press, 1973), 46–50; Walter Wilfall, "El Shaddai or 'El of the Fields," *Zeitschrift fur die Altestememtliche Wissenschraft*, 1980, 24–32. The debate centers on whether the term *shaddai* means "mountain" or "field." In addition to a refusal to admit the possibility of various "truths" in the text, such an approach illustrates the denial of female experience possible in a supposedly "objective" process of inquiry.

21. Savina J. Teubal, *Sarah the Priestess: The First Matriarch of Genesis* (Athens, OH: Swallow Press, 1984), 93.

22. Steve Davies, "The Canaanite-Hebrew Goddess," in *The Book of the Goddess Past and Present: An Introduction to Her Religion* (New York: Crossroad, 1985), 73.

23. The nursemaid is mentioned, though not by name, when Rebekah leaves the household of her mother (Gen. 25:59).

24. Setel, *Sadday.*

25. Mara Lynn Keller, "The Eleusinian Mysteries of Demeter and Persephone: Fertility, Sexuality, and Rebirth," *Journal of Feminist Studies in Religion 4*, No. 1, (1988): 33.

26. Erich Neumann, *The Great Mother: An Analysis of the Archetype,* translated by Ralph Manheim (Princeton, NJ: Princeton University Press, 1972), 267. However, the single reproductive function between the bees may also have inspired the special sexual unions of the priestesses, which scholars refer to as "sacred marriage."

27. Note that with the other two matriarchs, Sarah and Rachel, the *shifhah* bears sons first, before they do. Zilpah's sons may also have been born before Leah's. That these sons bore the names of divinities could be significant. Also notable is the statement "Leah stopped bearing" after her last son, Judah. This would make Judah her youngest son. It is only after she presents Zilpah to Jacob that she gives birth again, herself. There seems to be some distortion in this section of the Leah story that deserves further analysis.

28. It is because of the power in naming that the P school inserted phrases claiming Abraham named Ishmael (Gen. 16:15) and Isaac (Gen. 21:3).

29. *The Interpreter's Dictionary of the Bible* (Nashville: Abingdon, 1962) Vol. 2, 335.

30. *Ibid.,* Vol. 1, 90.
    Ibid., 251.

31. Robert Graves and Raphael Patai, *Hebrew Myths: The Book of Genesis* (New York: McGraw-Hill, 1963), 218. Is there any connection between Asherah as symbol

of happiness, and the repeated references to Sarah's laughter in Asherah's terebinth grove at Mamre?

32. See *Treasures of the Holy Land: Ancient Art from the Israel Museum* (New York:
Metropolitan Museum of Art, 1986), 175.

33. Rabbi Dr. H. Freedman and Maurice Simon, trans. *Midrash Rabbah, "Genesis,"*
Vol. I (London: Soncino Press, 1951), 468.

34. Raphael Patai, *The Hebrew Goddess* (New York: KTAV, 1967), 35.

35. Avraham Negev, ed., *The Archaeological Encyclopedia of the Holy Land* (Nash-
ville:Thomas Nelson, 1986), 45–46.

36. Frank Moore Cross, *Canaanite Myth and Hebrew Epic: Essays in the History of the
Religion of Israel* (Cambridge: Harvard University Press, 1973), 29–30.

37. Jo Ann Hackett, "Sadday in Its Ancient Near Eastern Context," paper delivered
at the American Academy of Religion Convention, Epigraphy Section, Society
of Biblical Literature, Anaheim, California, 24 November 1985. I thank Dr.
Hackett for furnishing me with a copy of her paper soon after the conference.

38. John Van Seters, *Abraham in History and Tradition* (New Haven and London:
Yale University Press, 1975), 311. Van Seters questions the existence of an ex-
tensive E source in the Pentateuch, allocating most of it to an early J and a later J.

39. *Ibid.*

40. Martin Noth, *A History of Pentateuchal Traditions,* translated by Bernhard W. Anderson (Englewood Cliffs, NJ: Prentice-Hall, 1972), 20.

41. Edgar Innes Fripp, *The Composition of the Book of Genesis, with English Text and
Analysis* (London: David Nutt, 1892), 47.

42. Thomas L. Thompson, *The Origin Tradition of Ancient Israel* (Sheffield: JSOT
Press, #55, 1987), 89 shows the obverse, how verse 1 establishes the required
central motif, the question of *Abraham's* childlessness. He totally overlooks the
matriarchs' need or even desire for heirs.

43. As translated in *The Torah: A New Translation According to the Masoretic Text*
(Philadelphia: Jewish Publication Society of America, 1962), 34. I am using this
translation throughout my text because it is a good example of an androcentric
bias.

44. This phrase is variously translated "consort with my maid." *Ibid.,* 25; "Go, sleep
with my maidservant," *The NIV Interlinear Hebrew English Old Testament,* edited
by John Kohlenberger III, Vol. 1, (Grand Rapids, MI: Zondervan Publishing
House), 34 and expressions to that effect. However, Trible's translation is accurate: Phyllis Trible, *Texts of Terror: Literary-Feminist Readings of Biblical Narratives*
(Philadelphia: Fortress Press, 1984), 11.

45. This phrase is seen as belonging to the J source by Fripp, *Composition,* 47. However, in the continuation of the Sarah/Hagar of theE strand, Hagar is still with
Sarah (Gen. 21). I contend that a reason had to be devised for Hagar's departure.
Sarah's harshness became the motive for Hagar's flight. But Sarah's anger is directed at Abraham, not Hagar (see chapter 4).

46. Westermann, *Genesis,* 244–45, comments: "v.9 is regarded as a compensating
addition of the redactor. CH 21 presupposes that Hagar and Ishmael are with
Abraham and Sarah; so they must have gone back; the messenger's advice in v.9
brings Hagar back. But a mere redactional explanation is not enough. The redactor must have had something in mind with this advice. He indicates thereby his
own interpretation of the Hagar narrative: He understands God's intervention
after Hagar's flight as the fulfillment of Sarah's original plan; if Hagar goes back,

Sarah can have a son by means of her." Westermann fails to explain why Ishmael is never portrayed as Sarah's son even though Hagar returned to her.

47. According to Fripp, *Composition,* 47, "In spite of 'Iahveh' in verses 9, 10, the v.v. 8–10 do not belong to the original Iahvistic narrative. Observe the bad literary style of 9–11 'and the angel of Iahveh said to her . . . etc." In some instances I find Fripp's adjudication of sources closer to my own than I do those of later scholars.

48. John Skinner, *A Critical and Exegetical Commentary on Genesis* (Edinburgh: T. & T. Clark, 1969). Skinner arbitrarily makes the connection of Genesis 15, the promise of a bodily heir to Abram with Genesis 18, or 17, the promise of a son through Sarah, even though it seems quite clear to me that, in this instance, the text indicates a connection with the desert son, Ishmael.

49. Genesis 15 is a difficult passage throughout. Fripp, *Composition,* 46, believes that "there is no evidence that any Iahvistic (sic) material lies at the root of either 1–6 or 7–12." Speiser, *Genesis,* 110, suggests E as the questionable but possible author of verse 5.

50. Jacob M. Myers, *I Chronicles: Translated with Notes and Introduction* (Garden City, NY: Doubleday, 1965), 180.

51. Westermann, *Genesis,* 245, again attributes the promise of descendants to the Matriarch to the Patriarch; "The author is saying something about the significance of Abraham, the father; he is the father of many peoples, not only of Israel."

52. *Ibid.*

53. *Ibid.*

54. The Ishmaelites would have been called Abrahamites. In fact there is no genealogy of Abraham in the Bible (see below).

55. The episode itself does not give the reader any idea as to the age of the son of the *shifḥah* until he is banished. Only then are we told that: Early next morning Abraham took some bread and a skin of water and gave them to Hagar. He placed them on her shoulder, together with the child. This sentence makes it seem as though Hagar's son was not much older than his half-brother who had just been weaned. This insinuation, that the sequence deals with two small children, is what obscures the reason for Sarah's decision to separate the boys. (See chapter 9.)

56. As translated in *The Torah: A New Translation According to the Masoretic Text* (Philadelphia: Jewish Publication Society of America, 1962), 34.

57. Any more than Pharaoh's daughter seemed concerned about the ethnic background of Moses being different to her own.

58. Emery, *Archaic Egypt,* 39.

59. Kamil, *Sakkara,* 34.

60. Emery, *Archaic Egypt,* 203–205.

61. *Interpreter's Dictionary,* Vol. 3, 512.

62. Sir Alan Gardiner, *Egypt of the Pharaohs* (London: Oxford University Press, 1961), 412.

63. Emery, *Archaic Egypt,* 42.

64. *Ibid.,* 65.

3. Hagar the *Shifḥah:* Neither Slave nor Concubine

1. Savina J. Teubal, *Sarah the Priestess: The First Matriarch of Genesis* (Athens, OH: Swallow Press, 1984), 36.

2. E. A. Speiser, *Genesis: Introduction, Translation and Notes* (Garden City, NY: Doubleday, 1964), 116.

3. *Ibid.*

4. John Skinner, *A Critical and Exegetical Commentary on Genesis* (Edinburgh: T. & T. Clark, 1969), 284.

5. T. K. Cheyne and J. Sutherland, eds., *Encyclopedia Biblica: A Critical Dictionary of Literary, Political and Religious History, The Archaeological Geography and Natural History of the Bible,* Vol. II (London: Adam and Charles Black, 1899), column 1933.

6. See for example: Raphael Patai, *The Seed of Abraham: Jews and Arabs in Contact and Conflict* (Salt Lake City: University of Utah Press, 1986), 21; *The Interpreter's Dictionary of the Bible,* Vol. 2 (Nashville: Abingdon, 1962), 508; John Van Seters, *Abraham in History and Tradition* (New Haven and London: Yale University Press, 1975), 88.

7. Skinner, *Commentary on Genesis,* 285.

8. Phyllis Trible, *Texts of Terror: Literary-Feminist Readings of Biblical Narratives* (Philadelphia: Fortress Press, 1984), 10.

9. Rabbi Dr. Charles B. Chavel, trans., *Ramban (Nachmanides), Commentary on the Torah, Genesis* (New York: Shilo, 1971), 211.

10. Trible, *Texts,* 22–23.

11. J. J. Finkelstein, trans., *The Ancient Near East: A New Anthology of Texts and Pictures,* edited by James B. Pritchard (Princeton: Princeton University Press, 1975), 31.

12. *Interpreter's Dictionary,* Vol. 4, 385–86.

13. *Ibid.,* 383.

14. *Ibid.*

15. *Ibid.*

16. Carol Meyers, *Discovering Eve: Ancient Israelite Women in Context* (Oxford: Oxford University Press, 1988), 9–10.

17. Skinner, *Commentary on Genesis,* 285. This is a good example of the assumption that a slave is also a concubine.

18. The Rabbis were concerned that Hagar is stated to have conceived twice (Gen. 16:4 and 16:11). Jacob Neusner, *Genesis Rabbah: The Judaic Commentary to the Book of Genesis, A New American Translation* (Atlanta: Scholars Press, 1985), 151.

19. *Ibid.,* 148. Since the *naditu* priestesses were to avoid pregnancy they must have been well versed in the most favorable and unfavorable times of fertilization in their menstrual cycles. It may have been due to this knowledge that the matriarchs seem to have chosen specific times for their sexual unions.

20. Teubal, *Sarah the Priestess,* 52, 94.

21. See, for instance, Genesis 30:9, which the Jewish Publication Society of America translates: "When Leah saw that she had stopped bearing, she took her maid Zilpah and gave her to Jacob as concubine," 53. In fact, in verse 16 Leah says to Jacob, "You are to sleep with me, for I have *hired* you with my son's mandrakes." This does not indicate a "master's" sexual dominance over his wife or her handmaid.

22. William A. Ward, *Essays on Feminine Titles of the Middle Kingdom and Related Subjects* (Beirut: American University of Beirut, 1986), 60–61.

23. *Ibid.,* 59.

24. Van Seters, *Abraham,* 88.

25. Genesis 17:1, 6, 16, 20 where El Shaddai blesses with fertility Abraham, Sarah, and Ishmael.

26. F. Brown, S. R. Driver, and C. A. Briggs, *Hebrew Lexicon of the Old Testament* (Oxford: Clarendon Press, 1951), 1046.

27. *Ibid.*

28. *Ibid.,* 51.

29. *Ben Yehudah Dictionary and Thesaurus of the Hebrew Language; Complete International Centennial Edition,* Vol. 3 (New York: Thomas Yoseloff, 1959), 7380.

30. C. Umhad Wolf, "The Terminology of Israel's Tribal Organization," *Journal of Biblical Literature 65,* (1946): 47.

31. Michael C. Astour, "Tamar the Hieroduk: An Essay in the Methods of Vestigal Motifs," *Journal of Biblical Literature 85* (1966): 186.

32. See Joshua's description of the organization of Bnei Israel (nation); *mth, shbt* (tribe), *mshpahah* (clan), *bait ab* (household or family) (Josh. 7:14).

33. *Interpreter's Dictionary,* Vol. 4, 699.

34. *Ibid.*

35. See Teubal, *Sarah the Priestess,* 60 ff.

36. Leah bore four sons and "Then she stopped bearing" (Gen. 29:35). Since Judah became preeminent, I believe he must originally have been Leah's youngest son. The episode of the mandrakes (verses 14–16) must have been added to account for the twelve tribes of Jacob. *Interpreter's Dictionary,* Vol. 4, 704-703.

37. In G. F. Moore's commentary on Judges he concludes that in the technical language of the Priestly code *mishpahah* was subdivided into households, which were the "houses of the mother['s father]" (*beit ab imo*), 243.

38. Teubal, *Sarah the Priestess,* 71.

39. *Ibid.,* 54 ff.

40. Louis Ginzberg, *The Legends of the Jews,* translated by Henrietta Szold (Philadelphia: Jewish Publication Society of America, 1909), 108.

PART II. THE SILENT TEXTS

Phrases taken out of context and incorporated into a different context constitute a "silent text." By altering their context such phrases convey a message radically different from their original intent.

The events in Hagar's life are told in three stages in the biblical narratives:

1. The conception of her child.
2. The rejection of her child.
3. The prophecy of her destiny.

Each of these stages in the life of Hagar has been incorporated into the context of the life of the patriarch Abraham with the intent of connecting him to her son, thus obscuring the position of Hagar and confusing the identity of her son.

To discover the original intent these stages, the silent texts, must be isolated from their present framework in the received text. Once the silent texts become evident, we can recover the objective of their message.

The Hagar accounts occur in two different geographical areas: in the household of Sarah in Hebron and in the deserts of Beer-sheva and Shur. As we shall see, the stories of each region reflect two independent traditions: that of Hagar the Egyptian and that of the Desert Matriarch. Each is an account of the genesis of a people: the Hagarites and the Ishmaelites.

4. Hagar Conceives: The Genesis of Transformation

Genesis 16

To past commentators the pivotal issues in the Genesis 16:1–6 story are twofold: The first is the friction and hostility between the two matriarchs, Hagar and Sarah. The second, and more important, is the conception of Abraham's firstborn, Ishmael, by the patriarch's concubine.

But to regard these as the dominant issues creates a distorted emphasis. The real underlying theme of the passages in question concerns the challenge posed to Sarah's method of acquiring an heir through Hagar: the acquisition by one woman of another woman's child. The passages explain both Sarah's loss of her expected heir and the basis on which Hagar came to retrieve possession of her child. We will come to see that the provocation for this loss does not stem from a conflict between Sarah and Hagar, but between Sarah and Abraham. It is the patriarch who instigates the dispute and its consequences: the eventual separation of the two women.

The sequence is written by J, whose deft strokes create a story of intensity and mounting interest. J's technique, while highly effective, sacrifices the delineation of character and omits essential details that could have contributed to a clearer understanding of the account. Filling these lacunae, an act of interpretation, is risky because it attempts to recreate from a subjective viewpoint elements for which there is no documentation.

Yet one of the most poignant episodes in the Genesis narratives is that of the relationship between these two women.

Initially called "Sarai," Sarah is childless. She presents Hagar to her husband, Abraham (then Abram), "That I may be built up by her" (16:2)—that is, the child of Hagar would become Sarah's heir/ess. Abraham fulfills Sarah's request; Hagar becomes pregnant. But the *shifḥah* becomes insolent to Sarah, Sarah reprimands her harshly, and Hagar runs away. The story is told as though surrogate motherhood was commonplace in that era. The vital issue would thus seem to be the nature of the attitudes of the women toward each other.

Indeed, potential conflicts arising between a prospective mother and substitute mother emerged as issues in the ancient Near East thousands of years ago.[1] The military ruler Hammurapi attempted to deal with them in the eighteenth century BCE.[2] Various contracts defining the particulars of the concerned parties in surrogate parenting have been unearthed in our century in the Middle East.

Like the biblical story, the Hammurapi regulation (CH 146) is concerned with the rights of the childless (*naditu*) priestess. No rights are given to the mother, who is a slave and may be punished for misconduct (CH 146). There is thus no question as to who acquires the future child: It belongs to the priestess. The Genesis narrative, however, is less clear. Sarah demands her rights when the conflict becomes intolerable to her (Gen. 16:5). But although she is rewarded, in that she can discipline the offender (16:6), she does not, as in the Hammurapi case, acquire the heir. Hagar, the mother, retains the child as her own (Gen. 21:10).

Conventionally, the issues that center on the mother problem in the story of Sarah and Hagar are deflected to the emotional attitude of the women. Robert Alter refers to the theme of Genesis 16 as being "only a special variation of the recurrent story of bitter rivalry between a barren, favored wife and a fertile co-wife or concubine."[3] And what seems to be the specific "special variation" to so many scholars about Genesis 16 is that "Abram plays a rather unfortunate role between these two stubborn women," as Claus Westermann puts it.[4] A. E. Speiser is perhaps the master at voicing the established message: "According to xvi 5, Sarah's hatred of Hagar stemmed from the concubine's tactless behavior toward her childless mistress; and Abraham was either unable or unwilling to intervene in the bitter rivalry between two headstrong women."[5]

Implied in this assumption of "bitter rivalry" is the view that the women are competing for Abraham's approval by producing offspring for him. The scholars do not even consider the possibility that the women's emotion might stem from a source other than *maternal pride* or *mutual jealousy*. Nor do they give attention to the predicament of the future mother. Even Hammurapi's design in CH 146 is to focus on the circumstances of women's behavior with each other, as though the question of status would take precedence over a mother's rights or emotions. Consideration of a mother's rights regarding her child is not even broached by Hammurapi. However, in the biblical story the women's rights are discernible, though veiled.

As is characteristic of any well-written account, a statement of the core issue appears in the opening sentence of Genesis 16.[6]

She [Sarai] had an Egyptian *shifhah* and her name was Hagar; so Sarai said to Abram, "See how it is, YHWH kept me from bearing; pray go into my *shifhah* perhaps I may be built up by her. (16:2).

The active participant is the matriarch Sarah; the patriarch is passive. The story continues until a crisis is reached in verse 5:

**So Sarai said to Abram, "The wrong done me is on you! I myself put my *shifhah* into your arms; now that she sees she is pregnant, I am despised in her eyes.
May YHWH judge between me and between you!**

At this point, then, Sarah is the central figure in the story; she has a concern: childlessness. She attempts to overcome it, providing herself with a substitute. Her effort is thwarted.

But by whom? In answering this question the original intent is shifted.

J does not recognize that the focus of this episode is about two women's effort to procure succession for themselves. Instead, he draws attention to Sarah's feelings about Hagar's behavior. From this point of view Phyllis Trible seems right: In the biblical account Sarah never speaks to Hagar nor utters her name because, Trible maintains, "For Sarah, Hagar is an instrument, not a person."[7] But Trible's emphasis is erroneous. Rather than chiding her *shifḥah* for insolence, Sarah surprisingly ignores her and turns on her husband instead. The discord arose only when Hagar knew she had conceived: only then did she become disrespectful. Moreover, we need to keep in mind that there was no hint of disunity between the women when Sarah suggested to Abraham that Hagar represent her. Sarah, then, does not blame Hagar; rather, she harshly reprimands her husband. What is the reason for this?

We will come to see that Sarah is angered, not primarily because of a personal slight, and certainly not because of "female jealousy," as traditional gloss has it. Rather, she is angered because Hagar's disposition flouts the laws that Sarah honors.[8]

THE CONFLICT

Sarah utters two phrases that help to elucidate the problem (Gen. 16:2 and 5). Significantly, both remarks contain formulas.[9] Anyone listening to or reading the narrative in ancient times would certainly have recognized the legal tone. In her first exchange Sarah uses what may be a standard formula, one that will be repeated by Rachel in Genesis 30:3 in a related context.[10]

Go now into my *shifḥah* that I may be built up by her. (Gen. 16:2)

CH 146 concerns a *naditu*/priestess acquiring descendants for her husband and herself. But Sarah, like Rachel after her, is anxious to have an heir of her own.[11] And she seeks the heir in what appears to be a ritually or legally prescribed manner.

The biblical text continues:

And Abram listened to the voice of Sarai and he went into Hagar and she conceived. Gen. 16:2-4).[12]

Because the sexual act is immediately followed by the conception, the rabbis understood that Hagar conceived from her first intimacy with Abraham.[13] The immediacy of conception as described in the text supports the notion that this was, indeed, a ritual union rather than the beginning of lengthy period of concubinage.

And when she saw that she was pregnant her mistress was despised in her eyes. (Gen. 16:4)

Note that the biblical account does not actually tell us how Hagar expressed her contempt for Sarah, or even *if* she addressed it to Sarah, nor does Sarah reprimand Hagar.

Instead, the matriarch turns to Abraham and voices her second significant phrase:

The wrong done me is on you! I, myself put my *shifḥah* in your arms; now that she sees that she is pregnant I am despised in her eyes.[14] (Gen. 16:4)

The fact that Sarah addresses her husband with vexed indignation denotes culpability on his part. Sarah has obviously seen the conflict as one between herself and Abraham, not between herself and Hagar. It is almost as though she were saying to him, "All these years things have been fine between Hagar and me; but now because of you, she has turned against me. You are to blame!"

It is crucial to understand that, according to the received text, in the cultural system they brought with them from

Mesopotamia none of these people had options. Sarah could not have descendants except through Hagar. Hagar was to deliver a child for Sarah but not bear children for herself.[15] Abraham's position was similar to that of Hagar's: His role was to provide heritage for Sarah's lineage in a preordained way, using a traditional method that did not recognize him or the substitute wife as parent.[16]

Apart from this there must have been a prior understanding—an oral or written agreement—between the participants in the ritual, which both Sarah and Hagar were duty-bound to honor and which was witnessed by the divinity. Furthermore, in her capacity as *shifḥah* of Sarah, Hagar is beholden to the goddess or god of Sarah (the deity who witnessed the agreement between Hagar and Sarah), even as Abraham's household was obligated to the command of his god (Gen. 17:12). In other words, Hagar had made an agreement with Sarah that Abraham had promised to honor. Abraham broke his part of the agreement threatening Sarah's acquisition of an heir/ess through Hagar. Hagar, as *shifḥah* of Sarah, was bound to her position and could not change it. But her attitude toward Sarah, after her association with the patriarch, showed that Abraham was the catalyst that established a new chain of events to challenge the status quo.

REASSESSING THE CONFLICT

To understand what happened in the episode in Genesis 16, we must take a closer look at Sarah's second pronouncement. The matriarch's first words of admonishment to Abraham are *ḥamasi aleḥa,* "my fury is against you!" The Hebrew root of the first word, *ḥamas,* is a strictly legal term denoting lawlessness and injustice. Speiser comments that "The same force is reflected in the Akkadian verb *ḥabalum* "to deprive someone of his legal rights."[17] The Code of Hammurapi explicitly states that women of whatever rank who are to bear children may not claim equality with the childless women they will represent. To do so would have legal implications.

Hamasi aleḥa is more than an invocation of Sarah's legal rights, however, because the phrase is a kind of curse. What Sarah is actually saying to Abraham is: "That I am deprived of my rights is on you!" (on your head).[18] A malediction, among other things, was designed to protect the terms of a contract by being directed at a future violator of a treaty or agreement.[19]

East Semitic curse formulations rely on the deity to execute the desired effect.[20] Sarah duly ends her malediction with the formula[21] "YHWH decide between me [*beini*] and between you [*u-beineḥ*]!" Rashi points out that *beinḥ* is second person feminine and should not be vocalized as masculine.[22] Rashi's insight is corroborated in Genesis 31:49–50, where both YHWH and Elohim are invoked as witnesses to an agreement between Laban and Jacob, on penalty of injury (Gen. 31:52). The "between me and between you" of this section is in the masculine form, *beini u-beinḥa.* Sarah then, in her last phrase, addresses *Hagar,* and forces a decision, saying in effect, "Let YHWH (who was witness) decide which one of us the child will be heir to." Since the main theme in the Hagar and Sarah stories pertains to the reorganization of the relationship between the matriarchs and their offspring, it seems much more appropriate to perceive the demand addressed to YHWH as a reference to the mother and the social mother rather than to Sarah and Abraham, as traditionally understood.[23]

Sarah's use of formal terminology, leaving the decision to the witnessing deity, indicates that her method of acquiring an heir also had the force of legal statutes behind it. Consequently, Abraham's course was tantamount to breaking the law in Sarah's eyes, and license for rebellion in Hagar's.

What did Sarah blame Abraham for? Sarah's anger is in direct relation to Hagar's behavior: claiming equality regarding motherhood. What link was there between Hagar's claim and Sarah's motherhood? What connection was there between Hagar's claim and Sarah's anger directed at her husband? Although Abraham's infraction is not clearly defined, the text seems to indicate that Abraham's behavior generated doubt

regarding Sarah's claim to Hagar's child. Sarah's severe re-
proach must have stemmed from the terms of an accord or
contract that Abraham had breached. Abraham's offense, deserving of malediction, was his intent to override the authority of the matriarch by instigating the rebellion of Hagar, *thus
attempting to deprive Sarah of her legal right to an heir.*

To determine the outcome Sarah relies on the curse formula, in which a divinity is called upon to resolve the issue.
Abraham, perhaps fearing the curse (of a priestess?) gives no
accounting to Sarah in regard to his conduct.[24] Instead, his
**"See your *shifḥah* is in your hands, do with her what is
good in your eyes"** admits a lack of authority on the patriarch's part vis-à-vis Sarah, and a distancing of himself from
the *shifḥah*.

This is far from a confrontation of jealousy between two
women. There is a great deal at issue:

1. At Abraham's instigation, Hagar's harmony with Sarah
   has been challenged.
2. Furthermore, Sarah's practice of having a woman bear a
   child for her is being contested.
3. Sarah is at risk of losing an heir/ess because of this
   changed attitude.

Sarah's fury is nevertheless aimed at Abraham for permit-
ting an alternate course to develop, a reorganization so profound that only the decision of a divinity could resolve it.

A tremendous transformation has taken place from the initial direction of the narrative. In this episode Sarah is losing
an heir; Hagar (with Abraham) is gaining one.

This new interpretation of the story of Genesis 16 shows us
that the two matriarchs, Hagar and Sarah, were initially not in
conflict with each other over the issue of acquiring an heir/ess
for Sarah. Hagar has spent close to a decade in the company of
Sarah, neither marrying nor becoming a mother.[25] Sarah requires Hagar's service on only one occasion. There are no
signs that Hagar rebelled or dissented in any way when Sarah

suggested she allow the patriarch to impregnate her. It could very well have been an honor to bear the heir of a priestess. The tenor of their relationship changes only after Hagar's association with Abraham, and it is the patriarch who is the focus of Sarah's anger, not Hagar, making it clear that the change was initiated by Abraham. It is presumably Abraham's attitude that causes a situation in which Sarah is (*tekal*) "lowered in her [Hagar's] esteem."[26] The patriarch then defers to Sarah's reaction: **"Your *shifḥah* is in your hands. Deal with her as you think right,"** he 'says to her. As Westermann acknowledges, "It is striking that Abraham's decision is completely in favor of Sarah."[27] Westermann presumes that a *decision* is made by Abraham, who "gives expression to the judgment of God who takes care of the interests of the disadvantaged."[28] But the decision is "striking" if the only culprit is Hagar! Abraham is simply acknowledging that he has no rights in regard to the *shifḥah* of Sarah, or in the resolution of the issue at hand.

"May YHWH decide between me and between you" then, questions the custom of a Mesopotamian priestess of acquiring an heir through her *shifḥah,* rather than a depiction of the friction and hostility between two matriarchs.

THE LOST BIRTH STORY

The conception of Ishmael is described twice, suggesting it was an event of some consequence. The birth of Hagar's son was clearly a meaningful event in the lives of Hagar, Sarah, and Abraham. Why, then, was it excluded from the accounts?

The absence of a birth-story deprives us of a clear accounting of the Hagar-Sarah record. Certainly, the circumstances surrounding the actual birth would be enlightening: Had there been a precise description of the birth of Hagar's son, we would have had a better insight into the relationship between Hagar and Sarah and the status of the son. The manner in which the child was born established his or her social position. If Hagar's son had been born "on Sarah's knees"—the prescribed method for a priestess to acquire heirs—we would have had the assurance that he was Sarah's heir. A description of the birth scene is critical because the method of giving birth in this context would establish both the status of the child being born and the social context in which the event occurs. A specific procedure was followed when a priestess acquired the child of her companion, whether sister priestess, sibling, or slave: The woman acquiring the child—that is, the priestess—took part in the birth process (Plate 7). Without the knowledge of how Hagar's son was born the sequel to the story is obscured.

J describes the annunciation of the birth of Ishmael (Gen. 16:11) in a desert scene following the pregnancy of Hagar in Sarah's household (Gen. 16:4). This section ends with a standard P formula announcing the birth of a son to Abraham, his naming of the son, and the patriarch's age at the time of the event. Immediately following that statement P inserts the covenant and circumcision sequence (Gen. 17), in which the patriarch circumcises both himself and his son, Ishmael, who is now thirteen years old. Missing between Hagar's conception of her son (Gen. 16) and the circumcision of her then thirteen-year-old (Gen. 17) is a narrative account of the birth of this son.

The exclusion of the birth scene of Hagar's son creates a dramatic transformation in the record of Hagar's life story. Without the story of the birth much is unclear: Was Hagar's son born in Sarah's household or in the desert? Did Hagar claim the child as her own, or did he remain the heir of Sarah?

Initially, Hagar's child was to "build up" Sarah's lineage. Sarah had said to Abraham, **"Go into my *shifhah, ulai ibane mimena,"*** often translated "perhaps I shall have a son through her," although the accurate rendition would be "perhaps I can be built up (that is, build a family) through her."[29] Sarah is indicating here that the heir/ess will be her's, not Abra-

PLATE 7. "This specific procedure was followed when a priestess acquired the child of her companion." *Birth group. (Cyprus eighth century CE). Published by permission of the Director of Antiquities and the Cyprus Museum. Nicosea, Cyprus.*

ham's. Rachel's first conception by way of her *shifḥah* corresponded to Sarah's: *"ve-ibane gam anoḥi mimena"* (that perhaps I too can be built up [Gen. 30:3]). Rachel uses almost the same terminology as Sarah and acquires a child by means of her *shifḥah* because she is also childless, implying a prescribed practice. In Rachel's case, however, the method of bearing the child is spelled out *veteled al birkai,* "so that she [Bilhah] can bear on my knees."

The expression to *bear on one's knees* is used in the Bible in reference to men as well as women, though with different connotation. Genesis 50:23 records: "Joseph lived to see children of the third generation of [his son] Ephraim; the children of Machir son of Manasseh were likewise born upon Joseph's knees." The biblical texts seem to corroborate the need of Babylonian men to legitimize their offspring.[30] Jacob "adopts" Joseph's sons, Ephraim and Manasseh, into his clan by taking the children on *his knees* (Gen. 48:5, 12), a general symbol of adoption.[31] In this case the children were sons of Joseph's Egyptian wife, the unnamed daughter of the priest Poti-phera. Jacob must have regarded these sons as their mother's descendants and was therefore obliged to observe an established custom before they could be acknowledged as members of his *mishpaḥah.*

With women, on the other hand, "bearing on one's knees" was literal. The mother who gave birth would sit between the legs of the woman who would become her child's social parent while the midwife assisted in the delivery. If this specific procedure was followed when Hagar gave birth to Sarah's presumptive heir, it presents a dramatic image of the intimate relationship necessary between the two women. If the clay group from Cyprus (Plate 7) is illustrative of a ritual birth as experienced by Hagar in Canaan, Sarah would have held Hagar in her arms and probably assisted in the birth process from behind. Sarah's function would be intimately connected to Hagar's experience. They may also have sought a safe and easy delivery from a same protective divinity.

One biblical account suggests that, indeed, Hagar gave birth to her son "on the knees" of Sarah. A statement made by Sarah (Gen. 21:10) implies that Hagar's son enjoys the same status as the son of the *shifḥah* and is therefore still Sarah's heir, even after her own son has been born:

She said to Abraham, "Cast out that salve-woman and her son, for the son of that slave shall not share in the inheritance with my son, with Isaak."

This implies equality between the sons. If the sons have the same status regarding the inheritance, Sarah must still regard Hagar's son as her heir after the birth of Isaak. If Hagar's son is Sarah's heir, the birth must have been carried out in the prescribed manner. But without a description of the birth the status of Hagar's son is left unclear. It is necessary to establish (1) that Hagar's son was not born in the desert but "on the knees" of Sarah, and (2) that the second reference to conception means that a different son was born to the Desert Matriarch.

Apart from that, the close participation between the women has been severed from the account. It is important to note that Hagar is not separated from her child, nor are Bilhah or Zilpah from theirs; all remain within the family unit, the *mishpaḥah,* to give suck and bring up their own children, even though these children were officially heirs of their social mothers. The children too would have enjoyed the love and attention of both women. It was only in later times, with the formation of elite nuclear family units, that mothers were separated from their kin, their companions, and also their children, in cases of adoption.

It is also important to remember that the women's association with each other usually began with the marriage of one of them and lasted a lifetime. The perplexing notice of the death of Deborah, the "nurse" of Rebekah, and her burial under a sacred tree (Gen. 35:8) is probably an indication of a long association between Rebekah and her companion. Rebekah is the only matriarch who lacks a *shifḥah*. The misplaced notice of the death of Deborah (Gen. 35:8), described as Rebekah's wet-nurse, must have occurred sometime during the twenty years between Rebekah's marriage and the birth of her twins.[32] Deborah was buried under a sacred tree, an indication of her distinctive status.

Although Abraham's intention and Hagar's rebellious behavior incite Sarah's anger, there is nothing in the narratives to suggest that Sarah disinherits Hagar's son until after she has conceived, borne, and weaned her *own* child. On the contrary, since Sarah maintains that Hagar's son enjoys the same status as her own son Isaak (Gen. 21:10), both women must have taken part in the ritual delivery of Hagar's son, who became and remained Sarah's heir.

Since Hagar's son was not born in the desert but in Sarah's household, both women with their children continued to share the same abode for a considerable length of time, indicating a continued relationship of the mothers and the son.

Although occasional antagonism between the women cannot be overruled, there is no evidence in the narratives that it existed as an ongoing condition. The reason for Sarah's later decision to separate the two boys was not based on hostility between the two women but, as will become evident, on the (divinely directed) destiny of the two sons.

Nothing further in the J narrative directly relates to the association of Hagar and Sarah, and we are left with the impression that their lengthy alliance has been severed irreparably. Yet this is not the case. The decision of YHWH—that Sarah bear her own child—does not immediately affect the relationship between the two women. It ends, years later, when a pathway is opened for Hagar to seek her own future.

5. Sarah Conceives: The Miracle in Laughter
Genesis 18

The previous episode ended with Hagar and Sarah awaiting divine judgment, almost as if Sarah has challenged the deity to take sides. In desperation, Sarah had exclaimed to Hagar: "May YHWH judge between me and between you!" (Gen. 16:5b). If the lot falls to Sarah, Hagar's offspring will be Sarah's heir, as planned. If the lot falls to Hagar, Sarah will remain childless and without a successor. Her line will die out. The tension in the story mounts to an unbearable crisis. Clearly, neither Sarah, Hagar, nor Abraham has the authority to resolve the conflict. It has been left, so to speak, in the hands of providence.

In the biblical narrative as it now stands, however, the force of Sarah's demand "May YHWH judge between me and between you!" is lost because it is not immediately resolved. The reader's attention is suddenly directed to the desert conception of Ishmael (Gen. 16:7–16) and to the covenant and circumcision episode, interposed by P, in which the promise of succession is directed at the patriarch (Gen. 17). In neither of these does the deity implement a solution specifically to the Sarah/Hagar predicament.[1] However, divine resolution does come: in J's story in Genesis 18. There we find a promise not to Abraham, but to Sarah. Both Genesis 16 and 18 focus on Sarah's house being "built up" (*ibbane* [Gen 16:2]).

ANDROCENTRIC INFLUENCE

Moses ben Nahman (Nachmanides) saw in Genesis 18 the fulfillment of YHWH's promise to Abraham in Genesis

17:21: "But my covenant I will maintain with Isaak, whom Sarah shall bear to you this season."[2] Skinner, however, suggests that Genesis 18 is an immediate sequel to Genesis 13:18, "And Abraham moved his tent and came to dwell at the terebinths of Mamre which are in Hebron; and there he built an altar to YHWH." Skinner sees this as part of a "legendary cycle which fixes the residence of Abraham at Hebron."[3] He proposes that the Abraham of this series is different from the Abraham of a Genesis 16 cycle. But to my knowledge no scholar has connected the promise of a son to Sarah in Genesis 18 with Sarah's demand in Genesis 16.

Skinner views the two parts of Genesis 18—the "visitors" passage and the annunciation—as part of the same episode. "In the course of the conversation which naturally follows a meal," he writes, "an apparently casual question leads to an announcement which shows superhuman knowledge of the great blank in *Abraham's* life, and conveys a first intimation of the real nature of the visitors [italics mine]."[4] Westermann, on the other hand, sees that "two narratives have overlapped and been fused into one: (a) the promise of a child to a childless couple (or childless wife), and (b) the visit of a divine messenger(s) of a god(s) who rewards the reception and hospitality with a gift, in this case, the birth of a child."[5]

If the gift of a child is the reward for hospitality, however, that same gift of the child cannot be connected to a prior promise to Abraham or to Sarah of progeny. In fact, the sequence of the "three visitors" is a prelude to the annunciation of the birth of a child to Sarah.

SEPARATING THE SECTIONS

The episode in question is considered to be one of the most obscure in Genesis:[6]

YHWH appeared to him by the tents of Mamre; he was sitting at the entrance to the tent as the day grew hot. Looking up, he saw three men standing near him. (Gen. 18:1–2)

Abraham dozes under the terebinths of Mamre at the entrance of the tent when YHWH appears. But in the next verse Abraham is described as lifting up his eyes and seeing *three men* suddenly standing beside him. He runs toward them from the entrance of the tent and bows to the ground. The sequence continues with Abraham inviting the three visitors to a meal. After the meal YHWH, alone, announces the birth of a son to Sarah.

This story is most perplexing. It commences with YHWH appearing alone, followed by Abraham seeing and entertaining three visitors, and then YHWH alone foretelling the birth of a son to Sarah. The episode ends with Abraham escorting *three visitors* toward Sodom, which they are planning to destroy.

Were there three gods? One god and two angels? Three angels? Did Abraham recognize the supernatural character of his guest(s)? It would seem that he did not, until YHWH identifies himself toward the very end of the episode.[7]

Once again I believe that there has been a commingling of texts, but this time the sections are both by J.[8] There are actually three episodes: The first describes a meal, the second an annunciation, and the third the destruction of Sodom. The first two episodes concern Sarah's future. The third has no relevance to Sarah or her future; it describes the part two visitors play in the destruction of Sodom and the deliverance of Lot.[9] This sequence has nothing to do with Sarah's storyline, the future annunciation of the birth of Isaak.

To intertwine these strands was an editorial decision. This was easy because both incidents involved three figures—the visit to Mamre refers to *three* men and the Sodom incident alternates between men (Gen. 18:22) and three supernatural beings, YHWH and two angels (Gen. 19:1).

It is not immediately apparent (particularly in the English version), however, that sentences which describe a plurality of visitors partaking of a meal are consecutive and encompass one theme.[10] The second theme begins with verse 1, but its sequel describing the annunciation of a child to Sarah is not taken up until verse 9. The subject of the patriarch's entertaining three visitors has been woven with the primary concern of the episode, the annunciation to Sarah of her conception of a son. Westermann suggests that "It is likely that in the course of transmission the narrative of the promise (and birth) of a child as deliverance from distress was joined with a narrative variant in which this same promise was the gift of those whom the childless couple received as guests."[11]

The Genesis 18 episode can thus be divided into two separate narrative strands, one containing references to a sole deity and the other to three men.

EPISODE OF THE THREE VISITORS TO MAMRE

Let us review the strand in which there are three visitors. In this sequence the patriarch is the dominant actor in the story:

18 2 Looking up he saw, three men (*anashim*) standing near him. As soon as he saw them he ran from the entrance of the tent to greet them and, bowing to the ground, 3 he said, 4 let a little water be brought; bathe your feet and recline under the tree, 5 and let me fetch a morsel of bread that you may refresh yourselves; then go on, seeing that you have come your servant's way. They replied, "Do as you have said." 6 Abraham hastened into the tent to Sarah and said, "Quick, three seahs of fine flour. Knead and make cakes (*ugot*)! 7 Then Abraham ran to the herd, took a calf tender and choice and he gave it to the servant-boy (*ha-na'ar*), who hurried to prepare it; 8 He took curds and milk and the calf that had been prepared, and set these before them; and he waited on them under the tree while they ate.
9 "They said to him, Where is your wife Sarah?" And he replied, "There, in the tent."
16 When they got up from there the men (*ha-anashim*) turned their face toward Sodom . . .

A NOTE ON THE "CAKES" SARAH MADE

Once we separate the story of Sarah's encounter with YHWH from this account (verses 1, 3, 10–15), we make the surprising discovery that there is no mention of divinity in this section. Abraham, (whose name is not even mentioned until verse 6) is startled to see three *men (anashim)* appear before him. The patriarch hastens from the entrance of the tent and humbly offers them refreshments, which turn out to be nothing less than a feast. Abraham's conduct indicates that these are people of some standing. There is a great deal of preparation. The calf must be killed and dressed and cooked. Sarah must knead, prepare, and bake cakes. When all is ready Abraham brings "butter and milk and the calf of the herd that he had prepared and placed it before them" and he himself stands under a tree while they eat. Since convention perceives the men to be three angels, or one god and two angels, discussion has focused on whether such superhuman beings would partake of food. According to a Midrash, the statement should be taken figuratively, as if the angels "appeared to be eating" or perhaps pretended to do so out of courtesy.[12] But once the two stories are separated this difficulty disappears. The visitors are clearly *men (anashim)* who partake of the meal.

Significantly, the meal Abraham places before the visitors does not include Sarah's cakes *(ugot)*. What then is the meaning of Abraham's urgency that Sarah "knead and make cakes" with three measures *(seah)* of the finest flour *(gemah)*? Three measures amounts to twenty-eight cups—the equivalent of nine loaves of bread—an incredible amount for three or four people.[13] Skinner concludes that it is "The preparation of a genuine Bedouin repast, consisting of hastily baked cakes of bread, flesh, and milk in two forms" (Plate 8).[14] He does not comment on the exclusion of the cakes from the repast. Their omission is nevertheless highly significant, because such cakes would suggest the special nature of the meal.

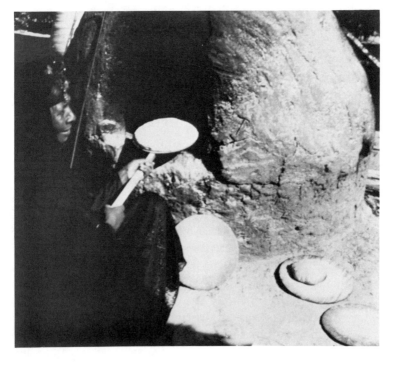

PLATE 8. "Such cakes would suggest the special nature of the meal."
Woman baking cakes (Luxor). Photo Myra Riddell.

PLATE 9. "The Goddess Hat-Hor. Her shrines were even more numerous than those of Horus."
The Mighty Hat-Hor (Dendara). The Egyptian Museum, Cairo.

Bread, or cakes of bread, were common cultic offerings made by ancient Near Eastern devotees and quite frequently appeared in ancient ritual. Egyptians pleaded with the "Lady of the Holy Land" (that is, the Underworld), who provided the deceased with food, "Let me have power over cakes, and let me eat of them under the leaves of the palm tree of the goddess Hat-Hor, who is my divine lady."[15] The mighty Hat-Hor was not only the Goddess of Love. She was by turns a cow, a cat, and a vulture: The stars on her belly indicate she was the cosmos itself.[16] Although most often shown as a cow, she is usually portrayed with her characteristic hairstyle— pulled behind her cow-ears and down to her shoulders (Plate 9). According to Wallis Budge:

The texts prove that the worship of Hathor was also universal, and that her shrines were even more numerous than those of Horus. She was, in fact, the great mother of the world, and the old, cosmic Hathor was the personification of the great power of nature which was perpetually conceiving, and creating, and bringing forth, and rearing, and maintaining all things, both great and small.[17]

Her cult centers were many but principally at Memphis, Thebes (Luxor), and Dendara. Each year she journeyed up the Nile to reenact her sacred wedding to the elder Horus. The nuptials were attended by thousands of well-wishers and seekers of favors.

In the community of the ancient past, in which only a small portion of the population was literate, tradition was transmitted orally. Myth, legend, and sacred history were not recorded in the pages of a book, on papyrus, or on clay tablets. Narratives were recited at festivals, told in the marketplace, or enacted during religious ceremonies, where a tale would be acted out in the form of a play at seasonal religious festivals. The actors were usually priestesses, priests, royalty, shamans, or the like.

A priestess, for example, would take on the part of a goddess. She did not simply play the part: she was literally understood to transmute her person into that of the goddess. And her audience knew this. They would see her arrayed in the splendor of a goddess with that deity's characteristics. If the priestess wore a mask with cow-ears, for instances, the worshipers would recognize in her the cow-goddess Hat-Hor (Plate 9) because the wearer of the mask *became empowered* by the deity. In this way the priestess and the audience would create a communal spiritual experience.

The story the priestess enacted may have been about a goddess's birth, marriage, the birth of her child, the death of her husband, and so on. If a priestess and a priest or king enacted the wedding of a goddess and a god, it would have included the sexual union of the deities; during the ceremony the sexual union would have been carried out by their human representatives. The act of copulation has been designated by scholars the *"hieros gamos"* or sacred marriage.

This pious and venerable ceremony was later described as *sacred prostitution* by patrilineal cultures. Patriliny, descent in the male line, required male control of the reproductive process in order that they might claim their biological heirs. Recognition of the father's biological function was central to the social structure. The generative reality of the life-giving female was slowly shifted to the intellectual creative power of the male: the Word (Gen. 1:3–24). This tenet, however, could not be enacted. The "word became flesh," so to speak: The dogma was transmitted by means of "sacred writings," or scriptures.

According to Leviticus 2:4–5 the absolute requirement for an offering was that the bread be made of unleavened dough. The flour was kneaded into unleavened dough *(batzek)* in a special trough, formed into large flat discs, and then baked on hot stones. As in Sarah's case the ingredients did not include leaven, but, interestingly, *batzek* comes from the root meaning "to swell." And the term *ugot* comes from the root meaning "to be round" (Plate 10). Sarah's *ugot* differed in this instance from the *lehem,* the bread given to Hagar before she wandered in the desert (Gen. 21:14), or the *lehem* offered by Abraham to denote a humble meal (Gen. 18:5).

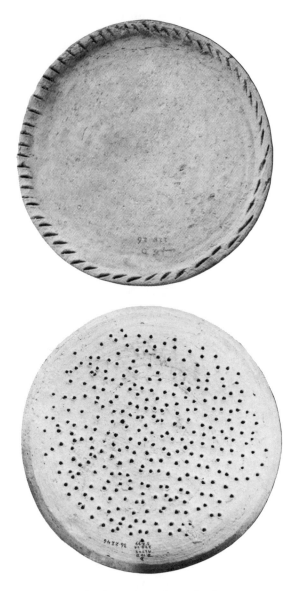

PLATE 10. "The bread must be formed into large flat discs . . ."
(Tell ed-Duweir [Lachish] shrine). Courtesy of the Israel Department of Antiquities and Museums.

PLATE 11. "The women knead dough to make cakes for the Queen of Heaven." *Egyptian woman kneading dough. Egyptian Museum, Cairo.*

Ugot are mentioned as being made of the manna that fell from heaven to the Israelites as they wandered in the wilderness with Moses (Exod. 12:39), and as being provided by an angel to Elijah who was starving in the desert (1 Kings 19:6)—both supernatural events. Jeremiah (ca. 609–608 BCE) provides us with a closer parallel.[18] The word came to the prophet from YHWH: "Stand in the gate of YHWH's house and proclaim this word . . . to all who enter by these gates to worship YHWH" (Jer. 7:1–2).

Among the many things that anger YHWH, as reported by Jeremiah, is an oft-quoted verse, "Don't you see what they are doing in the cities of Judah and in the streets of Jerusalem? How the children gather wood, and their fathers kindle fire, while *the women knead dough to make cakes for the Queen of Heaven,* and how they pour out libations to other gods in order to spite me?" [emphasis mine] (Jer. 7:17–18).[19] The "kneading" both by Sarah and the women of Jerusalem must have had some particular significance connected with the goddess (Plate 11), as in the cakes of Hat-Hor. Like the sacred cakes *(kavanim)* offered to the goddess (who, according to Raphael Patai, may have been Anat[20]), Sarah's cakes were not eaten. Indeed Leviticus 2 demands that the offerings be presented to YHWH, offerings that the priests "turn into smoke" as an "offering by fire of pleasing odor to YHWH" (Lev. 2:9). Such offerings obviously possess a sacred value and have no place in a festive meal.

THE FEAST BEFORE THE ORACLE

Let us now turn to some significant questions: What was the initial purpose of the narratives with which we are concerned? How did a childless priestess come to bear a child?

I have proposed in *Sarah the Priestess* that because Genesis 18 contains elements characteristic of a sacred nuptials ceremony, a *hieros gamos* is suggested here.[21] It has, in fact, many similarities to a particular Ugaritic text that describes the wedding of the goddess Nikkal to the god Yarih. This text was translated by C. H. Gordon who explains that it is a *hieros gamos*. In it, the moon-god Yarih pays the intermediary one thousand shekels of silver before the ceremony.[22]

I sing of Nikkal and Ib
Hrhb, king of Summer
Hrhb, Estival King,
When the Sun sets
The Moon rises
A virgin will give birth,

. . .

Lo a maid will bear a son

. . .

Hear, O Ktrt goddesses
. . . for his love, she is
for her lord . . .
Dagan . . .
Hear, O Ktrt!
Daughters of shouting
The Moon, illuminator of heaven, sends to Hrhb, King of Summer,
'Give Nikkal!
Moon would wed Ib
Let her enter his house.
And thou shalt get her for marriage by paying her father
A thousand shekels of silver
A myriad of gold.'

This bard ends his song with a hymn to the goddess, which begins:

> To Nikkal and Ib do I sing.
> The Moon is bright
> And may the Moon shed light on thee![23]

These two elements, the annunciation of the birth of a son and the thousand silver shekels, are found in the biblical story of Sarah and YHWH and Sarah and Abimelech.[24] Gordon notes that "Such annunciations are common in Ugaritic and Biblical literature. The earliest one in Scripture is that by an angel to Hagar, predicting the birth of Ishmael" (Gen. 16:11).[25] This ceremony differs from the Mesopotamian parallel in that in the Ugaritic version *the bride is destined to have a son.*

The Mesopotamian version celebrates the wedding of the goddess Inanna to the god Dumuzi but the fruit of the union is not a child but abundance for the land.

> The people of Sumer assemble in the palace,
> The house which guides the land.
> The king builds a throne for the queen of the palace.
> He sits beside her on the throne.
> In order to care for the life of all the lands,
> The exact first day of the month is closely examined
> And on the day of the disappearance of the moon.
> On the day of the sleeping of the moon,
> The *me* are perfectly carried out
> So that the New Year's Day, the day of rites,
> May be properly determined,
> And a sleeping place set up for Inanna.

Inanna (that is, the priestess) then descends from heaven to take part in the ritual union with the king. The king then bids the people enter the great hall. The people bring food and offerings.

The king embraces his beloved bride.
Dumuzi embraces Inanna.
Inanna, seated on the royal throne, shines like daylight.
The king, like the sun, shines radiantly by her side.
He arranges abundance, lushness, plenty, before her.
He assembles the people of Sumer.

The musicians play for the queen:
They play the loud instrument which drowns out the southern storm . . .
They play songs for Inanna to rejoice the heart.

After the feasting and festivities in which

> The people spend the day in plenty
> The king stands before the assembly in great joy.

Inanna returns to her abode in heaven.
The bard ends the song:

My Lady looks in sweet wonder from heaven.
The people of Sumer parade before the holy Inanna.
The Lady Who ascends into the Heavens, Inanna, is radiant.
Mighty, majestic, radiant, and ever youthful—
To you, Inanna, I sing.[26]

In this ritual the king or ruler was elevated to the status of a divinity; he became both king (man) and god. *Sarah the Priestess* also suggests that King Abimelech of Gerar was one of the three men who came to Mamre. In fact, the succession of events in Genesis 18 parallels those of the sacred nuptials to a considerable degree:

Before entering the holy nuptial chamber (where the mysteries of the union took place), the priest-king was seated upon a throne to mark his elevation to the status of royalty and divinity, facing the enthroned Goddess. It was apparently in this room *(gipar)* that the nuptial pair feasted during the time they remained in seclusion, their food being an omen of abundance which would result from the felicitous union. The future welfare of the whole community depended on the faultless accomplishment of every detail of the ceremony, and it must have been with great joy that the people were notified of the satisfactory fulfillment of the rites.[27]

There are two important parallels between this depiction of the preparations for the sacred nuptials that precede the oracle, on the one hand, and the section on the visitors and YHWH's annunciation in Genesis 18, on the other. Both posit a feast before an oracle. The scene takes place in a sacred area: In the Mesopotamian ceremony it takes place in the *gipar* (which, before it developed into a room in the temple complex, had been a sacred grove); and in the biblical account the sacred grove of Mamre is the residence of Sarah.

In preparation for the festivities the bride made provisions of every kind. She was assisted by her priests and servants, just as Sarah made cakes while Abraham and the servant prepared the meal. During the ceremony of the sacred nuptials the king and the priestess (regarded as the goddess incarnate) partook of a meal before the nuptials were consummated. Sarah's cakes, which were not consumed in the meal, were probably intended as an offering to a divinity. In the Babylonian version the union is consummated and the oracle is pronounced after the satisfactory fulfillment of the rites. In the biblical version the visitors ask the whereabouts of Sarah but the consummation of the union is not mentioned. Sarah's visit to Gerar, where King Abimelech gives Abraham one thousand shekels of silver for Sarah, is where the "wedding" takes place. I suggest that the oracle of YHWH (Gen. 18:10–15) came after the ceremony with Abimelech (Gen. 20). See appendix A.

There was one fundamental difference in the objective of the mystic nuptials in Canaan as compared to those of the early period in Mesopotamia. In an early period in Sarah's homeland, the participant in the sacred nuptials was to remain childless; if she conceived, the child when born was to be exposed to the elements.[28] In Canaan, however, the participant (who in an extant epic was the goddess Nikkal) *was destined to bear a child.*[29] In this light the conversation, Sarah's fear, and her exchange with YHWH are understandable, since the outcome of the ceremony was contrary to her expectations.

We can see now that the elements in the visit to Mamre are reflective of elements of a *hieros gamos* ceremony.[30] This permits us to surmise that these were emissaries from King Abimelech, or perhaps one of them was the ruler himself as a representative who would participate in the sacred nuptials. Here the king is still regarded as a mortal. Sarah's story should move from the nuptials with Abimelech in Genesis 20 to the annunciation, the satisfactory fulfillment of the rites in Genesis 18, in which the king has now been elevated to deity.[31]

That a similar sequence of events can be found in the Mesopotamian ceremony and in the biblical narrative gives the impression that the biblical writer attempted in every way to be true to the original material even while obscuring its primary intent. In the next section, the king assumes the guise of divinity.

THE PROMISE TO SARAH

The oracle-giving (that is, the annunciation of a birth to Sarah) after the ceremony of the *hieros gamos* is reflected in the sequence that follows the three visitors and the meal in Genesis 18.

If the sentences mentioning three visitors are omitted, the sequence of the annunciation would read as follows:

18 1 YHWH appeared to him near the oaks of Mamre, he was sitting at the entrance to the tent as the day grew hot. 3 He said, "My Lord ('*dny*) if it please you, do not go on past your servant, 10 and He said, "I will return to you when life is due, and your wife Sarah shall have a son."[32] Sarah was listening at the entrance of the tent, which was behind him. 11 Now Abraham and Sarah were old, advanced in years; Sarah had stopped having the periods of women. 12 And Sarah laughed to herself saying, "Now that I am withered, am I to have enjoyment with my husband so old?" 13 Then YHWH said to Abraham, "Why did Sarah laugh saying 'Shall I in truth bear a child, old as I am?'[33] 14 Is anything too difficult for YHWH? I will return to you, when life is due, and Sarah shall have a son."[34] 15 Sarah dissembled, saying, "I did not laugh," for she was frightened. He replied "But you did laugh."

21 1 YHWH took note (*p-q-d*=impregnated?[35]) of Sarah as he had spoken and YHWH did for Sarah as he had promised. 2 Sarah conceived and bore a son . . .

In this sequence the deity is identified by name: He is YHWH. The very first sentence, in which YHWH appears to Abraham as he dozes in the grove of terebinths of Mamre, belongs to the sequence that mentions only one god. This verse allows the hearer or reader to know the identity of the visitor. The next sentence with a single deity is verse 3, " '*dny*, if I have found favor in your sight, do not go past your servant." The word used for "my Lord," '*dny* in Hebrew, can also be read as plural; but the rest of the verse contains three unambiguous singulars, as Speiser accurately points out.[36] The word *'dny* can also be vocalized as *adonay,* "God." Abraham is commonly presumed not to have known the identity of the divine visitor, but since this sequence is indeed anthropomorphic Abraham must have recognized his guest. In fact the patriarch's initial words in verse 3, literally: "If I have found favor in your sight," were also used by Gideon when he encountered divinity (Judg. 6:17).

The next verse in the singular is verse 10, which begins the promise to Sarah, literally: "I will return . . . Sarah has a son." That the deity knew Sarah's name has been considered strange.[37] But this should not be surprising if he (YHWH— by means of—Abimelech) was to resolve the breach of agreement in Genesis 16. Verse 10 is usually translated: "I will return to you when life is due, and your wife Sarah shall have a son," following 2 Kings 4:16–17.[38] But the Hebrew *kaet haya* is interpreted by Rashi as: "at this season when the time comes around."[39] Nachmanides notes that "We do not find it recorded that at the set time He returned" (to Abraham).[40] But YHWH *did* return to Sarah (Gen. 21:1)! His promise must therefore have been directed to Sarah, not Abraham.

The second part of the phrase *ve-hine ben l'Sarah* (and behold/see, Sarah has/will have a son) is often compared to the *hoveket ben* of 2 Kings 4:16—which, however, is future tense, unlike *ve-hine ben,* "and she *has* a son," of Genesis. A more relevant comparison is Judges 13:5, "Actually you are already pregnant and bearing a son *(ve-yoledet ben)*"[41] The meaning is probably something like "you are definitely having a son."

The second part of verse 10, "Sarah was listening at the entrance to the tent *ve-hu aharav,*" is impossible to translate as it stands. It is usually rendered "which was behind him," but this is inexact. A closer paraphrase is "and he is, or will be, after him." *Ve-hu* refers to *ben,* son, in the previous sentence; that is, he (Sarah's son) will be after him (the god), and therefore should be interpreted as a thought of Sarah's as she hears the annunciation: "and my son will be his (Abimelech/YHWH's) descendant" (see below).

If this episode was meant to be an annunciation by a divinity that Sarah was to conceive a son, the foregoing would have sufficed. YHWH appeared, made his annunciation, and could have left. However, what follows seems to serve a different purpose. One objective is to explain the name "Isaak," connected to Sarah's laughter. The other intention is connected with Sarah herself, and her relation to the divinity. In this sequence the main characters are YHWH and Sarah; Abraham plays a minor role. Abraham's role as principal is picked up only after the annunciation of conception in the sequence about Sodom.

The "Abraham and the three visitors" section is conventionally viewed as an introduction to the stories of Abraham and YHWH, and Lot and two angels in the destruction of Sodom, because both sequences refer to three characters.[42] However, the three visitors in Genesis 18 have no names, and they are not angels but men *(anashim)*. The connecting phrase "when they got up from there the men turned their face toward Sodom" (Gen. 18:16) links two distinct accounts with different themes and characters.

QUESTIONING A TRADITION

The turning point in the Hagar-Sarah narrative is different for each woman, though for both it hinges on the judgment of YHWH. Their lives are still intertwined: Up to this point Hagar's son is still Sarah's successor. Nothing in the biblical narrative points to the obverse, particularly if the conflict in Genesis 16 is understood to have been between Sarah and Abraham rather than between Sarah and Hagar. Under these circumstances Hagar is still the *shifḥah* of Sarah, and her own prospects for descendants are virtually nil. Hagar, too, must await the "decision of YHWH." However, it is as yet not clear how, or even if, YHWH's decision will affect Hagar or her son. Since later in the story Sarah is still concerned with the status of the son of the *shifḥah,* the implication is that the priestess still envisioned him as her heir.

Here is what seems to have happened: YHWH's appearance at the terebinth grove in Mamre to resolve the conflict between Sarah and Hagar is the awaited oracle, the answer to Sarah's demand. YHWH foretells the birth of a child to Sarah. Sarah is incredulous and laughs because she knows that a priestess of her station cannot become an ordinary mother like Hagar. The "sexual vigor and laughter" associations relate to her in her role as goddess incarnate.

The sequence of events would be as follows:

1. Genesis 16: The question of "motherhood" between Hagar and Sarah
2. Genesis 18: The annunciation and beginning of the ceremony of the *hieros gamos*
3. Genesis 19: The interpolation of the destruction of Sodom
4. Genesis 20: The *hieros gamos* with Abimelech and conception of Isaak
5. Genesis 18: The oracle, the decision of YHWH
6. Genesis 21: The birth of Isaak, Sarah's successor
7. Genesis 21: The resolution for Hagar and her heir

Sarah's case is complex because her lineage will eventually come from her own biological descendant. It is thus necessary that she modify the custom and tradition required of women of her religious affiliation and rank. This is no small reformation for Sarah and must have brought with it a great deal of heart searching before she made her decision. This decision must also have involved acceptance of a new deity, a frightening experience (implied in her laughter and exchange with "YHWH"). Of course, we have no idea of the identity of this deity whom J calls YHWH. But he is the precursor of the god of the Hebrews.

WHY SARAH LAUGHED

The symbolism of Sarah's laughter is perhaps the most profound aspect of her story. It marks her transition from Mesopotamian priestess to Hebrew matriarch. Her son's name is significantly an expression of this experience: laughter as the mediator of transformation.[43]

The name "Isaak" is embedded in Sarah's story on two occasions:[44] "So she laughed to herself *(va-tetzehak)*" (Gen. 18:12); and "Sarah said, Elohim made a laughing stock *(tz'hok asah)* of me; everyone hearing will laugh *(yitzehak)* at me!" (Gen. 21:6).

Why is Sarah's laughter so important that it should become the designation of her son? In the first place the deity tells her *that she has already conceived!* This miraculous event is confirmed by Sarah's own observation in the comment that she had stopped menstruating, as is usual with women who have conceived.[45] She laughed to herself, thinking, "Now that I am withered am I to have (sexual) delight and *adoni* (my Lord or God) is so old?"[46] Westermann informs us that "Only in Genesis 18:11 [by J] and 17:17 [by P] is there mention of the age of the childless couple; according to extrabiblical parallels this belongs to another narrative variant"; and "The parenthesis [regarding age] interrupts and disturbs the flow of the narrative."[47] I would add that Sarah's concern about age and her future sexual activity, the conventional view, distorts not only the flow but the intent of the narrative; it is not sexual activity in old age that Sarah is concerned about. If this is the only passage in which age is mentioned by J, why would this writer attempt to hide, perhaps not a young, but certainly not an aged Sarah?

Sarah's disbelief in her conception can be understood only in terms of her belonging to a religious order such as that of a *naditu* priestess, who simply could not envision herself as becoming pregnant. After all, it had been for this reason that Sarah had been so dependent on Hagar for a successor. Sarah's fear of conceiving was not limited to the practice of childlessness observed by these women; surely a greater fear was in the consequences of pregnancy. As previously mentioned, at a certain period in Mesopotamia if a priestess conceived, allowed her pregnancy to come to term, and delivered a child, that child was to be exposed to the elements at birth. A famous inscription describing the birth of Sargon of Agade, the founder of Akkad, illuminates this practice:

I am Sargon the mighty king, king of Agade
My mother was a high-priestess, I did not know my father . . .
My city was Azupiranu, set on the banks of the Euphrates.
My priestess-mother conceived me, and bore me in secret,
She put me in a basket of rushes, she caulked my lid with bitumen,
She put me into the river, which did not rise over me,
Akki the irrigator drew me out as he dipped his pail . . .[48]

When YHWH asks her, "Why did you laugh?"[49] Sarah answers, "I did not laugh, I was afraid." Afraid of what? Of being pregnant? More likely, of being a pregnant priestess! But YHWH insists, "No, [but] you did laugh." This curious exchange gives the impression that this deity was not that familiar to Sarah, even though he knew her name (verse 9). It also gives the impression that he was a divinity who did not know the laws that governed the profession of her homeland, and that she could not believe he was able to change those laws, even though he had previously given his credentials ("Is anything too difficult for YHWH?"). The deity then proves his attributes: "Now YHWH visited (impregnated) Sarah just as he had said and he did for Sarah just as he had promised" (Gen. 21:1). YHWH, at any rate, was true to his word and Sarah bore a son. The son's name, in turn, is true to his mother's experience.

That J had trouble with this portion of Sarah's story becomes evident when he excludes her calling and makes Sarah's age the cause of her disbelief and laughter instead. Later, the Priestly school went even further. Unable to accept the connection between Sarah's experience and Isaak's name, these theologians turn Isaak into Abraham's son and have the patriarch name him in relation to an experience of his own.

To this end they add references connecting Abraham to the annunciation. In one reference Abraham is told in an oracle that his wife Sarah will bear him a son, "And Abraham threw himself on his face and laughed; and he thought, 'Shall a child be born to a hundred year old man?' " (Gen. 17:17). Note that this verse includes three elements essential to the priests: the patriarch's humble acceptance of the situation, his laughter rather than Sarah's, and Abraham's age—an important factor for the priestly source. The P school intensified their contention with a flat statement: "Abraham gave his new-born son, whom Sarah had borne to him, the name of Isaak" (Gen. 21:3). But this association of Isaak's name to the patriarch was not entirely convincing. Rashi attempted to further eliminate any ambiguity as to whose laughter was implicit in Isaak's name. "Abraham had faith and *rejoiced* while Sarah *sneered;* hence God was angry with Sarah but not with Abraham," he assures us.[50]

The apparent effort to conceal any positive association between Sarah's laughter and her son's name gives the impression that the ancient editors had something to hide. In a cuneiform text from the period of the first dynasty of Babylon of the second millennium, there is an inscription dedicated by Hammurapi to Aṣratum (the Akkadian rendition of Asherah). In it she is described as *kallat ṣar ṣami,* "bride of the king of heaven," and *belet kuzbi u ulṣi,* "mistress of sexual vigor and rejoicing."[51] Since both these elements—the reference to sexual pleasure or delight, and rejoicing or happiness—appear in the biblical text regarding Sarah, does this denote an association between Sarah and the Canaanite goddess Asherah in whose grove she resided?[52]

WHO WAS YHWH?

Who was YHWH? How did he affect the relationship between Sarah and her personal deity? Let's take another look at the text.

The two sentences beginning "YHWH visited Sarah . . ." in the extant text are the introductory sentences to Genesis 21, the narrative in which the deity is Elohim. An E episode cannot have begun with "*YHWH* visited Sarah as he had spoken and *YHWH* did for Sarah as he had promised." The promise to Sarah is part of J's account, not E's. That Sarah had conceived and had borne a son was due to the intervention of YHWH, not Elohim. In Genesis 21, the core E narrative, Sarah's son Isaak is being weaned. He is already a few years old. Furthermore, these J sentences are the resolution to the climactic conclusion of Genesis 16, "YHWH decide between me and between you."

How did they get there? *They were dislodged from the end of Genesis 18 to form the introduction to the E account in Genesis 21, in an effort to weaken the impact of YHWH's fulfillment of his promise to Sarah.* To further render impotent the direct relationship of YHWH and Sarah, P includes the patriarch's name: "and Sarah bore a son *to Abraham* in his old age." And of course, as is usual with P, he has Abraham circumcise the child and name him. Finally, the patriarch's age is announced—all in good Priestly tradition.

I contend that the principal story, the annunciation of Isaak's birth to Sarah, is the awaited divine intercession on Sarah's behalf after her conflict with Abraham.[53] The resolve of the oracle is also YHWH's answer to Sarah's **"May YHWH decide between me and between you."** In his wisdom YHWH establishes a new social order for the women. The deity does not divest either woman of a successor. Instead, YHWH grants descendants to both of them.

This is not an announcement to Abraham that he will have a son; the son is Sarah's in replacement of Hagar's. Westermann concurs: "In an older form the promise of a child could have been directed to the woman, as in the majority of parallels."[54] Significantly, all but one of the women in the parallels who are spoken to by a deity (or angel) have no name. They are Hannah, Samuel's mother (1 Sam. 1:20); the Shunamite woman (2 Kings 4:16); and Samson's mother, Manoah's wife (Judg. 29:5); the Desert Matriarch, mother of Ishmael, can also be included in this list. It becomes obvious that the story in Genesis 18 is Hagar's as well as Sarah's and that the issue addressed to YHWH was a question concerning motherhood between Hagar and Sarah and not that of the birth of a son to an aged patriarch—particularly since the name of the future child reflects incidents in the life of the Matriarch.

In my view Genesis 18 has various important functions: First, it explains how Sarah became impregnated during the ritual of the sacred nuptials; and it explains the means by which the conception of Isaak became endorsed by Sarah, a priestess who had lived by a code of childlessness. Sarah had been forced to acknowledge the miraculous power of a new deity in order for this transformation to be divinely sanctioned.

It also seems clear that the appearance of a divine being to Sarah opened the way for J's introduction of YHWH as the deity of promise to Sarah. That this deity was made to be the sole god of the entire Sarah cycle obliterated the dramatic impact of Sarah's profound transformation.

It could not possibly have been the same divinity who witnessed and approved Hagar's function in providing an heir/ess to Sarah and who then changed his mind and decided that each should bear her own child. The first deity approved of Mesopotamian custom, having witnessed the agreement, and must have therefore been Sarah's personal diety, who came with her from her homeland.

Sarah came from the city-state of Ur (see Map I), whose protector deities were Nanna-Sin and Ningal. She then resided in Haran, in northern Mesopotamia. Haran enjoyed the protection of the same deities as those of Ur, Nanna-Sin and Ningal. Unlike most Sumero-Akkadian deities, the lunar goddess Ningal was also revered in Canaan and Egypt; she is known in Ugaritic literature as Nikkal Ib or Nikkal and Ib.[55] Was this perhaps the deity who came with Sarah to Canaan? Is this the goddess Sarah represented in the sacred nuptials ceremony as suggested earlier in this chapter?

After the episode of the three visitors (Abimelech and his courtiers?) Sarah is visited by YHWH, who tells her that she has conceived. Sarah knows that she has stopped menstruating but she laughs inwardly at the idea that pregnancy is the cause of it. However, YHWH insists that this is the expected oracle in answer to the ritual. Sarah has good reason to fear the oracle. It is when the oracle is given that Sarah has that strange exchange with YHWH/Abimelech: He said, "Why did you laugh . . . and so on," and Sarah answers, "I did not laugh," for she was frightened. YHWH/Abimelech insists, "But you did laugh." This sequence ends abruptly with no resolution. It would seem, however, that Abimelech attempted to rectify Sarah's problem. "I herewith give your brother a thousand pieces of silver; *this will serve you as a covering of the eyes before all who are with you, and you are cleared before everyone.*" Sarah's predicament stemmed from the ritual usage customary to *her* congregation, not Abimelech's. The thousand shekels of silver proffered by the king symbolized sanction of the local ritual being performed by a Mesopotamian priestess; she was cleared of all responsibility for *his* ritual and its consequences. Therefore, **"YHWH *impregnated (p-q-d)* Sarah as he had promised, and YHWH did for Sarah as he had spoken. Sarah conceived and bore a son."**

Genesis 18 records details of a portion of the sacred nuptials that took place between Sarah and a representative of the divine bridegroom, probably Abimelech. Sarah's response to the outcome of the oracle, her laughter, is the pivotal point in the account. Because of this her experience is immortalized in the naming of her son.

On another level there are tremendous implications to this story. When she accepts the oracle that results in her pregnancy Sarah must have severed her affiliation to the Mesopotamian institution she has been associated with all her life. The disbelief and fear expressed in Sarah's laughter now take on a magnitude of meaning difficult to comprehend. The decision of YHWH, that Sarah bear her own offspring, overrules Sarah's deity (Ningal?) for whom she remained childless. Who is the "YHWH" of this sequence? Is it perhaps the moon-god Yarih who wedded Nikkal who, like Abimelech, pays one thousand shekels of silver to a family member for her?

We cannot be sure who the deities were in the Sarah cycle. However, it is clear that the attempt (by J?) to infuse a polytheistic story with a monotheistic overtone erased a dramatic turning point in Sarah's life.

Did Sarah realize that on a deeper level she may have been relinquishing control of her sexuality and pregnancy to a new divine order? Sarah's fear and YHWH's blunt retort, "But you did laugh," gives the impression that Sarah had no choice but to accept YHWH's decision. In relinquishing her status as a Mesopotamian priestess Sarah is able to disengage herself from her previous position to become the mother of a people, symbolized in her laughter. But it also implies acceptance and loyalty to a new divinity. Whether this deity is Yarih, Elohim, El Shaddai, or some other divinity subsequently erased from the records, we may never know. Nevertheless, Sarah's decision to accede to so tremendous a transformation lay the foundations of a community on which future Hebrew priestesses and Hebrew mothers were able to build, for generations and generations.

The story, of course, does not end here. Hagar's story is so intimately entwined with that of the priestess that any alteration in the destiny of Sarah involves a change for Hagar as well. The induction of that change is already apparent early on. If Rashi is correct in his reading of *"beini u beineh"* as referring to Hagar and Sarah rather than Abraham and Sarah (with which I concur), the "between me and between you" has Sarah placing Hagar on an equal standing with herself when she addresses the deity. That Sarah later concedes that the two sons are in equal positions regarding the inheritance factor indicates that the conventional characterization of those involved is indeed questionable.

Hagar's life seems to be as much the concern of a deity and her future as much under the protection of divinity as any other biblical character. If Sarah becomes absolute as a person, not dependent on Hagar, Hagar too is to become her own person, independent from Sarah. Whether this emphasis on individuality is favorable—with each woman going her own way, left to fend for herself with exclusive divine protection—is debatable, since it was at the expense of companionship and communal cooperation.

Hagar's independence, as we shall see, was conditional on her departure from Hebron. Her sad and lonely exile is beautifully depicted. Nevertheless, Sarah too is to be bereft of companionship. She too will be left alone. Because of "YHWH's" decision, both women are left with only their sons, on whom they will in future become dependent.

6. Determining the Inheritance
Genesis 21:16–21

THE NON-NUCLEAR BIBLICAL FAMILY

Families living in biblical times did not have the structure and assumed relationships of Western society. It is important that we free ourselves from the paradigm of the nuclear family so we are not tempted to compress the biblical family into that structure.

Certainly, at least some ancient Near Eastern societies did not hold our concept of nuclear family entirely: that is, father (head of household), mother, and children, with inheritance through the male line.[1] "In most societies the nuclear family is a derivative and secondary unit . . . taking our own rather peculiar system as the norm leads only to confusion," as Robin Fox points out.[2] Similarly, in Canaan at that time, we are dealing with a period of transition between the unit of a (matrifocal) clan *(mishpaḥah),* to that of a people (tribe, *shevet*), or a nation (which itself was only later to be composed of nuclear units).

In biblical times children were heirs of their (social) mother's estate apart from that of their father's. This is evident in the biblical literature as well as in the Babylonian material. Sarah's story commences with her search for an heir: *"ulai ibbane mimmena"* (perhaps I will be built up through her) (Gen. 16:2). Her story also ends with the same theme, "The son of that slave will not inherit with my son" (Gen. 21:10). It seems difficult to presume that Sarah did not enjoy a contract specifying that *"henceforth, the children will be her heirs."*

Similarly, the exasperation evident in the outcry of Rachel and Leah points to an analogous prior agreement (breached by their father Laban), "Have we still a share in the inheritance of our father's house? . . . Truly, all the wealth that Elohim has taken away from our father *belongs to us and to our children*" (Gen. 31:14, 16). This disclosure of the sisters permitted Jacob to leave the homeland of his wives and take them to Canaan. It is after this that Laban chases after them, in search of "his" *teraphim,* the religious images he does not find because Rachel had concealed them in her saddlebags.

Before Laban returns home and Jacob proceeds on the journey, Laban institutes a pact with Jacob that sounds like a codicil to a marriage contract: "May YHWH watch between me and between you *(beini u-beinḥa);* when we are separated from one another, if you mistreat my daughters, or if you take other wives besides my daughters, even if there is no-one there, remember Elohim is witness between me and between you!" (Gen. 31:50). The reference here to "other wives" is also a confirmation that Bilhah and Zilpah are not associated with Jacob in what we understand as a conventional marital relationship of any sort; here Laban states that Jacob's wives are exclusively Rachel and Leah.

We cannot simply assume that the relationships of Sarah, Hagar, Abraham, and the two sons to each other were analogous to those of a later period. We must also beware of applying kinship terms to quite a different system. Carol Meyers relates that "the variety of family configurations that ethnographers report strongly suggests that environmental and social constraints figure prominently in the way families take shape."[3] That Sarah was "wife" of Abraham does not necessarily mean that their relationship follows present conventional marriage observances.

The special circumstances of their marriages is perhaps more evident in Rachel's case. Rachel's sister Leah bore four sons; Rachel's *shifḥah,* Bilhah, bore two; Leah's *shifḥah,* Zilpah, bore two more; and Leah again bore two sons and one daughter before Rachel conceived her first child. Jacob's legendary love for Rachel makes it difficult to accept that they spent close to a decade without having sexual relations, but the case of the *shif-*

ḥah possibly bears this out. Leah had borne four sons before Rachel's *shifḥah* conceived. It is possible that the handmaids of priestesses were also to remain childless for a certain period. At least according to the biblical records both Hagar and Bilhah, like the matriarchs, were "barren" for a considerable period of time. There is no indication that these women had sexual relations with the patriarchs other than to conceive.

Women not only regulated the sexual activity of their handmaids with their husbands but their own as well. This authority is clearly described in Genesis 30:14–16:

Once, at the time of the wheat harvest, Reuben came upon some mandrakes [reputed to induce human fertility] in a field and brought them to his mother Leah. Rachel said to Leah, "Please give me some of your son's mandrakes." But she [Leah] said to her, "Was it not enough for you to take away my husband, that you would also take my son's mandrakes?" Rachel replied, "Then let him lie with you tonight, in return for your son's mandrakes." When Jacob came home from the field in the evening, Leah went out to meet him and said, "You are to sleep with me, for I have hired you with my son's mandrakes." And he lay with her that night.

I am not convinced, for instance, that all priestesses who were to remain childless, and who were "wedded" to rules, had sexual relationships with their husbands as well.[4] It has been argued that priestesses "could avoid impregnation only by using abnormal methods of intercourse," since "castration or sterilization were unknown and technically unfeasible in antiquity."[5] This is an incredible statement from an author who in this same essay makes a case for the knowledge of *coitus interruptus* in antiquity. Furthermore, other contraceptive techniques, such as abortion, herbal brews, and so on, are known to have been used in that period.[6] However, enigmatic descriptions were made of priestesses, such as "the *naditu*-priestesses, who let their womb live in wisdom," which may not refer to contraception.[7] It may very well be that certain priestesses had intercourse exclusively with a priest or king who was elevated to the status of royalty and divinity, but only at certain times and possibly for specific reasons. This certainly seems to be the case with the biblical matriarchs.

The pattern of the family structure is fundamental to its inheritance regulations. In the narratives *the matriarchs have authority over the sexual activity of their husbands and sons, and over that of younger or subordinate women.* The domestic sphere of the matriarchs, then, includes control of their own bodies and that of their *sh'faḥot.* In other words, male sexual activity is regulated by their wives and mothers. This can be a significant distinction for the lives of women. Incest, rape, and sexual harassment could be highly curtailed if the social values of the biblical matriarchs were taken as seriously as those of the patriarchs.

The theme of Genesis 21:9–13 is ostensibly Sarah's challenge to the legitimacy of Ishmael as beneficiary of a legacy (which would change the destinies of two future patriarchs, Ishmael and Isaak). The disputed legacy is presumed to be Abraham's, but its nature or the content of Ishmael's threat to it are not explicit.

Although Genesis 21:9–13 is sometimes considered to be no more than a variant of the same tradition used by J in Genesis 16, it contains some important distinctions.[8] Genesis 16 was about the procurement of heirs; at stake in Genesis 21 is the future of the women's two sons. Sarah's admonition to Abraham—"Get rid of that slave-woman and her son, for the son of that slave-woman will never inherit with my son" (with Isaak)—results in the banishment from Hebron of Hagar and her son. The question here is not of motherhood (Sarah now has her own child), but rather the fate of the legacy.

Conventional interpretation of the passage, that it is Sarah's maternal jealousy that excites her and prompts her cruel demand, or that "God gives Sarah her way . . . because he [Ishmael] is only the son of the maidservant," is subverting a significant issue.[9]

Also, there are many enigmas in this passage. What legacy is Sarah referring to: land rights? cattle? social status? the legacy of her position? Whose legacy are we talking about, Abraham's or Sarah's? Would the son of a slave-woman inherit equally with a son of the master? What conditions would require the eviction of the concerned parties?

On the basis of Genesis 25:5 ("Abraham willed all he owned to Isaak") it would seem that the legacy Sarah is wresting from Hagar's son is Abraham's—"For the son of that slave shall not share in the inheritance with my son." But we must not forget that these people adhere to Mesopotamian custom. In Babylonia the inheritance customs for the husband were quite different from those of his priestess wife. Children acquired by a *naditu* from another woman, whether a sister, a *sugetu,* or servant, became the *naditu*'s legal heirs. *A Babylonian man, on the other hand, had to legitimize or adopt any heir he wished to have.*[10]

That fathers were required to adopt their offspring seems reasonable in a matrilineal setting in which children were reckoned in the descent line of their mothers even though the biological function of the father was acknowledged. There is evidence in Genesis that this custom was practiced by at least one patriarch: Jacob "adopted" the grandchildren of Rachel as his heirs (Gen. 48:14–16). Furthermore, the Testament of Jacob (Gen. 49:1–27), recognized as one of the oldest poems in the Bible, may well be a relic of an adoption ceremony by Jacob of his sons before his death.[11] In this Testament Jacob "chooses" (that is, adopts) those tribes that are to become the twelve tribe amphyctony. In the biblical sequence the Testament follows Jacob's adoption of his grandchildren, inferring that these two sections chronicle a sole theme.

A man's adopted/legitimated children, in the Babylonian view, enjoyed the same status as biological children.[12] However, the mere act of acceptance (by the would-be father) did not include rights. Adoption was established solely by contract.

If the father did not fulfill the contract (for example, if the adopted person was treated as a slave), this was a breach of contract. The natural parents then had the right to reclaim the child (unless this was prevented by the contract), or the person could return to the parents' home. If succession was established by contract, the person who was "adopted" gained the same rights as a natural heir. Legitimated children of a man's slave-woman inherited equally, at his death, with his natural children.[13] This regulation applies only to the children of the *man*'s slave, not the woman's.

It is significant that while a man needed to legitimate his own heirs, Hammurapi regulations consistently mention women having sons *for the husband*. These contradictions suggest that the general attempted to introduce patriliny into the society: Women were to produce sons who became their father's heirs without the husband needing to legitimize them. However, "There is no evidence in contemporary legal documents that the provisions of the Hammurapi Code were ever carried out" in the general's lifetime.[14]

From the pre-Hammurapic point of view, then, Abraham's legacy is separate from that of Sarah's, and he had to legitimize any son he intended to acknowledge as heir. The main reason for adoption by childless parents was to obtain heirs who would provide the proper offerings of drink and food at their tomb.[15] (The Babylonians may be assumed to have drawn no distinction between adoption of natural sons by the father and the legitimation of them.)[16] P indirectly implies that Abraham adopted *both* Ishmael and Isaak, since they both bury him in Sarah's tomb (Gen. 25:9). Also, the circumcision of Ishmael by Abraham may have been an attempt by P to circumvent the issue of adoption.

Whatever the case, it is not Abraham's estate but her own that Sarah is concerned with at the time she determines the futures of Hagar and her son. In fact the issue of a legacy of Abraham's does not even materialize in the episode of Genesis 21; the patriarch is saddened at the loss of the boy's presence in Hebron, but he mentions nothing of the loss of an heir. This is not to say that the patriarch had no legacy to leave and no heir to leave it to. It is saying that the issue in Genesis 21 does not concern the patriarch's legacy.

We have been led to believe that Sarah relinquished her hold on Hagar's son when she bore her own child. Why, then, is there any question as to who will inherit?

It has been argued that Sarah's demand that the two sons be separated followed the ancient Mesopotamian law #25 of the ruler Lipit-Ishtar (ca. 1934 BCE).[17] This law states: "If a man married a wife, and she bore him children and those children are living, and the slave also bore children for her master (but) the father granted freedom to the slave and her children, the children of the slave shall not divide the estate with the children of their (former) master." But this is an incorrect analogy. To begin with, this regulation is directed at a man, his wife, and his slave; whereas the biblical story is about a woman (who is a priestess) and her *shifḥah* (Gen. 21:11). Lipit-Ishtar is concerned with the children of the husband.

Genesis 16 makes it clear that Hagar's child is Sarah's heir. Nothing in the subsequent story gives any indication that Sarah rejected that relationship with Hagar's son. In fact Sarah's statement "the son of that slave will not share in the inheritance with my son" (Gen. 21:10) indicates the equality of the status of the sons, at least in Sarah's eyes.

The following verse, however, asserts that Abraham is distressed at the imminent departure of Hagar's son, "For it concerned a son of his." If Abraham is so distressed about "his" son, by what authority could Sarah demand that this son leave Hebron?[18] This is the first time we hear that Abraham has claimed the *shifḥah*'s son as his; did he "adopt" him in Babylonian fashion? But why then would it have been in the matriarch's power to decide whether the son would or would not inherit from Abraham, even if he were forced to leave? Despite the references to Abraham's relation to Hagar's son, the account indicates that the "inheritance" is Sarah's, since she has authority over it, and that Hagar's child is still her heir, since he has the same status as her son Isaak. Hagar's destiny is also in Sarah's hands, since it is she who demands that Abraham dismiss her.

That Abraham had no recourse is indisputable. Unable to contradict the priestess, the Patriarch turns to Elohim. But Elohim supports Sarah's decision that Isaak, not Hagar's son, will be the sole beneficiary of the legacy. "Whatever Sarah tells you, do as she says," he admonishes Abraham (Gen. 21:12b). As an ancient Near Eastern priestess, what legacy did Sarah have to confer on her successor?

THE LEGACY OF A PRIESTESS

During the second millennium a woman received a substantial portion of her inheritance from her parents on her initiation into the priesthood or on her marriage. Babylonian information concerning marriage and inheritance is complex because there are no general rules that could apply to anyone, as in the Hammurapi Code. Instead the parties concerned drew up individual contracts to suit each specific event and circumstance. Different customs must also be gleaned from marriage contracts, which themselves vary according to the status and circumstances of the people involved. A breach of contract was resolved by community elders, religious or secular judges, or by oracles, as in the case of Hagar and Sarah.

In the ancient Near East marriage contracts were drawn up for the benefit of the bride. A contract was executed for each woman at her marriage, presumably because the dowries of priestesses could be substantial.

The highest rank of the priesthood was the *entu,* which in the Sumerian form describes her as "the divine bride" or "sister of the god."[19] The Akkadian *en/entu* is a loan word coined from the ordinary Sumerian word for "lord/lady, master/ mistress/ owner," indicating a reordering by the Akkadians of the direct relationship the Sumerian priestess enjoyed with divinity. These priestesses remained childless, and it was regarded as boding disaster to the land if under certain astronomical conjunctions men had intercourse with these women.[20]

Following the *entu,* decreasing in rank, were the *naditu,* the priestess; the *qadistu,* the holy woman; the *kulmasitu,* the votaress—all of whom remained childless—and the *sugetu,* the lay-sister/ priestess. It is important to remember that even though the titles of these women were the same in all of Mesopotamia, their functions and privileges may have varied from temple to temple and from region to region. So when I suggest that Sarah and Rachel were *naditu* priestesses or question whether Leah (and perhaps even the *sh'fahot*) may have been *sugetu* priestesses, I am implying rank rather than function.

Even though Akkadian was the language of the Code of Hammurapi, circa the eighteenth century BCE, titles of priestesses were always written with an ideogram in the Sumerian language.[21] This indicates that the profession of women dedicated to the service of a deity had its origin in the pre-Babylonian civilization of Mesopotamia, a presumably revered tradition.[22]

In two post-Hammurapi marriage contracts, the *seriktu* (dowry) is called a *nudunnu.*[23] This is a much larger dowry, and was given to a *naditu* of Marduk and a *sugetu,* both women belonging to religious orders.[24]

One of these contracts gives evidence that two sisters could remain together on the betrothal of one of them; that they received handmaids and slaves as well as property and money when they married; and, most importantly, their children become their heirs.

In this contract the bride, a *naditu,* is also a *kulmasitu.* The *nudunnu* given her consisted of a large number of objects, but also included the bride's sister (who would probably bear children for her *naditu*-sister), two female salves, and someone by the name of Qisti-Ilabrat. The contract ends with:

all this, the dowry of Liwir-Esagil, *naditum* of Marduk and *kulmasitum,* the daughter of Awil-Sin her father, the son of Imgur-Sin, was given her on bringing her into the house of Utul Istar, the priest of Istar, the son of Azag-Istar for Warad-Šamas his son. When the ½ maneh of silver, her bridal gift, has been bound to her girdle [making it her absolute and personal property] and restored to Utul-Istar her father-in-law, *henceforth the children are her heirs.*[25] [Emphasis mine.]

Hammurapi changed that.

Elements in the contract apply surprisingly well to Rachel and Leah, who are also concerned with their inheritance and seem to accuse their father of a breach of contract (Gen. 31:14–16). As priestesses Rachel would be the *naditu,* her sister Leah the *sugetu.* In not wanting to give his daughters their inheritance (Gen. 31:14–15), Laban may have been attempting to follow Hammurapi—particularly as it was his sons, the interested parties, who complained (Gen. 31:1).

We also learn in one of these contracts of a woman giving her personal slave to her daughter. Interestingly, this contract provides that Damiqtum, the *sugetu* who receives her dowry from her father Ili-ma-ahi and her mother Belitum, also receives her mother's handmaid Taram-Agade, "after Belitum's god has called her away" (that is, after her mother's death). I think that the flavor of these marriage contracts can tell us more about a woman's experiences than the dry rulings of a lawmaker. The usual reason that a woman was given a slave at her marriage was because she was a *naditu* or a *kulmasitu,* who were not envisioned as bearing children. Belitum, the mother who had the handmaid, may herself have been a priestess, and her child, Damiqtum, actually the daughter of the handmaid, Taram-Agade. It is possible, then, that the social mother Belitum was providing, after her death, for the natural mother, Taram-Agade, to remain with her daughter.

The relationships between women, the mother and social mother, need not be one of hostility, as we have been led to believe in the biblical account of Sarah and Hagar. This contract also accentuates the lengthy relationship between a woman and her handmaid.

What is most relevant to the biblical story is that, according to these marriage contracts, it is consistently specified that a sister, handmaid, or slave would bear the priestess her heirs. Once the contract is signed and the dowry given, *henceforth the children are her heirs.*

SARAH'S LEGACY

If she was married the legacy of a priestess would include her dowry *(šeriktu)* (to which her husband had no claim), and the bridal-gift *(terḥatu)*, which was usually a sum of money.[26] However, the *naditu* also had what was called her "ring-money" *(ina semiris)*: money that she herself had earned and of which she had free disposition. Ring-money also consisted of property bought by the priestess, including land and slaves, which was administered by her husband.[27]

We know that Sarah had earned the considerable sum of one thousand shekels of silver, which King Abimelech handed to Abraham.[28] If this was the *ina semiris* from the king of the small territory of Gerar, how much more would the powerful king of Egypt have given Sarah for similar services? "And Abram was treated well, for her [Sarai's] sake he was given sheep, oxen, asses, male slaves and *sh'faḥot,* she-asses and camels" (Gen. 12:16). However, when they returned from Egypt to the Negev, "Abram was very laden with livestock and the silver and the gold *(b'kesef u-b'zahav)*" (Gen. 13:2). The definite article *b'* would imply that silver and gold had already been mentioned.[29] However they were not a part of the gifts given to *Abram* by Pharaoh in Genesis 12:16; the silver and the gold must then refer to Pharaoh's gift to the priestess Sarai. Again, that *Abram* is laden with wealth (that includes assets of the priestess) reflects Babylonian custom, where the husband administered the possessions of his *naditu*-wife. So even if she had earned nothing else, Sarah would certainly have owned her *šeriktu* (dowry) and the *(ina semiris)* gift/payment from Abimelech and perhaps from Pharaoh also—more than sufficient to buy Sarah's tomb, for which Abraham negotiated (for the presumably exorbitant price of four hundred shekels), with plenty left over for the future heir to inherit. What does seem clear, then, is that Sarah was concerned about a considerable inheritance.

It is also possible that some form of contract had been drawn up by Hagar's parents relinquishing her to Sarah, and that a portion of the riches received by Sarah and Abraham from Pharaoh were destined to become the property of Hagar or her offspring. Unfortunately, we have no idea whether Hagar could have been "adopted" by Sarah. Had she been a young child when she first became associated with Sarah, this could explain why it took ten years before she conceived Sarah's child. Unfortunately, too much of Hagar's story has been lost to us, leaving only a couple of tantalizing lines with which to both pose and resolve the problem of inheritance in relation to Hagar.

THE DEATH OF SARAH

One question that to my knowledge has been overlooked is the timing of Sarah's decision to dismiss Hagar and her son. Her immediate motive, as we shall see in the next chapter, concerns the *"metzahek"* incident: something in the behavior of Hagar's son that prompts Sarah's resolve. But after the determination has been settled, Sarah dies.

Two episodes (Gen. 21:22–34 and 22:1–9) and a genealogical notice on the birth of Rebekah (Gen. 22:20–24) separate the *metzahek* incident from Sarah's demise. The first records an agreement reached after a dispute between Abraham and Abimelech over ownership of a well. The second, the *akedah,* is the story of Abraham's near-sacrifice of Isaak. Both of these episodes are self-contained units that, as Gunkel points out, "begin with a distinct introduction and end with a very recognizable close."[30]

The two episodes in question begin with "At that time (Abimelech and Phicol . . . said to Abraham)" and "Sometime afterward (God put Abraham to the test"), respectively. "At that time" follows the story of Hagar and the Desert Matriarch in the desert. The episode ends, "And Abraham resided in the land of the Philistines a long time." This episode is followed with the story of the *akedah,* the binding of Isaak, which ends, "Abraham then returned to his servants, and they departed together for Beer-sheva; and Abraham stayed in Beer-sheva." Finally, Rebekah's genealogy is registered prior to the death of Sarah. Since these are obviously self-contained units they should be omitted from the Sarah and Hagar narrative and Sarah's death should be reinstated where it belongs, before the departure of Hagar, where it, too, would become "a very recognizable close."

Hagar's text ended: "God said to Abraham, 'Do not be distressed over the boy or your slave; whatever Sarah tells you, do as she says, for it is through Isaak that offspring shall be continued [for you].' " But the last sentence of this episode should include: "Sarah's lifetime—the span of Sarah's life—came to one hundred and twenty-seven years. Sarah died in Kiriath-arba—now Hebron—in the land of Canaan; and Abraham [and Hagar] proceeded to mourn for Sarah and bewail her. (Gen. 23:1–2). And then Abraham buried his wife Sarah in the cave of the field of Macpelah, facing Mamre—now Hebron—in the land of Canaan (verse 19)."

It seems reasonable to believe that Hagar mourned the loss of her companion of over half a century (see Plate 12). Thus the story of Hagar and Sarah would conclude with Hagar facing her new destiny—and Sarah, hers. Accordingly, the *metzaḥek* incident and Sarah's resolve to dismiss Hagar and her son can be understood as her deathbed testament (see appendix A).

PLATE 12. "Hagar mourned the loss of her companion."
Kneeling mourner. (Egypt, Fourth or Fifth Dynasty ca. 2500–2150 BCE). Courtesy of the Israel Department of Antiquities and Museums. The Norbert Shimmel Collection. Photo Zeev Radovan.

7. The Possible Beneficiaries

That Sarah's legacy was substantial makes the designation of a beneficiary crucial. Furthermore, as we have seen, a child inherited its mother's social status. In the case of a priestess this heritage would have had serious implications. Marriage alliances, for example, were an important factor in ancient society. Sarah's designated heir would not only receive her tangible assets, but would be in line to headship: *the heir would attain authority as "head-of-family" or clan.*

Part of the "inheritance" both boys shared equally was the right to management. This inheritance is not exclusively the transmittal of material wealth (which would be after her death), but rather the reason for which a priestess acquired an heir in the first place: to care for her in her old age; to manage her possessions (of which they would presumably inherit all or part eventually); and *to perform the appropriate ritual at her death.* Neither son is recorded as having cared for her in her old age, managed her possessions, or performed a ritual at her death.

Since lament for the dead had its original setting in the family, it is most interesting that neither Hagar's nor Sarah's son is mentioned in the mourning and burial of Sarah. This section originates with P. But neither J nor E report the matriarch's death. However, J must have recounted it at some point, because he alludes to Sarah's death at a later date, when Rebekah arrives in Canaan to marry Isaak:

Then Isaak brought her into the tent [of] his mother Sarah and he married Rebekah and so she became a wife to him; and he loved her and Isaak was comforted after his mother['s death].[1]

With little or no mention of Sarah's death or legacy in the narratives of J and E it is difficult to establish exactly what Hagar and her son were disinherited from.

According to Genesis 24:36 Abraham gave everything he owned to Isaak before his death. The wealth is enumerated: sheep and cattle, silver and gold, servants and maidservants, camels and asses. It seems strange that Abraham would give Isaak "all that he has" when he was still alive. Moreover, the inheritance Isaak received is exactly what Pharaoh gave to Abraham "because of Sarai" (Gen. 12:16), including "the silver and the gold" (Gen. 13:2). It seems unlikely that Abraham had received this sizable gift from Pharaoh, considering he had deceived him. The magnitude of the gift seems much more in accordance with the large sum of silver Abimelech gave to Abraham for Sarah.

Although being the beneficiary of wealth is of considerable significance, was this Sarah's principal concern? At the very beginning of the story, when Sarah proposes to acquire an heir by way of Hagar, she gives her reason to Abraham: *ulay ibbane mimmena,* "perchance I shall be built up through her." Hagar's son is to be regarded as her descendant.

What did this mean to Hagar's son? As we have seen, the legacy of a priestess included: (a) her material possessions, (b) the right to administer her holdings, (c) the duty to care for her in her old age, and (d) to perform important ritual libations at her death. We know too that a child inherited the status of its mother. In the case of a priestess, a female heir would inherit the rank of her religious affiliation as well. A male heir, on the other hand, would occupy a position of authority within their matrilineal descent group.[2]

The successor of a childless priestess who had not previously adopted anyone was provided for her by a woman whom she acquired when she married, and who was, as far as we know, associated with her for the purpose of providing her with offspring. This heir enjoyed the same rights as a family member. Women, particularly priestesses, who adopted heirs did not need to clarify the status of the inheritance by contract, although they often did for the purpose of stipulating specific instructions.[3]

With so much at stake we need to discover who was eligible to be Sarah's heir, and why she appointed who she did.

HAGAR AS THE POSSIBLE HEIR OF SARAH

If Hagar were truly a daughter of Pharaoh's "house" it would seem more realistic that she was presented to Sarah in the position of companion, more handmaid than slave; at least this would be in accordance with the concept of *shifḥah* who was looked upon as part of the *mishpaḥah.*

Is there any possibility that Hagar (and subsequently her son) could have had a claim on Sarah's legacy? Van Seters contends that "an ordinary concubine could not give to her son the rights of inheritance suggested here."[4] But he does not go on to question the status of the person described as *concubine:* If a concubine could not give her son rights of inheritance, which the text suggests he has, was she perhaps not a concubine?

Priestesses who lived in cloisters were also known to adopt the daughter of a sister or a junior *naditu* to care for them in their old age (after retirement).[5] The daughter then became the heir of the *bîtum epsum,* the house within the cloister, given to the priestess by her parents. The religious motive for adoption (of which the Hammurapi Laws significantly make no mention, but which appears in at least one contract) maintains that when the adoptive mother dies the adopted daughter "shall offer a libation of water for her"—a reference to a funerary rite, perhaps one related to the worship of ancestors. "The stipulation requiring the adoptee to maintain the adoptive parent is found in cases of adoption by females and some males."[6] Is there any biblical reference of an association between a woman, her *shifḥah,* and her legacy?

Proverbs 30:21–23 reads, under the heading *Four Intolerable People,*

> Under three things the earth shudders,
> there are four it cannot tolerate:

A slave who has become king;
An obstinate fool when he is filled with food;
An unpopular woman when she gets a husband;
And a slave girl who supplants her mistress.[7]

R. B. Y. Scott comments: "The slave girl . . . supplants her mistress probably by bearing her *master* a child when her mistress is barren. The contempt of Hagar for Sarah in such circumstances is noted in Gen. 16:1–6."[8] Scott's paraphrasing, however, is quite inaccurate.[9] The Hebrew text of this proverb actually claims that an intolerable person is: "*a* shifḥah *who is to inherit* (tyirash) *from her mistress.*"[10] Scott was correct in recognizing a reference to the Hagar-Sarah episode, but he was forced to mistranslate the proverb in order to accommodate it to traditional interpretation. Nevertheless, this warning demonstrates that there was a phase in which a *shifḥah* inherited from her mistress. This implies two things in the story of Hagar and Sarah: (1) Sarah had a legacy (2) in which Hagar (and consequently her son) had an interest.

If the legendary background of Hagar has any validity, she may indeed have originally been intended as Sarah's heir. However, as daughter of Pharaoh Hagar would be an Egyptian princess.[11] It would be unlikely that a king of the stature of a pharaoh would give his daughter in servitude to the wife of a wandering nomad, as the patriarchs are customarily portrayed. Furthermore, ancient Egyptian society was matrilineal and the priests took every precaution to safeguard the purity of succession.[12] An Egyptian monarch would not have approved a daughter's marriage with a foreigner.

Nevertheless, according to this legend the Egyptian king, because of his deep love for Sarah, wrote out a contract deeding her all he owned in the way of gold and silver and male and female slaves. Besides all of this he also gave her the province of Goshen (Map II), "the province occupied in later days by the descendants of Sarah, because it was their property." Most remarkable of all, Pharaoh gave Sarah his own daughter Hagar as servant, for he preferred to see her as the servant of Sarah to matron of another house."[13] On the other hand, since *sh'fahot* were included in Pharaoh's gift, Arab lore has Pharaoh insist on the matriarch choosing one of his *handmaids;* Sarah selects Hagar, "for whom she had conceived a liking," as her *shifhah*.[14]

If Sarah's primary intent regarding Hagar was to acquire a child of hers, in what way would Hagar be contemplated as heir? Since Hagar was not given to Sarah at her marriage in order to produce a successor, it is possible that Sarah, as priestess, may initially have "adopted" Hagar with the intention of making her the heir. *Naditu* priestesses are known to have adopted the woman who was to bear her children as sister. The stipulations in the contracts seem to bond the women together with the implication that, should the husband wish a divorce, he must divorce both women.[15] If there were children they would remain with the women. It is no less likely that Sarah would choose as her heir someone with whom she had a close relationship over at least a decade and who was to bear her children, than it would be for Abraham to have expected Dammeseq Eliezer (Gen. 15:2), one of his household servants of whom we know nothing, to be his successor.

I think this point is important because it shows that women also bonded to other women to insure their futures and the futures of their heirs and successors. Hagar was intimately involved in Sarah's lineage and legacy, particularly since her Egyptian heritage prescribed descent through the female line.

Since both Sarah and Hagar belonged to matrilineal descent systems, both of them must have hoped for daughters. Each, however, had only one son. Since Sarah had no sisters, her female next of kin was her uterine brother's daughter, Milkah (see Table 1).

Before Sarah's death a notice appears, giving the parentage of Rebekah: She is the grandchild of Milkah (Gen. 22:20), although she may very well have been Milkah's daughter.[16] What is important here is that Sarah is being apprised by her kin of the availability of a daughter for her son: "Milkah too has borne sons . . . and [Bethuel the father of] Rebekah." The placement of this notice in the biblical sequence is suspect.[17] "Milkah too" refers back to Sarah. Since Hagar had a son, and Sarah did not expect to conceive herself, the intention must have been that Rebekah was to marry Hagar's son, Sarah's heir.

In other words Sarah could have adopted Hagar as her successor. But since Hagar had a son, a female heir from Sarah's matrikin became a necessary component of the descent group.

THE METZAḤEK INCIDENT

The chronology of events in Genesis 21 creates the impression that Isaak is an infant at the time of the separation of the two sons. The episode, as we have seen, includes the conception and birth of Isaak, which belongs to Genesis 18. In reality, then, this episode begins with the weaning of Isaak, at which time Abraham gave a great feast.

It is significant that the feast was for the weaning of Isaak, not for his circumcision, which P states occurred when Isaak was eight days old (Gen. 21:4). It is highly unlikely that infants ever underwent the operation.[18] It is almost certain that Isaak did not—particularly if, as I contend, his mother was a Babylonian priestess and his father was the Philistine Abimelech, since neither the Babylonians nor the Philistines practiced circumcision.[19]

In antiquity, as in many contemporary communities, infant mortality was high. Extended lactation practices helped to insure infant survival. The weaning of a child was akin to rebirth; its chances of living into adulthood were maximized if it had survived the first few years. This was the reason for the feast given at Isaak's weaning. It could very well be that the feast was, in part, an acknowledgment to the nurturing goddesses who helped provide rich and nourishing mother's milk. The many figurines of goddesses and women with their breasts cupped in their hands (Plate 4) may have been used for sympathetic magic.

The sequel to the weaning feast describes an incident that manifestly elicits a forceful reaction in the matriarch Sarah: "Cast out that slave-woman and her son, for the son of that slave shall not share in the inheritance with my son Isaak," she demands of Abraham.

This episode is from the E strand, composed in the northern kingdom of Israel circa the ninth century BCE. E was geographically removed and probably close to a century later than the southern Judean J, author of the first Hagar-Sarah episode. Their vision of Hagar is equally miles apart. That Hagar evolves from the *shifḥah* of Sarah to the slave of Abraham should not surprise us.

Although the question of inheritance is a direct sequel to the weaning story, there is nothing to certify that this event happened at the same time as the feast.[20] I strongly suspect it did not because the *metzaḥek* incident, as we shall see, could only have occurred when the sons were of marriageable age.

According to the chronology of P (which is all we have), Hagar's son was fourteen years old when Isaak was born. At the time of the *metzaḥek* incident, however, sometime after the weaning feast (which must have at least been anywhere from two to four years after Isaak's birth), Hagar's son would have been between sixteen and eighteen years old. Since we do not know how much time elapsed between the weaning and the *metzaḥek* incident, he could have been even older. But Isaak too would have been much older. This would be the time when Hagar's son, now a man, had reached the marriageable age. Sarah had at least one, if not two, heirs old enough to have gained that position; one was certainly Hagar's son.

It is Hagar's son whose behavior *(metzaḥek)* convinces the matriarch Sarah that the two children should not inherit equally. Sarah's license for her decision is that "the son of this *amah* (slave) will not be heir with my son." Westermann sees the question of inheritance as "merely symptomatic," because, he says, "the future of a woman lay with her own son and nowhere else."[21] Conventional interpretation of the passage, that it is Sarah's maternal jealousy that excites her and prompts her cruel demand, is subverting a significant issue.[22]

Van Seters points out that in the first half of the story (Gen. 21:8–13) "the only tension seems to be between Sarah and Abraham over the demanded expulsion of Ishmael, but this is finally resolved by Abraham's compliance." Abraham's compliance is significant. It seems quite out of character for the patriarch, as he is traditionally portrayed, to allow Sarah to banish not only Hagar, but his own (and only natural) son. But Van Seters does not pursue the reason for Abraham's compliance, accepting, perhaps, Westermann's view that "the question of 'inheritance' is merely symptomatic," or that "God gives Sarah her way . . . because he is only the son of the maidservant."[23]

Why is Sarah so incensed at Hagar's son that he should lose the inheritance because of his *metzaḥek* behavior? The biblical verb (m)*s-h-k* used by Sarah as the motive for her demand is unclear and difficult to translate. It is variously rendered "playing," "mocking," or "amusing." None of these terms can justify Sarah's banishing Hagar and her son from Hebron. The use of these English terms give us the impression that Hagar's son was young and blameless, and that Sarah's action was due only to a mean and spiteful personality.

The Hebrew term is used in Genesis 19:14, 26:8, and 39:17, as well as 21:9. Each of these verses are contained in passages related to sexual activity. In Genesis 26:8 the term is used in reference to the "conjugal caresses" between Rebekah and Isaac, also from the E source.[24] The term is again used in Exodus 32:4–6, from the J strand, again in a relevant context: While Moses is on the mountain receiving the tablets, Aaron, his priest-brother, makes a calf-mask (*egel masehah:* of the goddess Hat-Hor?), builds an altar, and proclaims, " 'Tomorrow shall be a feast to YHWH!' Early next day, the people offered up burnt offerings and brought sacrifices of well-being; they sat down to eat and drink, and then rose to *make merry (letza-*

ḥek)." Nevertheless, Rashi comments that "This implies incest (uncovering of nakedness as is stated in Genesis
39:17)."[25] It is interesting to note that *metzaḥek,* and Isaak's
name in Hebrew, *Yitzḥak,* come from the root *tzaḥak.* This
play on words must have had some significance in the context
of the story as it was originally told, but is now lost to us.

If *metzaḥek* has a sexual connotation, as I suggest, it refers
to religious or social behavior that is of concern to Sarah.[26]
The sexual implication in *metzaḥek,* then, refers to sexual maturity. Sarah saw the son of Hagar "showing sexual maturity." Sarah realized that Hagar's son was now adult enough to
marry.

One of the underlying themes in the Genesis narratives is
the emphasis placed on the choice of marriage partners. Interestingly, both Isaak and Jacob, their mother's chosen successors, marry into their mother's descent group by way of their
mother's brothers, Harran and Laban. In matrilineal descent
groups a woman bears children who perpetuate her own but
also her brother's group.[27] A man looks to his sister, not his
wife, to provide him with heirs. Ideally, descent in the female
line would require the sisters to bear daughters. But both
Sarah and Rebekah each have only one pregnancy (which
may be due to their status as priestesses) and they bear only
sons. Since both Hagar's son and her own were male, Sarah's
spiritual successor would be a carefully chosen bride for her
successor from her own matrikin.

A section is dedicated to the background and events leading
up to the betrothal of Rebekah and Isaak. When she arrives in
Canaan Isaak symbolically introduces Rebekah to her new
station in life by consummating their union in his mother's
tent (Gen. 24:67). Legend supplies the magnitude of this
event:

You find that as long as Sarah lived, a cloud hung over her tent (sig-
nifying divine presence); when she died, the cloud disappeared; but
when Rebekah came, that openhandedness returned. As long as
Sarah lived, there was blessing on her dough, and the lamp used to

burn from the evening of the Sabbath to the evening of the following Sabbath; when she died, these ceased, but when Rebekah came, they returned. And so when he saw her following in his mother's footsteps, separating her *hallah* in cleanliness and handling her dough in cleanliness, straightway, and Isaak brought her into his tent.[28]

This, more than anything, exemplifies what Sarah meant by *ibbane*, "being built up." But the *metzahek* incident describes Sarah's anguish when she realizes that Hagar's son, her first heir, had been the recognized future husband of Rebekah.

Sarah's determination that Hagar and her son leave must have derived from three major causes: First, the son was still Sarah's heir (since she refers to the status of both sons as equal) and is now of marriageable age (Gen. 21:10b). Second, Isaak must have been too young to marry or Sarah could have arranged for his matrimony at that time. Third, she was obviously unable to do this before her death. It is only after Sarah's death that Abraham sends for Rebekah (Gen. 24:2).

SARAH'S CHOICE

The question still remains as to why Sarah was able to disinherit Hagar's son in favor of her own when, according to Babylonian custom, the son of the *shifhah* would have been regarded as the son and heir of the priestess. I think that there are several reasons for this.

In the first place, unlike historical Babylon, the norm in Genesis is ultimogeniture, the succession of the youngest.[29] Isaak is Sarah's youngest, and therefore her "chosen" son.

In the second place, the circumcision of Hagar's son would have been an issue. The rite of circumcision could certainly have been a serious factor for Sarah, if, as P claims, Abraham had circumcised Hagar's son. The circumcision of Abraham at age ninety-nine is symbolic of the patriarch's initiation into a new covenant community with Elohim and a rejection of his

Mesopotamian heritage. There would have been no conflict for Hagar over the circumcision of her son, since it was an ancient custom among the Egyptians. Was Hagar the Egyptian introducing religio-cultural customs to Abraham and her son that were unacceptable to Sarah?

Finally, Isaak was conceived during the ceremony of the sacred nuptials, when both his parents—Sarah and Abimelech—embody divinities.[30] Isaak, like the Mesopotamian rulers Gilgamesh and Shulgi before him, could claim he was divinely conceived. Not so the son of Hagar and Abraham, who was conceived by mere humans. As Sarah's acquired heir Hagar's son would have inherited a certain status from his social mother, but this would not compare to the divine status of his half-brother. It is to Sarah's youngest son, the divinely conceived son, that Sarah wishes to bestow succession.

Sarah's reason for her decision would not have been alien to Hagar; she would have recognized the special divine status of Isaak. The god of Egypt

took upon himself the form of the reigning king of Egypt, and he visited the queen in her chamber and became the actual father of the child who was subsequently born to her. When the child was born it was regarded as a god incarnate, and in due course, was presented, with appropriate ceremonies, to Ra or Amen-Ra, in his temple, and this god accepted or acknowledged it to be his child.[31]

Traditionally, Isaak is Abraham's youngest also, but the relation between Isaak and Abraham has been forced in the genealogy. After Abraham's death comes the usual list of begetting, which start with the customary introduction: *ve-ele toledot,* "this is the genealogy"; but what follows is the list of Ishmael's descendants (Gen. 25:12), not Isaak's. Isaak's genealogy is even stranger. It too starts with *ve-ele toledot,* "this is the genealogy" of Isaak, son of Abraham; but it then goes backwards, reversing the descent line by stating: "Abraham begot Isaak." There is nothing in the genealogy about Isaak's descendants either. Instead, Isaak and Rebekah's genealogy commences with the narration of the birth of Esau and Jacob.

Scholars call this an "expanded genealogy." The absence of customary genealogy and the elusive accounts of Isaak may be due to the special circumstances of his conception and birth.

The profound transformation has now taken place: Sarah, who was to only have an acquired son, is now mother of her own biological child, Isaak. As her spiritual heir and beneficiary of her assets, Isaak is free to marry Sarah's successor, Rebekah.

Yet the transformation that benefits Sarah deprives Hagar of her status as mother of Sarah's heir, and all that might have entailed. But Hagar is not left destitute. She is now free to leave Hebron and seek out her own destiny and that of her son. That the "sexual maturity" of Hagar's son was an important component in Sarah's decision, and that Hagar is now in control of her life and her son's, is evident from the fact that *she* chooses a wife for her son from her Egyptian homeland (Gen. 21:21), despite the paternity of Abraham.

More important, Hagar, who was destined to have no child she could call her own, is now the acknowledged mother of her own biological son. But this son, whose destiny had been to inherit the awesome wealth and power of a priestess, is left destitute, and is the major loser in this changed situation.

Significantly, Hagar's son did not acquire a name until he was identified with the son of the Desert Matriarch (see Table 2). In confusing him with Ishmael the biblical writers, as we shall see, granted the son of Hagar and Abraham the semidivine status enjoyed by the son of El-ro'i.

8. The Desert Matriarch

Genesis 16:7–15 and Genesis 21:14–21

Two desert sequences in the Genesis narratives are accredited to the life story of Hagar the Egyptian. These desert sections comprise only sixteen verses. As we shall see, however, only four of these verses apply to Hagar. The remainder belong to the story of the figure I have identified as the Desert Matriarch.

Since the two sections of Genesis 16:7–15 and 21:14–21 belong to the story of the same woman, it will be necessary to reassemble and then disentangle the stories, so that the individual accounts of the two women, Hagar and the Desert Matriarch, can become evident.

THE TWO DESERT NARRATIVES

Significantly J's desert sequence (Gen. 16:11–14) is out of context. It does not belong after the conception of Hagar's child in verse 4. P's connecting phrases—which have Hagar flee Sarah's wrath and then return to her by command of the "angel of" YHWH—should be excluded, together with P's reference to Abraham at the end (verses 15–16), thereby leaving this desert story intact.[1] Once these phrases have been omitted, as discussed in chapter 2, we are left with the text of a nameless woman in the desert, whom I call the Desert Matriarch. This text, Genesis 16:11–14, must first be reconnected to the desert text in Genesis 21:14–21, both of which contain the theme of a miraculous well or spring. Furthermore, the second desert story in Genesis 21, compiled by the E source, includes material that belongs exclusively to the Hagar source.

So we are dealing first with a Desert Matriarch text that was divided into two sections; and second with a separate portion of Hagar's story in which she too has a sequence in the desert, but which has been interwoven with the second Desert Matriarch text.

First, let us combine the two complete desert stories, the first by J and the second by E.*

16   7 An angel of YHWH found her by a spring of water in the desert, the spring on the road to Shur
11 And the angel of YHWH said to her
"Behold you are pregnant
and shall bear a son
You shall call him Ishmael
For YHWH has paid heed to your suffering
12 He shall be a wild ass of a man
His hand against everyone
And everyone's hand against him,
And in defiance of all his kinsmen he shall take over (rule)."
13 And she called the Lord who spoke to her, "You are El-ro'i," [the all-seeing god] by which she meant, "Even here I have seen after I have seen?"
14 Therefore he called the well Beer-lahai-ro'i. It is between Kadesh and Bered.

21   14 Early next morning Abraham took some bread and a skin of water and gave them to Hagar. He placed them on her shoulder, together with the child, and sent her away. And she wandered about in the desert of Beer-sheva.
15 When the water was gone from the water-skin, she left the child under one of the bushes,
16 and went and sat herself down across [from him], a bow-shot away, for she said "Let me not look on the death of the child." And she sat across and she cried out loudly.
17 God heard the cry of the lad, and an angel of Elohim called to Hagar from heaven, "What troubles you, Hagar? Fear not, for Elohim has heard the voice of the lad wherever he may be.
18 Come, lift up the lad and hold your hand on him, for I will make a great nation of him."

---

*Again, J's story is in boldface type, E's is underlined.

19 Then Elohim opened her eyes and she saw a well of water. She went and filled the skin with water and let the boy drink.

20 And Elohim was with the boy; and he grew up he dwelt in the desert and became a bowman.
21 He lived in the desert of Paran, and his mother got a wife for him from the land of Egypt.

Once the two episodes have been combined, discrepancies become obvious.

To begin with the episodes mention two different locations in the Sinai Peninsula: Shur and Beer-sheva/Paran (see Map IV). The location in Genesis 16 is the Way to Shur, where the Desert Matriarch was found (verse 7) between Kadesh and Bered (verse 14). The site of Bered has not been determined: but Kadesh (Kadesh-Barnea) is a thirty-six mile walk from the desert of Beer-sheva of Genesis 21. Kadesh and Kedesh are used for cities that were ancient sanctuaries in the land of Canaan.[2] "Barnea" is coupled with Kadesh to distinguish it from other sacred sites. The site of this Kadesh-Barnea, which has been equated with the location of Genesis 16, has been identified with the ancient oasis known in Arabic as *'Ain el-Oudeirat*. Kadesh-Barnea is distinctive because it has the largest of three brooks and the only one that flows all year.[3] But this latter classification makes an argument against Kadesh-Barnea/'Ain el-Qudeirat as the site, since the Desert Matriarch's anguish was due to lack of water.

Abraham too is said to have journeyed "from there to the region of the Negev and settled between Kadesh and Shur" (Gen. 20:1). However, the story continues, "While he was sojourning in Gerar . . ." but Gerar is not on the way to Kadesh-Barnea or Shur (see Map III). At any rate Genesis 20:1 must have been misplaced because the "from there" makes no sense in its present context.

The location of the Desert Matriarch between Kadesh and Bered must have been somewhere south of the Brook of Egypt on the Way to Shur (Map IV). It seems more likely

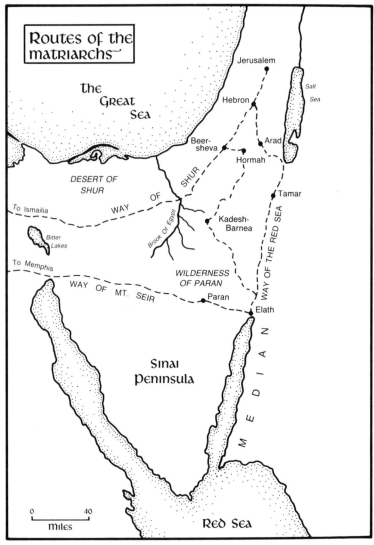

Routes of the matriarchs

The Great Sea

Jerusalem

Salt Sea

Hebron

Beer-sheva

Arad

DESERT OF SHUR

SHUR

Hormah

WAY OF SHUR

To Ismailia

Brook Of Egypt

Tamar

Bitter Lakes

Kadesh-Barnea

WAY OF THE RED SEA

To Memphis

WILDERNESS OF PARAN

WAY OF MT. SEIR

Paran

Elath

MEDIAN

Sinai Peninsula

0   40
miles

Red Sea

Mary McArthur, Cartographer.

Map IV

that the location would be closer to the Desert of Shur, three days' journey from Egypt, where Moses and the children of Israel traveled and found no water (Exod. 15:22).

The wilderness of Beer-sheva, on the other hand, extends eastward toward Hormah and Tamar in the Negev and the Wilderness of Paran, west of Elath. So, to begin with, we are dealing with two different locations at which different events happened to two distinct matriarchs; one who was "found" on the Way of Shur, the other who "wandered about" in the Wilderness of Beer-sheva.

Second, there is a discrepancy in the portrayal of the son in Genesis 21, which is more striking in Hebrew than in English. The expression for the son alternates between "child," *yeled* and "lad," *na'ar;* English translations use "boy" throughout, or "child" and "boy," making the distinction trivial.[4] I suggest that *yeled,* child, describes the son of the Desert Matriarch, whose birth took place in the beginning of her story. Hagar's son is more likely the *na'ar,* the youth for whom she found a wife in her Egyptian homeland.

Also striking is the fact that in the biblical text the miracle of the well and its naming is told before the near death of the child. One would expect this miraculous appearance of the well to happen when the child is dying of thirst, and then be followed, as in the first episode, with the naming of both the miraculous well and the god who caused it. But neither the god nor the well receive names in the second episode.

I would argue, then, that the lad *(na'ar)* sentences and those about a child *(yeled)* belong to two distinct narratives. If the "lad" *(na'ar)* passages belong to Hagar's story, and the "child" *(yeled)* phrases are the Desert Matriarch's, the two accounts become discernible (Hagar's phrases are set in bold type, the Desert Matriarch's in Roman):

21   14a Early next morning Abraham ... sent Hagar away
14c And she wandered about in the Wilderness of Beer-sheva.

16 7a "An angel" of YHWH found her by a spring of water in the desert, the spring on the Way of Shur.

21 14a (He) took some bread and a skin of water and gave them to (her)

14b He placed them on her shoulder together with the *child (ha-yeled)*.

15 When the water was gone from the water-skin, she put the *child (ha-yeled)* under one of the bushes, and went and she sat herself across [from him], a bow-shot away; for she said, "let me not look on the death of the *child (ha-yeled)*." And she sat across and she cried out loudly.

21 **17 Elohim heard the voice of the *lad (ha-na'ar)* and a messenger of Elohim called to Hagar from heaven and said to her, "What troubles you Hagar? Fear not, for Elohim has heard the voice of the *lad (ha-na'ar)* wherever he is.**

18 Come, lift up the *lad (ha-na'ar)* and hold your hand on him, for I will make a great nation of him."

21 19 Then Elohim opened her eyes and she saw a well of water. She went and filled the water-skin with water and let the boy *(ha-na'ar)* drink.

20b he dwelt in the desert and became a bowman [archer].

21 **20a Elohim was with the *lad (ha-na'ar)* and he grew up**
21 He lived in the wilderness of Paran; and his mother got a wife for him from the land of Egypt.

It becomes evident in this classification of the texts that a few passages that applied to Hagar have been interwoven with a portion of the story that belongs to the Desert Matriarch. In separating the two stories it becomes clear that they are quite distinct and refer to two different episodes.

The text can now be analyzed as follows:

1. The two sons are clearly contrasted; one is a child or infant, the other a young lad. This distinction is corroborated in the text, in that Hagar's son is called the *lad (ha-na'ar)*, except in verse 14; and the Desert Matriarch's son, the *child (ha-yeled)*, except in verse 19. There is one problematic note in this accounting of the Hagar desert story:

that Abraham, among other things, gave Hagar a skin of water at her departure but it is the Desert Matriarch who remains without water in the skin. But, as we know, much of this material was reworked to link the patriarch to the matriarchs and their descendants.[5] Thus I think it is safe to assume that it was originally the Desert Matriarch rather than Hagar who went off into the desert with her son on her shoulder together with the water-skin, because the son is described as *yeled* in this phrase. It is also the mother of the *yeled* who is left without water in the skin later on in the story.

Because of the confusion between two sons of different ages, it became problematic for commentators to accept that a youth was set on the matriarch's shoulder; it caused many speculations to surface.[6]

2. That the Desert Matriarch's son is referred to as *ha-na'ar* in verse 19 must be a scribal error, since it concerns the child dying of thirst.

3. The "Way of Shur" becomes the location of the epiphany of the Desert Matriarch, and Beer-lahai-ro'i the site of the miraculous well; whereas Beer-sheva/Paran is the locale of Hagar's experience. Since the Desert Matriarch was found by the deity on the Way of Shur, where her story begins, she is not connected to Hebron or Beer-sheva. Hagar, on the other hand, leaves Sarah's abode in Hebron, travels to Beer-sheva, and wanders about in the wilderness there.

4. The reference to the mother being "a bow-shot away" is compatible with her child's destiny as a bowman. These terms may originate with the Desert Matriarch's clan identification of archers or hunters . . . but also of warriors. A wall relief in the temple of Ramses III (1182–1152 BCE) at Medinat Habu shows the king and his archer attendants (Plate 13). Hundreds of specimens of various types of arrows were found in Sakkara tombs. Their size and lightness confirms the comparative small-

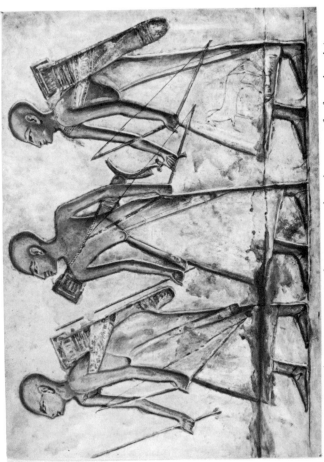

PLATE 13. "The Desert Matriarch may never have been very far from her dying child."

Egyptian archers, Temple of Ramses III (Medinat Habu, Egypt 1182–1151 BCE). Courtesy of the Oriental Institute of the University of Chicago. Photo Alfred Bollacher.

ness of the bow.[7] The Desert Matriarch may never have been very far from her dying child. Westermann points out that this is the first and virtually the last time a weapon is mentioned in the patriarchal story.[8] This supports the strong possibility that the Desert Matriarch's story belonged to separate Ishmaelite lore. The symbols for virile manhood were the bow and arrow in ancient Israel, and sexual potency is compared to arrows in the quiver of a mighty man.[9] Masculinity, then, was seen as comprising sexual potency and military prowess. The matriarchs' sons are each divinely endowed with one of these two elements: Hagar's son, with sexual potency, would become instrumental in founding a nation; and the Desert Matriarch's son, with military prowess, would put his hand against his enemies, with the bow and arrow. In other words he would identify with the clan characteristics of his mother's.

5. A distinction is made between the *Matriarch who cried out* and was heard and rescued by YHWH (Gen. 16:11) and Elohim hearing and answering the *cry of the lad* (Gen. 21:17).

6. The two endings "and he lived," verses 20a and 21, in this rendering become attached to their own records. The first—"he [Ishmael] lived in the desert and became a bowman"—belongs to the locale of Shur, where El-ro'i/YHWH found his mother; it presumably refers to his mother's clan of archers, since she measured distance by the length of a bow-shot. The Desert Matriarch was on the "Way of Shur" between Kadesh and Bered; the "Way" is identified as a road that runs north of Kadesh-Barnea to Ismailia (Map IV). The site of Bered is unknown.

7. Hagar, on the other hand lived with her son in the desert of Paran and "got a wife for him from the land of Egypt." It is Hagar's son, *ha-naʿar,* now a "sexually mature" young man, who is old enough to be married.

The Wilderness of Paran is mentioned ten times in the Bible, but its location does not always appear to be in the same region.[10] However, since Hagar takes a wife for her son from her homeland, I believe the accurate site in this instance is the site mentioned in 1 Kings 11:18, in which Hadad the Edomite and his retinue flee from Edom south to Midian (Map III), and from there west through Paran to Egypt. The Wilderness of Paran referred to here must have stretched across the mountain range west of the gulf (of Aqaba), incorporating the Way of Mt. Seir, which crossed the Sinai Peninsula to Memphis (see Map IV). Hagar could have taken the route from Hebron through Arad to the Way of the Red Sea; or she may have gone first to Beer-sheva and from there to Kadesh-Barnea and from there found her way to Egypt through Paran.

The different topography of the locations is also worthy of mention. Although the biblical term for the three locations, Shur, Beer-sheva, and Paran, are all referred to as *midbar* (desert), they are very different; the English terms "desert" and "wilderness" do them more justice. The Desert of Shur is sandy with an occasional barren rock jutting from it. Had the Desert Matriarch crossed the Brook of Egypt, and continued in a westerly direction, she could easily have lost her way in the sandy desert. The Wilderness of Paran, on the other hand, consists of a striking range of high rock mountains that are completely barren. It is certainly a long way to Egypt from Hebron via the wilderness of Paran: over two thousand miles. Hagar may have wandered on the outskirts of Beer-sheva on her way to Hormah or Tamar, where she could have joined a caravan that would have taken them to Egypt, perhaps by the Way of the Sea of Reeds. It was therefore not Hagar's son who was in danger of dying of thirst in the desert; it was the Desert Matriarch's son, Ishmael.

MIRACLE IN THE DESERT:
THE DESERT MATRIARCH TEXT

The originally separate narrative of the Desert Matriarch is about the miraculous appearance of a well and the mystery of the birth of her son, Ishmael. The core material was used by both J and E, who employed different portions of it in their narratives. Because of this the well could receive its name before the near death of the Desert Matriarch's child.

I suggest that the original material went something like this:

THE DESERT MATRIARCH TEXT

16 **7 (An angel of) YHWH found her by a spring of water in the desert, the spring on the road to Shur and said, 11b "See, you are now pregnant and you will have a son. 12 and he will be a wild ass of a man his hand against all and everyone's hand against him and against the face of all his brothers will he rule.**

21   14b And he [Elohim] gave her bread and a skin of water setting them on her shoulder with the child. 15 When the waters were gone from the water-skin she left the child under one of the bushes 16 and she went and she sat herself across [from him], being like [the distance of] the shooting of a bow, because, she said, "I cannot look on the death of the child," and she sat across [from him] and she cried out loudly. 19 Then Elohim opened her eyes and she saw a well of waters so she went and filled the water-skin and she gave the child to drink.

11a and [the angel of] YHWH told her further, "you shall call his name Ishmael for YHWH heard your suffering

16   13 And she called the name of [YHWH] the one speaking to her "You are El-ro'i," because, she said, "Even here I have seen after I have seen." Therefore he called the well Beer lahai-ro'i.
It is between Kadesh and Bered.
20   19 He dwelt in the desert and became a bowman.
25   17 And these are the years of Ishmael: one hundred and thirty-seven years; then he breathed his last and was gathered to his kin.

In this rendering of the text the narrative of the Desert Matriarch can be appreciated fully. I have omitted verse 10—"And the angel of YHWH said to her 'I will greatly increase your offspring and they shall be too many to count.' " As Van Seters rightly points out, "It is quite incompatible with v.11 for it talks about Hagar's offspring before mentioning the birth of the child and the whole perspective is quite different from what follows in vv.11–12," in which the prophetic oracle speaks of only one descendant.[11] Also, as mentioned previously, this prophecy attempts to associate the Matriarch's epiphany with the promise to Abraham in Genesis 15:5.

The Desert Matriarch experiences the mystery of impregnation by a desert god. This god is neither YHWH, as J maintains, nor Elohim, as suggested by E. He is an unknown desert god whom the Matriarch later names El-ro'i. This god reveals the mystery of her impregnation to the Matriarch in verse 11a, and foretells the child's destiny to her in verse 12: "He will be a wild ass of a man." (This is not an uncommon description. Samsi, an Arab queen, is compared to a "wild ass-mare."[12]) A notice of the birth of Ishmael has been omitted, as was the birth of Hagar's son. The birth of Ishmael could not be recorded because it occurred in the desert. The birth of Hagar's son could not be recorded because it would have challenged the hostile relationship between Hagar and Sarah and would have emphasized the fact that the child was Sarah's heir, not Abraham's.

The last part of the couplet of verse 11, the naming of the child Ishmael, "El-heard," was out of place in the original section because it referred to the Desert Matriarch's suffering before the crisis occurred. In fact the child is not named in the whole of E's section, which seems inconceivable if a name had been given to him previously. He was named after the crisis because his name is linked to his plight. The name Ishma-el is given in response to the intervention of the god El-ro'i who heard the loud cry of the Desert Matriarch when she thought her baby was dying of thirst. Furthermore, the name *El*-heard (Ishma*el*), incorporates the name of the God *El*-ro'i (not YHWH), who saved his life. "On certain occasions we are able to catch the name of a pre-Javistic God of the legend," Gunkel comments.[13] At any rate, this is certainly not a "YHWH" story and should not form part of the narrative of J that deals with Hagar.

This confusion of gods is somewhat clumsily resolved in verse 13, "And she called the name of YHWH the one speaking to her, you are El-ro'i." Van Seters believes that this verse may be considered suspect as an addition, and that the explanation of Ishmael's name in Genesis 16:11c is probably not original and is irrelevant to the story [of J]."[14] However, removing the name of YHWH, and placing the naming of Ishmael after the incident in which the god hears him cry, seems a more sensible solution.

SIGNIFICANCE OF THE DESERT MATRIARCH TEXT

The narrative of the Desert Matriarch tells the story of the miraculous birth of a hero and the materialization of a sacred well. The hero is the ancestor of the tribe of Ishmaelites who bear his name. The main protagonist, however, is not the son but the mother. It is the Desert Matriarch's story that contains the elements of a betrothal-type scene as defined by Alter and Fuchs, as discussed in chapter 2. It is she who becomes impregnated by a divinity, giving her son semidivine status. The god-bridegroom foretells the personal future of the child. This is not the prediction of a future nation but rather the personal forecast of a hero of a desert tribe of nomads.

The narration of the rescue of the child dying from thirst is told almost as though it were a separate story. The miracle of the well is told in very simple terms—"Then Elohim opened her eyes and she saw a well of water"—and yet this is the axis on which the narrative revolves. Because of the miraculous appearance to the Matriarch of the well of water, the god receives his name, the well receives its name, and the child receives his name.

The names are all connected to the Desert Matriarch: Ishmael, for the god's response to the woman's anguished cry; El-ro'i ("visionary god" or perhaps "god of my vision"), so called because of the woman's epiphany; finally, El-ro'i names the well Beer-lahai-ro'i ("well of one who sees and lives?") because of the woman's experience there.

The Desert Matriarch's experience at the well is not clear in the biblical rationalization. By giving the god the name "El-ro'i" she meant, the Bible tells us in an enigmatic phrase, *"hagam halom raiti aharei ro'i."* This phrase has elicited many interpretations, such as, "Have I gone on seeing after he saw me?" presupposing death after seeing god (Exod. 33:20; Judg. 6:23, and so on). The literal Hebrew words translate to: now-here-I-saw-behind (or after) seeing. The name given the well is also obscure: *Beer-lahai-ro'i* or "well-living/ One-seeing." Following my interpretation of the story, I would suggest this phrase meant something like, "She named him El-ro'i by which she meant 'now here, (in this spot) I saw (came face to face with) the god after (having) my vision,' and it is because of this that *he,* El-ro'i, named the spring, *well* of the *visionary* (woman who gave or gained) *life.*" In this instance the god also gives a name to his son in recognition of *his* experience; *El*(-ro'i) *heard* the cry of the afflicted mother, and called their son, Ishma-el.

The Desert Matriarch, like Sarah, is (1) a woman blessed with an epiphany (2) whose son becomes the manifestation of her vision. Like Sarah's son Isaak, who faces death at the hands of his father (Gen. 22), the son of the Desert Matriarch also experiences a symbolic rebirth. He, like Isaak after him, is saved from death by divine intervention. The abode of the Desert Matriarch becomes a sacred sanctuary, Beer-lahai-ro'i, as did the grove of the terebinths of Mamre, the abode of Sarah the priestess.

Perhaps most important, both matriarchs—the Desert Matriarch and Sarah—are recorded as participating in a theophany. Their direct interaction (with life-giving connotations) with the supernatural is the element that gives substance to the events. This exceptional situation is what has given their stories a factor of timelessness and secrecy, as though the revelation were too sacred to be imparted.

THE ISLAMIC TEXTS

Although Hagar is not mentioned in the Qur'an, the Holy Book of Islam, she has a significant role in tradition. Most of her story is culled from Genesis 21. An enactment of Hagar's plight, known as the *Sa'y,* is performed by devotees (though not a requirement) who make a pilgrimage to the Islamic sanctuary at Mecca (Map I).

Numerous collections of traditions have been prepared by different Islamic scholars. Some of these works have obtained almost canonical standing among later Muslims. But an official codification, which would be exclusively valid, has never been made.[15] The collection of al-Bukhari is recognized as particularly authoritative and is held in high esteem.[16]

According to the Islamic story Sarah's jealousy induced Abraham to decide to travel to Arabia with Hagar and Ishmael. "The party was guided by the *Sakina* [Hebrew, Shehinah] or, according to others, by Gabriel."[17]

Al-Bukhari gives the account of Hagar's story as follows:[18]
Abraham brought her and her son Ishmael, when she was suckling him, and placed them at the sight of the House [the Ka'ba, sanctu-

ary] under a tree, over Zamzam [a stream] on the place of the Mosque. And there was no one in Mecca at that time and no water. And he placed them there, and set down by them a vessel with dates, and poured water therein. Then Abraham took the trail to leave them. And the mother of Ishmael followed him, and said, O Abraham, Where are you going, leaving us in the valley where there is no human or anything! And she said that to him repeatedly, but he went on without turning to her. So she said, Did Allah command you to do this? He said, Yes! And she said, Then He will not forsake us. And Abraham went on until, when he was at the turn, where they could not see him, he turned his face toward the (place of the) House, and prayed this prayer: "O Lord! verily, I have caused my seed to dwell in this valley, without vegetation, by Thy Sacred House! O Our Lord, may they stand here in prayer; and make the hearts of some folk love them, and feed them with fruits so that they may be thankful!"

Then the mother of Ishmael began suckling Ishmael and drinking from that water, until what was in the vessel was exhausted; and she thirsted, and her son thirsted. And she began looking upon him writhing, or, as accounts say, kicking. And she went away, not liking to look upon him. And she found as-Safa, the nearest mountain in the land adjoining, and went upon it. Then she turned toward the valley to see whether she beheld anyone—and she beheld no one. And she came down from as-Safa. Then she raised the tips of her arms, and hastened with the haste of a person exerting himself, until she passed through the valley. Then she came to al-Marwah, and got up on it, and looked to see whether she beheld any one, and she did not behold anyone. And she did that seven times.

And when she ascended al-Marwah, she heard a sound, and said, Silence! (Meaning herself). Then she heard it again; and she said, I have heard you! If there is any help with you—! And behold, Gabriel was there at the place of Zamzam; and he scraped it with his heel (or, his wing) until water appeared. And she began damming it up, and catching it with her hand, thus, and putting it by handfuls into her vessel. And Ibn 'Abbas says: The Prophet [Muḥammed] said, Allah have mercy on the mother of Ishmael! If she had only left Zamzam, or if she had not caught the water with her hands, Zamzam would be a clear spring!

So then she drank and suckled her child. And the Angel said to her, Fear not being forsaken; for here is the (place of the) House of Allah, which the child will build up, with his father; and, verily, Allah does not forsake his people.

Two elements are immediately apparent in the Islamic version: (1) the woman is referred to as "the mother of Ishmael"; and (2) the woman has no part in the miraculous appearance of the spring. Like the Desert Matriarch, this woman has no name. Unlike the Desert Matriarch, her action—scooping up the water to save herself and her son—is scorned: Because of her the miraculous Zamzam spring is murky!

Nevertheless this matriarch's plight is linked to a rite. According to Ibbn 'Abbas, the Prophet said, For that reason the people on Pilgrimage hasten between the two mountains. In fact, the Qur'an ascribes special sanctity to the two mountains:

Behold! Safa and Marwa are among the Symbols of Allah,
So if those who visit the House in the Season
or at other times,
Should compass them round,
It is no sin to them. (*surah* [chapter] 158)

In a classic commentary on The Holy Qur'an, the sacred book of Islam, on *surah* 158, Abdullah Yusuf Ali remarks:

These are two little hills of Safa and Marwa now absorbed in the city of Mecca and close to the well of Zam-zam. Here, according to tradition, the lady Hajar, mother of the infant Isma'il, prayed for water in the parched desert, and in her eager quest round these hills, she found her prayer answered and saw the Zam-zam spring. Unfortunately Pagan Arabs had placed a male and a female idol here, and their gross superstitious rites caused offense to early Muslims. They felt some hesitation going around these places during the Pilgrimage. As a matter of fact they should have known that the Ka'ba (the House of God) had been itself defiled with idols, and was sanctified by the purity of Muhammad's life and teaching."[19]

The two hills near the Ka'ba in Mecca were sacred in pre-Islamic times and are said to have contained a male image on as-Safa and a female image on al-Mawra. Pilgrims ran back and forth between them seven times. The Prophet incorporated the ancient Arab ritual into Islam by linking it to the mother of Ishmael, or, conversely, the ritual originated with the *sa'y* of an Arab Desert Matriarch story, which the Prophet linked to Abraham. In fact, it is very likely that Muḥammed recognized the biblical Desert Matriarch story in Arab lore. He wisely left her nameless in the Qur'an so that she could be incorporated into the Sarah-Abraham-Hagar account.

The "place of the House" (the Ka'ba) was also a pre-Islamic sanctuary that contained an image of an Arabian god, Hubal, a stellar deity. The statue stood inside the Ka'ba, above the sacred well, which was thought to have been dug by Abraham. In the mural paintings of the pre-Islamic Ka'ba Hubal was represented as an old man holding arrows.[20] The practice of establishing a new faith by introducing new characters to ancient shrines seems to have been customary with all major religions.

ORIGIN OF THE DESERT MATRIARCH TEXT

We have no way of knowing the source of the Desert Matriarch text, since, to my knowledge, there are no extrabiblical texts similar to it or which allude to it. However, much in the text, as noted above, is associated with Arabian pre-Islamic religion.

But there is also much that hails from Egypt. Unique in the story of the Desert Matriarch is that she measures distance by a bow-shot and her son becomes a bowman. These elements are predominant in Egypt and Egyptian mythology. Both Egyptian women and goddesses are associated with bows and arrows.

The oldest and most characteristic symbols of the goddess Neith were two arrows and a bow or shield (indicating, in part, that she was a goddess of war, not only of the hunt).[21] At a very early period these became the recognized emblems, not only of Neith herself but also of Sais, the chief city in which her temple was situated, and for the nome (province or region) of which the city of Sais was capital.[22] Neith is one of the most ancient of Egyptian goddesses and her worship was widespread even in predynastic times (see Plate 14b). During the first four dynasties this goddess possessed sanctuaries in many parts of Egypt, and several of her priests and priestesses were buried in *mastaba* tombs in and near Saqqara.[23] According to Wallis Budge,

The cult of Nit, or Neith, must have been very general in Egypt, although in dynastic times the chief seat thereof was at Sais in the Delta, and we know that devotees of the goddess lived as far south as Nakada, a few miles to the north of Thebes, for several objects inscribed with the name of queen Nit-hetep have been found in a grave at that place.[24] . . . The hieroglyphic texts prove that in very early times Neith was the personification of the eternal female principle of life which was self sustaining, self existent, and was secret, unknown and all pervading. . . . and that she brought forth her son Ra without the aid of a husband.[25]

The Heliopolitan priesthood attempted to discredit Neith in favor of her son, their god Ra. But "it was found hopeless to attempt to substitute the Heliopolitan company of gods for Neith in the city of Sais, because there the worship of that goddess was extremely ancient and was very important. The fact that her name forms a component part of royal names very early in the Ist Dynasty proves that her worship dates from the first half of the archaic period, and that it is much older than the theological system at Heliopolis."[26] (See Map II.)

In fact there were at least three queens whose names contained the element "Neith" and whose symbols were crossed arrows: Neith-hotep, Her-Neith and Meryet-Neith (Plate 14a). These queens have been identified by their impressive tombs. It has been suggested that these queens were consorts of the first kings, but there is no evidence for this.[27]

On a different level, then, the story of the Desert Matriarch can be seen to incorporate the archetypal figure of an Egyptian goddess.

THE DESERT MATRIARCH AND THE GODDESS

The attributes of Neith, like those of other ancient goddesses, varied from time to time, as "priests attempted to harmonize every new religious system of belief with every one that had existed before it."[28] Contemporary scholars also believe that attributes of different goddesses were ascribed to each goddess; thus Neith, "who was believed to perform some important ceremonies in connection with the dead" is identified with Isis; or, "in late dynastic times was regarded as nothing but a form of Hathor, 'the cow who gave birth to Ra.' "[29] Although goddesses, with the help of priest manipulation, may have adapted aspects of each other, their similarities may originate from another source.

Neith, Hat-Hor, and Isis are cosmic goddesses. All three incorporate three aspects (three phases of the moon): maiden, mother, and crone. All three were looked upon as mothers of all the deities. But each also had only one son: Sebek, Heru-ur (Horus the Elder), and Horus (the Younger), respectively. These three goddesses are also cthonic deities, connected with the underworld. Neith, Lady of the West (Death), was believed to perform some important ceremonies in connection with the dressing, preservation, and protection of the dead which were of a magical character. It is in her aspect of crone, protector of the dead, that I would associate Neith's emblems of bow and arrow.

I suggest that the stories of the biblical matriarchs also contain archetypal aspects of the goddess: maiden, mother, and crone. Like Isis in her maiden aspect, Hagar and Sarah remain childless for a considerable period of time. Like the three goddesses (in the archaic period) in their mother aspects, Hagar and Sarah each have only one son. And like a cthonic goddess, the Desert Matriarch rescues her son from the underworld.[30]

Many elements in the story of the Desert Matriarch, as I have presented it, belie a link to the goddess Neith: the mention of arrows and the prophecy that her son would be a warrior ("His hand against everyone" [Gen. 167:12]; Neith's son Sebek was called "great king, the prince of the Nine Bow Barbarians");[31] the divine conception and birth of her son "without a husband" and the miraculous survival of her son from the grip of death have some correlation to the goddess Neith. The Matriarch's enigmatic description of herself—"Even here I have seen after I have seen, *(hagam halom raiti aharei ro'i)"*—evokes a reflection of Neith's description of herself, "I am what has been, what is, and what shall be." [32] (see Plate 14b.) It must be remembered too that the Desert Matriarch *named* the god, something even Moses dared not do!

Since Neith's importance and popularity extended over Upper and Lower Egypt, many myths must have circulated about her; the biblical story may very well reflect an archaic Arabian myth influenced by Egypt. The Sinai Peninsula, after all, was a great source of materials for Egypt, the most important of which were copper, malachite, and turquoise.[33] There the goddess Hat-Hor was worshiped long before the close of the Sixth Dynasty (2345–2181 BCE).[34] It is tolerably certain that Egyptian myth traveled with caravans that bartered merchandise across the Sinai Peninsula.

Conventionally, in her fusion with Hagar, the inclusion of the Desert Matriarch fulfilled the promise to Abraham in Genesis 17 that he will be a father of nations and that Ishmael will be fertile and his offspring exceedingly numerous and will be made into a great nation (Gen. 17:18–20). The maxim of the story being that "Israel's inheritance of the land is tied to the expulsion of non-Israelites."[35]

PLATE 14a. "The symbols of crossed arrows on a stela of Queen Meryet-Neith." *Stela of Meryet-Neith (3100–2800 BCE). Egyptian Museum, Cairo.*

PLATE 14b. Neith is one of the most ancient of the Egyptian goddesses, and her worship was widespread even in dynastic times. "I am what has been, what is, and what shall be."
The Los Angeles County Museum of Art. Gift of the Hearst Foundation.

The account collected by al-Bukhari, to some extent, supports this. After being saved by the angel Gabriel, Ishmael and his mother remained in Mecca:

until there came by a company of the Jurham, or people of a tribe who approached by such a way; and they encamped at the lower part of Mecca. And they saw a bird circling; and they said, Verily, this bird is circling about for water. We have carefully observed this valley and there is no water in it. So they sent a scout or two—and behold, water! So they returned and informed them about the water and they approached. And the mother of Ishmael was at the water. And they said, Will you allow us to settle here near you? And she said, Yes, but you will have no right in the water. They said, yes. So they sent word to their people, and they settled with them, until, verily, there was a number of households of them. And the child [Ishmael] grew to his youth, and learned Arabic from them, and was acceptable and pleasing to them when he became a young man. And when he reached maturity, they gave him a wife from among them. And the mother of Ishmael died.[36]

Here, then we have an account of the Islamic origin of the Arab people. Muḥammed used the same technique as the biblical authors: the adaptation of a myth familiar to the people of the region to create a sacred text. The biblical authors used an Egyptian myth to link Ishmael to Abraham. Muḥammed incorporated an Arabian myth of a local hero who was not an Arab (did not speak Arabic) but who became the eponymous ancestor of the Arabs. This myth, like the biblical account, is of a mother and son, alone in the desert, dying of thirst, who are saved by a miraculous well.

In the Islamic version Ishmael marries an Arabian woman and it is through *her* that the Ishmaelites are counted as an Arab tribe. In other words, although descent is matrilineal, the descent group is not matronymic. But neither is it patronymic. In both the Hebrew and Islamic versions the group is named after the son, Ishamel, not the patriarch Abraham to whom both stories were appended.

The Islamic version retains its local pre-Islamic elements and ritual in the Sa'y, the pilgrimage the mother made between the two hills, the Safa and the Marwah. Unfortunately the tradition of the Egyptian Matriarch was all but lost. It is therefore propitious that it can be recovered in the story of the Desert Matriarch.

9. Hagar the Egyptian: A Lost Tradition

THE HANDMAID'S TALE[1]

Hagar, as we have seen, was not a poor slave thrown out into the wilderness empty-handed, the "unwitting cause of Sarah's fury."[2] She leaves Hebron with her grown son, free to encounter a new destiny. The narrative does not describe her actions or feelings before her departure. With Sarah dead, there would have been no reason for her to remain in Hebron, had she had the choice. The thought of returning to her homeland in Egypt must have been appealing. Surely she made offerings at a local sanctuary (Plate 15) to ensure a safe journey and fortunate outcome before leaving. After all, the gods had not been unkind to her: She had her freedom and her son. Her venture is told in six critical sentences:

THE HAGAR DESERT TEXT

21 14a Early next morning Abraham . . . sent Hagar away
14c And she wandered in the Desert of Beer-sheva.
17 Elohim heard the voice of the *lad (ha-na'ar)* and a messenger of Elohim called to Hagar from heaven and said to her, "What troubles you Hagar? Fear not, for Elohim has heard the voice of the *lad (ha-na'ar)* where he is.
18 Rise, lift up the *lad (ha-na'ar)* and hold your hand on him, for I will make a great nation of him."
20a Elohim was with the *lad* when he grew up
21 He lived in the wilderness of Paran; and his mother got a wife for him from the land of Egypt.

That Abraham rather than Sarah takes leave of Hagar supports my contention that the notice concerning Sarah's death is misplaced. Genesis 23, the story of the purchase of the bur-

PLATE 15. "Surely she made offerings to a local sanctuary."
Maidservant carrying offerings, Tomb of Meketra, (Thebes, Ninth Dynasty, 2065 BCE). Egyptian Museum, Cairo.

ial cave of Machpelah, may in part have been authored by the Priestly strand. But "it seems probable that the narrative is based on some local tradition by which the form of representation has been partly determined."[3] It has also been considered "a midrashic expansion of a brief notice in that document."[4] The "local tradition" and the "brief notice" tell of Sarah's death at the age of one hundred and twenty-seven in Kiriath-arba, and her burial: "And then Abraham buried his wife Sarah in the cave of the field of Machpelah, facing Mamre—now Hebron—in the land of Canaan."

Having left Hebron, Hagar and her son wander in the Desert of Beer-sheva, a perfect metaphor for their psychological situation.

And Elohim heard the voice of the lad and he called out to Hagar (from the heavens) saying, "What troubles you Hagar? Fear not, for Elohim has heard the voice of the lad where he is."[5]

This is not the story of the near death of a child. It is the desperation of mother and grown son who have been deprived of what they had, for so long, considered their portion. For decades their destinies had been entwined with that of the awesome and powerful *naditu*. It is the young lad, however, who is inconsolable, for it is he who has been separated from his association with Sarah the priestess; and it is his voice that comes to the attention of the divinity. It is nevertheless to the mother that the deity gives the prophecy. It is significant that the deity does not question the emotional outcry of the youth, but directs his address to Hagar:

"Rise, lift up the lad and hold your hand on him, for I will make of him a great nation." Elohim was with the boy and he grew up. He lived in the desert of Paran; and his mother got a wife for him from the land of Egypt.

A difficulty in this interpretation for the traditional view is that Hagar, as the direct recipient of the oracle of the divinity, is integral to the story, therefore making the previous one to Abraham (verse 12) redundant. Predictably, Westermann makes Abraham the principal recipient of the promise—which then, he asserts, "must be promulgated to Hagar, because it is she who now takes the place of Ishmael's father."[6]

The insertion in verse 12 of Elohim's promise to increase the patriarch's seed through the son of Hagar functions to obfuscate one of the most startling events in Genesis: *Hagar is the only woman in the Bible who, protected by her personal god, receives the promise that* she *(via her son) will become a great nation.* Her son remains nameless because it is Hagar who becomes the eponymous ancestress of her future descendants, just as it is the Desert Matriarch who remains nameless because it is Ishmael, her son, who becomes the eponymous ancestor of his descendants. That Hagar is the ancestress is borne out by the fact that the Hagarites, descendants of Hagar (see below) dwelt in an area close to the Wilderness of Paran, whereas initially the Ishmaelites range was in the Desert of Shur (Map III), where Ishmael's mother conceived and bore him.[7] Throughout, this story is Hagar's not her son's; and her god's concern is with her, not her son.

This text states unequivocally that Hagar must "lift up the lad and hold [her] hand on him." This strange directive that Hagar should hold her hand on her son seems to mean that from now on Hagar should take command of him (her matrilineal prerogative), the implication being that her future and her son's are now in her own hands, not in Sarah's.

The second desert story by E records the only portion of a desert scene that is relevant to the Matriarch Hagar and the promise that her descendants (via her son and his wife), the Hagarites, will become a nation situated in the Wilderness of Paran.[8] Skinner points out that an Egyptian strain among the Bedouin of Sinai would be easily accounted for by the very early Egyptian occupation of the Peninsula.[9] Notably, Hagar's descendants are to be understood as predominantly Egyptian in the biblical text, since, besides being Egyptian herself, Hagar found an Egyptian wife for her son from Egypt.[10]

There is nothing in this text that makes the patriarch Abraham the center of the story. The theme refers very clearly to Hagar and her descendants.

A NOTE ON THE DESCENDANTS OF HAGAR

Scholars maintain that there is no decisive evidence that associates the peoples known as Hagarites (Hagri, Agrite, Hagarim), and "Sons of Hagar" to the only recorded matriarch of that name.

However, I believe that this contention stems from the androcentric interpretations of the texts and the efforts to confuse Hagar's son with Ishmael.

With the matriarch Hagar relegated to the status of slave/concubine and the focus of her story centered on the birth of Ishmael and the origins of the Ishmaelites, it is difficult to draw a connection between the Hagarites and Hagar. Nevertheless, once we have recognized that Ishmael was not the son of Hagar, and that her son remains unnamed, the connection is easily made; the descendants are matronymic (named after the mother).

There are various references to Hagar's descendants (as distinct from Ishmaelites) in the Hebrew Bible and the Apocrypha:

1. 1 Chronicles 5:10: In the time of Saul the [descendants of Joel] made war on the Hagarites *[hag'rim]* who fell into their hand and who then resided in their tents on the eastern frontier of Gilead.[11]

2. 1 Chronicles 5:18–22: The sons of Reuben, Gad, and the half-tribe of Manasseh had warriors, men armed with shield and sword, who could draw the bow and who were trained for war, to the number of 44,760 fit for service. They made war on the Hagarites, Jetur, Naphish (two sons of Ishmael), and Nodab. When they received support against them, the Hagarites and all their allies fell into their hand for they cried unto God during

the battle and he answered them because they trusted
him. They captured of their possessions 50,000 camels,
250,000 sheep, 2,000 asses, and 100,000 men. Because
the war was of God, many were slain. They continued
to live in their territory until the Exile [in 743 BCE].[12]

The Hagarites and the Ishmaelites are two obviously
quite powerful and distinct tribes.

3. 1 Chronicles 27:31: [A long list, and then] "Obil the
Ishmaelite was in charge of the camels and Jehdeiah the
Meronothite was in charge of the she-asses. Jaziz the
Hagarite [hag'ri] was in charge of the flocks. All these
were overseers of the property belonging to king
David."

In the early monarchy Ishmaelites and Hagarites are
also named separately.

4. Psalm 83:7: "Your [Israel's] assailants make an alliance:
The tents of Edom and the Ishmaelites, of Moab and the
Hagarites *[hag'rim]*."[13]

Here, the Ishmaelites and the Hagarites are clearly
mentioned as two quite separate peoples.

5. Baruch 3:23: "Sons of Hagar" are mentioned in connection with Teman and described as those "who seek after
wisdom."[14]

The passages above make it quite obvious that there were
two distinct tribes: the Hagarites and the Ishmaelites, with the
Hagarites descending from Hagar (and Abraham), and the Ishmaelites descending from Ishmael, the son of the Desert Matriarch. Eighth-century Assyrian texts make mention of a people
called Hagaranu and suggest a close association between the
Hagaranu and the Nabatu, similar to the link between Hagar
and Nebaioth in the genealogy of Hagar-Ishmael (Gen.
25:13).[15] I mention this simply to suggest the remote possibility that Hagar, like Sarah, could have come from the southern
region of Mesopotamia.

The Hagarites grew into a powerful people who played an
important role in the development of Islam. In their fascinat-

ing book *Hagarism,* Crone and Cook contend that Islamic tradition grew out of pre-Islamic sources:

Virtually all accounts of the early development of Islam take it as
axiomatic that it is possible to elicit at least the outlines of the process from the Islamic sources. It is however well-known that these
sources are not demonstrably early. There is no hard evidence for
the Koran in any form before the last decade of the seventh century,
and the tradition which places this rather opaque revelation in its
historical context is not attested before the middle of the tradition,
but whose faith was integrated into Islam, was known by various
designations, such as the Greek "Magaritai," the Syriac "Mahgre"
or "Mahgraye" and the corresponding Arabic term, *muhajirun.*[16]

Crone and Cook comment that "the 'Mahgraye,' as an early Syriac source informs us, are the descendants of Abraham
by Hagar." They conclude that "the 'Mahgraye' must thus be
seen as Hagarene . . . [whose] earliest identity of the faith . . .
was in the fullness of time to become Islam."[17] In later times
the term "Hagarenes" was applied by Christians to Muslims,
and from the name of Hagar the Syrians even formed the verb
ahgar or *ethhaggar,* "to become a Muslim," as well as the noun
Mahgraya, "a Muslim."[18]

In view of the fact that Hagar is the only biblical person
with that name, and that her story is specifically told, it seems
reasonable to maintain that she was the eponymous ancestor
of the Hagarites. We should not be surprised that the connection between a female ancestor and her people has been severed in an androcentric record.

SIGNIFICANCE OF THE HAGAR TEXT

I proposed at the beginning of this chapter that the author
interwove Hagar's text with the story of the Desert Matriarch
in order to focus the narrative on the patriarch Abraham.
How was this achieved?

Hagar is impregnated by Abraham in order that the priestess Sarah may acquire an heir. Hagar becomes pregnant but a

conflict arises in which Sarah blames Abraham for his breach of contract or agreement. Nevertheless, the biblical authors have Hagar flee from Sarah so that culpability could be ascribed to her. But her escape became a difficult problem for later interpreters regarding the identity of offspring. Difficult problems make for perplexing solutions.

In Genesis 16:4 Hagar is impregnated by Abraham at Sarah's request. But since the Desert Matriarch was identified with Hagar, her pregnancy became Hagar's also! This second pregnancy (Gen. 16:11a) became an obstacle for the sages. The phrase "Behold you are pregnant," we are told by Rashi, should not be interpreted in the present tense, for obviously Hagar was aware of her state: It plainly says in verse 4: *she saw she was pregnant.* Rather, Rashi is following his comment on verse 5, "May YHWH decide between me and between you," that as a result of Sarah's evil eye, Hagar miscarried. Accordingly, the angel now tells her that when she returns home she will conceive *again* and bear a son.[19] Most critics simply ignore the whole question.

Shortly thereafter Sarah conceives and bears her own child, and she dismisses the son of Hagar. Hagar and her son leave and go off on their own to fulfill a new destiny, a future that is promised Hagar *after* she leaves Sarah's household. Throughout the entire story Hagar's son remains either nameless or is misnamed Ishmael (the latter by the Priestly source).

The authors' design was to depict the patriarch as "the father of a multitude of nations," as predicted in Genesis 17:4–5 and the reason why the patriarch's name was changed from Abram to Abraham. The authors' criterion was twofold: One, they intended to include the Ishmaelites in the lore of Israel. (Ishmaelites are not always the enemies of the Hebrews or Israelites. During David's tenure his sister Abigail was married to Jether, an Ishmaelite; and Obil, also an Ishmaelite, was an official in the king's administrative organization [1 Chron. 2:17 and 27:30, respectively]). Two, they needed to establish that the descendants of Hagar, the Hagarites, were descendants of Abraham.

Too many problems would have arisen had Hagar been permitted her true story. First, Hagar's position as slave allowed for the structure of the nuclear family to remain intact, that is: father, mother, children (and concubine). Second, Abraham could be depicted as using Sarah's slave as a means for begetting a son for himself, in patrilineal tradition. Third, the bond between the women could be changed to the paradigm of hostility between mistress and servant. Finally, a woman's prestige as ancestress of a people could be invalidated.

The merging of Hagar's story with the Desert Matriarch's created an impression of a lost soul, manipulated by god and mistress, with no destiny but that of her son's and the father who begot him.

The story of the Desert Matriarch filled these requirements perfectly. Her story contains two important events—the birth of the ancestor of the Ishmaelites, recorded by J, and an explanation of the origins of the sacred site (of Beer-lahai-ro'i), which belongs to the E source. Neither source associates Hagar with the Hagarites. J used the birth of Ishmael story to relate the patriarch Abraham to the Ishmaelites by merging his mother with Hagar. E fused Hagar and the Desert Matriarch and their sons, obscuring the origins of the Hagarites by making Abraham the ancestor of the "sons." J ends the Desert Matriarch's story with a note about the Ishmaelite terrain, from Havilah, by Shur, to Asshur. This broken fragment was misplaced by the P source onto a genealogy of Hagar's son (Gen. 25:12) whom he, as usual, calls Ishmael.[20] Nevertheless, the Ishmaelite territorial range was West of the Brook of Egypt, whereas the Hagarites were eventually located East of the Jordan, Moab, and Edom (Map III). In effect, writers, editors, and redactors obliterate "mothers" of nations in favor of a "father."

The confusion of mothers also complicates the story of the life of Esau, Jacob's brother. Esau married Bas'math, daughter of Ishmael, sister of Nebaioth (Gen. 36:3). But Bas'math is also called daughter of Elon the Hittite (Gen. 26:34). However, since Nebaioth is clearly stated as the firstborn of Ishmael (Gen. 25:13), Bas'math, his sister, is also Ishmael's daughter. The Hittite reference must have been to her mother, one of Ishmael's wives of whom Rebekah complained (Gen. 27:46) and the reason why she sent Jacob to seek a wife from her kindred in Mesopotamia. The story continues, "Esau realized that the Canaanite women displeased his father Isaac. So Esau went to Ishmael and took to wife, in addition to the wives he had, Mahalath, the daughter of Ishmael, sister of Nebaioth" (Gen. 28:8–9). Mahalath and Bas'math are two women. Mahalath's father was the son of Hagar and Abraham; Nebaioth was the son of Ishmael and so was not Mahalath's brother. In other words, to please his father Esau married a granddaughter of Abraham, in patrilineal convention (see Table 3).

Keturah, mother of six Arabian tribes (of which the most prominent in the Hebrew Bible is Midian), is also identified as wife of Abraham. Thus the patriarch also became a father of "nations" other than of the Hebrews and the Ishmaelites. Eventually, Abraham came to be understood as the ancestor of all Arabs, even though, according to the genealogy, Joktan is the ancestor of the Arabs (Gen. 10:25–29).

The notion of a "father of a multitude of nations" was in principle, in the interest of David or his son, Solomon. As Gunkel points out, "The great growth which Israel experienced under the first kings probably yielded it the moral force to lay claim to the foreign tales and give them a national application."[21]

As far back as 1844 the association of Hagar to the Hagarites was succinctly acknowledged by the Reverend Charles Forster, one of the six preachers in the Cathedral of Christ, Canterbury, and rector of Stisted, Essex (as his attributes are quaintly described). Even though he accepted the traditional relationship between Hagar and Ishmael, he declared the following:

By his abandonment, although in compliance with divine command, of Hagar and her son, Abraham had clearly forfeited all natural claims as father. Hagar, in virtue of this act, became, as it were, the sole parent of Ishmael, and the rightful mother of his future progeny. That the progeny of Ishmael, therefore, should, among other national appellatives, preserve and perpetuate his mother's name and memory, would seem only a just consequence, and natural anticipation.[22]

THE ISLAMIC TRADITION

There are many stories in Islamic lore about Hagar (or, in Arabic, Hadjar), who is the wife, not the concubine of Abraham.

Ibn Ishaq says: Hagar was a maid-servant of goodly mien and beauty. And Sarah presented her to Abraham, saying, behold, I find her an obedient woman; so take her, and perhaps Allah will give you a son from her. For Sarah had been denied children, and had despaired of them. And Abraham had prayed to Allah to give him a worthy successor, and the prayer had long gone unanswered, until the age of Abraham had advanced, and Sarah was still barren. Then Abraham lay with Hagar, and she bore Ishmael.[23]

Ath-Tha'labi says: Sarah conceived Isaak at the time when Hagar conceived Ishmael and they bore them at the same time. And they grew up to boyhood and while they were one day vying with each other, and Abraham was watching over the contest, Ishmael won. And Abraham sat him on his lap, and sat Isaak at his side. Sarah was watching this, and became angry. And she said, You placed the son of the servant woman in your lap, but my son at your side! So the jealousy peculiar to women took hold upon her, and she swore that she would indeed cut a piece out of her, and would alter her neck, and would fill her hands with blood. But Abraham said, Take her and circumcise her [that is, clitoredectomy] and it will become a practice after you, and you will quit your oath. So she did, and it became a practice among women.[24] Others say that Sarah, with the intention of disfiguring Hagar, even pierced her ears; so this then became the fashion among women.[25]

Then Ishmael and Isaak fought one day, as boys are wont; and Sarah became angry with Hagar, and said, "You shall not live in the same town as me, ever!" And so she bade Abraham put her away. And Allah sent a revelation to Abraham that he should bring Hagar and her son to Mecca.[26] And al-Bukhari relates that Hagar was the first woman to adopt the trailing skirt, who adopted it to efface her tracks from Sarah.[27]

Abraham and Hagar, according to Muslim tradition, are buried in the *hidjir* of the Holy House, at Mecca, "a distinction they share with most of the prophets."[28]

Both the Hebrew, Christian, and Islamic accounts attempt to denigrate the characters of the matriarchs in favor of the patriarchs. This is not the "will of God" but the design of men.

Nevertheless, we can regard the wonder of Hagar's story in the description of her spiritual growth. Her story is a paradigm for a new social order. Hagar emerges from her initial experience as a dependent human being, whose vocation was to serve the needs of others, to the establishment of herself as an independent person, the mother of a people. However, it must not be forgotten that her success depended on her experience with Sarah; her training within community became the basis for the formulation of her own community.

NOTES

4. Hagar Conceives: The Genesis of Transformation

1. I use *substitute* rather than surrogate because the latter term has been mistakenly used to refer to the natural mother, the woman who gives birth. The true *surrogate* is the woman who takes over the role of mother from the woman who gave birth.

2. On a stela, now in the Louvre, Paris, known to us as the "Code of Hammurapi" (CH).

3. Robert Alter, *The Art of Biblical Narrative* (New York: Basic Books, 1981), 49.

4. Claus Westermann, *Genesis 12–36: A Commentary,* translated by John J. Scullion, S.J. (Minneapolis: Augsburgh, 1981), 241.

5. A. E. Speiser, *Genesis: Introduction Translation and Notes. The Anchor Bible.* (New York: Doubleday, 1964), 157.

6. The first sentence in J's account commences with verse 2. The extant first sentence I disregard because it is a gloss by P. See Westermann, *Genesis,* 237.

7. Phyllis Trible, *Texts of Terror: Literary-Feminist Readings of Biblical Narratives* (Philadelphia: Fortress Press, 1984), 11.

8. Savina J. Teubal, *Sarah the Priestess: The First Matriarch of Genesis* (Athens, OH: Swallow Press, 1984), 33–34.

9. Genesis 16:2 and 30:3. The latter translation is so completely distorted in the Jewish Publication Society of America's translation that it is not recognizable as a formula. In Hebrew the two verses Genesis 16:5 and 31:53 are practically identical, however.

10. See Westermann, *Genesis,* 239.

11. Teubal, *Sarah the Priestess,* 33 and 106.

12. Literally, "And Abram *heard* the voice of Sarai," which may indicate that the formula followed some form of oracular utterance.

13. Jacob Neusner, *Genesis Rabbah: The Judaic Commentary to the Book of Genesis, A New American Translation* (Atlanta: Scholars Press, 1985), 151. This comment supports my contention that Hagar was not Abraham's concubine and did not have a close relationship with him.

14. Speiser's translation/interpretation of verse 5, which is correct, reads *beikeha* as "lap" rather than the customary "bosom" or "arms." He quotes identical usage in the old Sumerian-Akkadian dictionary of legal expressions known as *ana ittisu* (B. Lansberger, MSL I, 1937): "he placed his daughter in [the other's] lap," Table 3, column iv, line 34. Sarah placed Hagar in Abraham's *arms* so that she may *bear* on Sarah's lap (actually knees). Correct reference to the lap can be found in regard to the biblical Rachel (Gen. 30:3). Speiser, *Genesis* (Garden City, NY: Doubleday, 1964), 118.

15. Hagar was under Sarah's jurisdiction for ten years. She had neither husband nor child in that time, nor was she associated to Abram in any way. Either she had an agreement with Sarah to bear children solely for her, or her status as handmaid forbid her to marry or conceive without Sarah's permission.

16. Genesis 15 makes it clear that Abram had no other recourse than to have his steward inherit from him. It is possible that Abram's authority lay with the children of his sister, if he had one (daughters were not counted as offspring by the biblical writers), as is customary with many matrilineal societies. This possibility

would in part explain why Lot was not counted as Abram's heir by the patriarch, since Lot was not a sister's but a brother's son, and was not a member of his *mish-pahah*. See Genealogy of the Mothers Table 1.

17. Speiser, *Genesis,* 117.
18. Gerhard von Rad's comment on this subject is revealing: "The 'cry' *hamasi aleika* cannot be translated, 'My wrong be upon you,' but rather 'My wrong is your responsibility,' i.e., you are competent and responsible to restore my right. The 'cry' was the customary legal formula with which one appealed for legal protection. Sarah goes the limit with her counterstroke: she appeals to the highest judge, who sees every secret thing." This scholar's preconceived notion of Sarah's subordination to Abraham distorts the Matriarch's stature by making her appeal to both the Patriarch and to God. See Gerhard Von Rad, *Genesis: A Commentary,* translated by John H. Marks (Philadelphia: Westminster Press, 1972), 187. It is this perspective that allows verse 6 to be interpreted as Abraham giving Sarah *permission* to punish Hagar: "As her mistress you exercise full control over her. If she mistreated you, punish her as you please." Rabbis Nosson Scherman and Meir Zlotowitz, eds., *Bereshis: A New Translation with Commentary Anthologized from Talmudic, Midrashic, and Rabbinic Sources* (Brooklyn, NY: Mesorah Publications, 1978), 545 n.6.
19. *The Interpreter's Dictionary of the Bible,* Vol. 1 (Nashville: Abingdon, 1962), 749.
20. *Ibid.,* 750. Similar phraseology is used in Genesis 31:53, where Jacob and Laban seal an agreement with God as witness.
21. See also Genesis 31:53; and possibly Exodus 5:21.
22. *The Pentateuch and Rashi's Commentary, Genesis*, Vol. I (Brooklyn, NY: S. S. & R. Publishing Company, 1949), 135.
23. Westermann, *Genesis,* 241.
24. See Teubal, *Sarah the Priestess.*
25. Abraham was seventy-five years old when he and Sarah left Haran (Gen. 12:4). After arriving in Canaan they immediately go to Egypt, where Hagar presumably joined them; "Abram had dwelt in the land of Canaan ten years" when he took Hagar to wife (Gen. 16:3). Hagar bore Ishmael when Abraham was eighty-six.
26. Alternately translated "despised" or "in contempt of."
27. Westermann, *Genesis,* 241.
28. *Ibid.*
29. See, for instance, *The Torah: A New Translation According to the Masoretic Text* (Philadelphia: Jewish Publication Society of America, 1962), 25.
30. See below, chapter 6.
31. John Skinner, *A Critical and Exegetical Commentary on Genesis* (Edinburgh: T. & T. Clark, 1969), 387.
32. Isaak was forty years old when Rebekah married him, and he was sixty when she gave birth.

5. Sarah Conceives: The Miracle in Laughter

1. Genesis 17 is concerned with the promise of a son of Sarah's for Abraham, "I, YHWH" will give *you* a son by her" (verse 16).
2. Rabbi Dr. Charles B. Chavel, trans., *Ramban (Nachmanides); Commentary on the Torah. Translated and Annotated with Index* (New York: Shilo, 1971), 233.

3. John Skinner, *A Critical and Exegetical Commentary on Genesis* (Edinburgh: T. & T. Clark, 1969), 299.

4. *Ibid.,* 301–302.

5. Clauss Westermann, *Genesis 12–36: A Commentary;* translated by John J. Scullion, S.J. (Minneapolis, Augsburgh, 1985), 274.

6. Skinner, *Genesis,* 302.

7. John Van Seters questions how it was that Abraham recognized the deity. John Van Seters, *Abraham in History and Tradition* (New Haven and London: Yale University Press, 1975), 211. The appearance of YHWH is only identifiable as YHWH if it is part of a separate sequence in answer to Sarah's petition to YHWH. Abraham's use of the same phrase terminology used by Gideon substantiates this contention; see below.

8. Against Van Seters, *Ibid.,* 202–203.

9. See Skinner, *Genesis,* 303–307, where the passage of Abraham's intercession is viewed as "the product of a more reflective age than that in which the ancient legends originated" (305). In other words, the story of the three visitors to Abraham is an introduction to the episode of the destruction of Sodom in which the three play a major role. The dialogue between YHWH and the Patriarch of "abstract principles and divine government" is not a part of the (J's?) original theme in the Sarah episode.

10. I thank Nurit Shein for pointing this out to me.

11. Westermann, *Genesis,* 275.

12. *The Torah: A New Translation According to the Masoretic Text* (Philadelphia: Jewish Publication Society of America, 1962), 122.

13. *Ibid.*

14. Skinner, *Genesis,* 300.

15. E. A. Wallis Budge, *The Gods of the Egyptians: Studies in Egyptian Mythology,* Vol. I (New York: Dover, 1969), 436.

16. Ian Portman, *The Temple of Dendara* (Cairo, Egypt: The Palm Press, 1984), 8.

17. Budge, *Gods of the Egyptians,* 431.

18. John Bright, ed., *Jeremiah: Introduction, Translation, and Notes. The Anchor Bible,* Vol. 21 (Garden City, NY: Doubleday, 1965), 58.

19. Translation by John Bright, 53.

20. Raphael Patai, *The Hebrew Goddess* (New York: KTAV, 1967), 32.

21. See Savina J. Teubal, *Sarah The Priestess: The First Matriarch of Genesis* (Athens, OH: Swallow Press, 1984), chapter 12, "Supernatural Conception," 123 ff. Of the various descriptions of nuptials between divinities or divinities and humans in ancient texts, there is never a reference to a ritual designated *heiros gamos* (that is, sacred), which is a contemporary but useful appellation.

22. Cyrus H. Gordon, *The Common Backgrounds of Greek and Hebrew Civilizations* (New York: W. W. Norton, 1965), 288. Yarih is the counterpart of the Mesopotamian moon god Nanna-Sin. Yarih, unlike Sin, had no consort until the advent of Nikkal, the Mesopotamian moon goddess.

23. Gordon, *Ugaritic Literature,* 63–65.

24. See my treatment of this theme in Teubal, *Sarah the Priestess,* 119 ff.

25. *Ibid.,* 64.

26. From the translation by Diane Wolkstein and Samuel Noah Kramer, *Inanna Queen of Heaven: Her Stories and Hymn from Sumer* (New York: Harper & Row, 1983), 107–10.

27. Teubal, *Sarah the Priestess,* 114–15.

28. *Ibid.,* 128.

29. *Ibid.,* 120.

30. *Ibid.,* 119–22.

31. *Ibid.*

32. Skinner, *Genesis,* 301 n. 10, rightly comments that "It is surprising that no one seems to suspect a reference to the period of pregnancy." I concur with his translation.

33. It is generally acknowledged that YHWH spoke directly to Sarah rather than Abraham, since the exchange is between YHWH and Sarah.

34. Or, as proposed by Skinner, *Genesis,* 301 n. 9, "According to the time of a pregnant woman."

35. Judges 15:1; also Teubal, *Sarah The Priestess,* 126.

36. Speiser, *Genesis,* 129.

37. Gerhard von Rad, *Genesis: A Commentary,* translated by John H. Marks (Philadelphia: Westminster Press, 1972), 202.

38. *The Torah,* 28 and note (b).

39. *The Pentateuch and Rashi's Commentary, Genesis* (Brooklyn, NY: S. S. & R. Publishing Company, 1949), Vol. I, 155. Rashi quotes 2 Kings 2:4 to corroborate his interpretation.

40. Chavel, *Ramban, Torah,* 237.

41. Robert G. Boling, *Judges: A New Translation with Introduction and Commentary. The Anchor Bible.* (Garden City, NY: Doubleday, 1975), 217.

42. See Van Seters, *Abraham,* chapter 10, 209 ff.

43. Carol P. Christ, *Laughter of Aphrodite: Reflections on a Journey to the Goddess* (San Francisco: Harper & Row, 1987), 6.

44. To conceal Sarah's active part in the annunciation and naming of Isaac, P resorts to having the Patriarch laugh in the (second) annunciation of the birth of Isaac. This was really helpful to twentieth-century scholars. In his 33 lines of excursus on the name of Isaak, Westermann, for instance, does not name Sarah once; in fact, with a great deal of fast double-talk, Westermann manages to have the name Isaak come from "El laughed, the father laughed or the child laughed!" cf. 269.

45. This is not an editorial comment as suggested by Robert Graves and Raphael Patai, *Hebrew Myths: The Book of Genesis* (New York: McGraw-Hill, 1963), 165, but is clearly a comment made by a woman to herself or others when explaining the circumstances. Rabbi Dr. H. Freedman and Maurice Simon, trans., *Midrash Rabbah, "Genesis"* (London: Soncino Press, 1951), 91, and others suggest the reading of "ended altogether" regarding Sarah's menstruation. See also, William T. Miller, *Mysterious Encounters at Mamre and Jabbok* (Chico, CA: Scholars Press, Brown Judaic Studies 50, 1984), 34.

46. The reference to old age refers to the one who will impregnate Sarah. It is not clear whether it refers to Abraham or the god's representative. I suggest it was the latter in Teubal, *Sarah the Priestess,* 127.

47. Westermann, *Genesis,* 280.

48. H. W. F. Saggs, *The Greatness That Was Babylon: A Sketch of the Ancient Civilization of the Tigris-Euphrates Valley* (New York and Toronto: New American Library, 1962), 403–404. This account is very reminiscent of the story in Exodus 2:2–3, in which the mother of Moses hides him for three months after his birth, but when she can hide him no longer she too places him in a reed basket, caulks it with bitumen and pitch, and puts it into the Nile.

49. Since Sarah answers the question it is obvious that verse 15 was addressed to her, not Abraham.

50. Rabbis Nosson Scherman and Meir Zlotowitz, eds., Bereshis: *A New Translation with Commentary Anthologized from Talmudic, Midrashic, and Rabbinic Sources* (Brooklyn, NY: Mesorah Publications, 1978), Vol. 2, 577.

51. John Day, "Asherah in the Hebrew Bible and Northwestern Semitic Literature," *Journal of Biblical Literature 105,* No. 3 (1986): 386.

52. The terebinth tree was sacred to Asherah. Mamre was a grove of terebinths.

53. Scholars (like Gunkel) have tried to connect Genesis 18:1 to 13:18, which would indicate that Mamre was a sacred place because Abraham built an altar there, and would be a continuation of a sequence that included Lot. But ignoring the importance of the Matriarchs leads to many problems. cf. Van Seters, *Abraham,* 203–204.

54. Westermann, *Genesis,* 275. To Westermann, of course, although the announcement is made to Sarah, the son will be Abraham's as well. The reverse is never true.

55. Cyrus H. Gordon, *Ugaritic Literature: A Comprehensive Translation of the Poetic and Prose Texts* (Rome: Pontificum Institutum Biblicum, 1949), 63 n.1.

6. Determining the Inheritance

1. "We are naturally tempted to claim that the nuclear or conjugal family is the most basic unit." Robert A. Oden, Jr., "Jacob as Father, Husband and Nephew: Kinship Studies and the Patriarchal Narratives," *Journal of Biblical Studies 102,* No. 2 (June 1983): 202.

2. Robin Fox, *Kinship and Marriage: An Anthropological Perspective* (Garden City, NY: Harmondsworth, Penguin, 1967), 99, 258–60.

3. Carol Meyers, *Discovering Eve: Ancient Israelite Women in Context* (Oxford University Press, 1988), 56.

4. At least before the advent of "reformers" like Hammurapi.

5. Michael C. Astour, "Tamar the Hierodule: An Essay in the Methods of Vestigal Motifs," *Journal of Biblical Literature 85,* (1966): II: 191.

6. Savina J. Teubal, "Women, the Law, and the Ancient Near East," in *Fields of Offerings: Studies in Honor of Raphael Patai,* edited by Victor D. Sanua (London and Toronto: Associated University Presses, A Herzl Press Publication, 1983), 306.

7. Astour, "Tamar," 189 n.27.

8. John Skinner, *A Critical and Exegetical Commentary on Genesis* (Edinburgh: T. & T. Clark, 1969), 285.

9. *Ibid.,* 322; Claus Westermann, *Genesis 12–36: A Commentary,* translated by John J. Scullion, S.J. (Minneapolis: Augsburgh, 1981), 344.

10. G. R. Driver and John Miles, eds., *The Babylonian Laws: Transliterated Text, Translation, Philological Notes and Glossary* (Oxford: Clarendon Press, 1955), 351.

11. The Testament of Jacob was so named by A. E. Speiser, *Genesis: Introduction, Translation and Notes. The Anchor Bible.* (New York: Doubleday, 1964), 370. According to Skinner (*Genesis,* 509) this document underwent successive modifications and expansions before it took final shape in the hands of a Judean poet in the court of David or Solomon.

12. Driver and Miles, *Babylonian Laws,* 351.

13. Code of Hammurapi #170.

14. D. Winton Thomas, ed., *Documents from Old Testament Times,* translated with Introductions and Notes by Members of the Old Society for Old Testament Study (New York: Harper & Row, 1961), 28.

15. Actually, the concept of adoption did not exist in Babylonia. The term *maru* means something like "acquired in sonship." Sons and daughters in sonship/daughtership were regarded as no different from natural children. Interestingly, there are no adoption laws in the Torah.

16. Driver and Miles, *Babylonian Laws,* legal commentary, 351.

17. Nahum M. Sarna, *Understanding Genesis: The Heritage of Biblical Israel* (New York: Schocken, 1970), 157. Sarna claims that "The matriarch was solely interested in safeguarding the material patrimony of her son." Sarna does not enlighten us on how he arrived at this conclusion.

18. "His" son is often translated "a son of his," implying he had more than one son; an effort to include Isaak as his offspring. It is interesting that Sarah's story commences with Abraham causing her the loss of an heir and ends with the matriarch depriving the patriarch of his. Could this be perceived as some form of retribution, or punishment?

19. Driver and Miles, *Babylonian Laws,* 361.

20. *Ibid.,* 364.

21. An ideogram is a Sumerian sign read as an Akkadian word. The Sumerian ideogram for "the bride of god," NIN DINGIRra, would be read *entu* in Akkadian, the Babylonian language. In my text I will use only the Akkadian terms.

22. Inheritance customs among women of the clergy may very well have survived in their pre-Babylonian traditional form despite the general incursion of patrilineal succession elsewhere. Driver and Miles, *Babylonian Laws,* 358.

23. In Old Babylonia the *nudunnu* was given by the parents to their daughter, the equivalent of the *šeriktu.* Later, in the Hammurapi Laws #171–172 and in Assyria it became a settlement by deed made by the husband on his wife for her maintenance during widowhood. See *Ibid.,* 265.

24. *Ibid.,* 257.

25. *Ibid.,* 254.

26. *Ibid.,* 258.

27. *Ibid.,* 365.

28. Savina J. Teubal, *Sarah the Priestess: The First Matriarch of Genesis* (Athens, OH: Swallow Press, 1964), 120–21.

29. Hebrew sages dealt with this problem as follows: "The definite article 'the' would seem to imply that he received these, too, in Egypt [although they are not mentioned among the gifts in 12:16]; or quite possibly he bartered the surplus of his other gifts for silver and gold." Rabbis Nosson Scherman and Meir Zlotowitz, eds., *Bereshis: A New Translation with Commentary Anthologized from Talmudic, Midrashic, and Rabbinic Sources* (Brooklyn, NY: Mesorah Publications, 1978), 457.

30. Hermann Gunkel, *The Legends of Genesis: The Biblical Saga and History* (New York: Schocken, 1964), 43.

7. The Possible Beneficiaries

1. The Hebrew text actually ends, "after his mother." But Speiser notes that the preposition *ahrei,* employed in this technical sense, is in complete agreement

with the Akkadian *arki,* which is both "after" and "after the death of." A. E. Speiser, *Genesis: Introduction, Translation and Notes. The Anchor Bible.* (Garden City, NY: Doubleday, 1964), 182.

2. David M. Schneider and Kathleen Gough, *Matrilineal Kinship* (Berkeley: University of California Press, 1961), 6.

3. G. R. Driver and John Miles, eds., *The Babylonian Laws: Transliterated Text, Translation, Philological Notes and Glossary,* Vol. I (Oxford: Clarendon Press, 1955), 396 n.5.

4. John Van Seters, *Abraham in History and Tradition* (New Haven and London: Yale University Press, 1975), 197.

5. Driver and Miles, *Babylonian Laws,* 359.

6. *Ibid.,* 385.

7. R. B. Y. Scott, *Proverbs-Ecclesiastes* (Garden City, NY: Doubleday, 1965), 179.

8. *Ibid.,* 181–82.

9. See Scott's "Note on the Problems of Translating the Bible," *Ibid.,* 29.

10. *Hebrew and English Lexicon to the Old Testament,* Francis Brown, S. R. Driver, Charles Briggs, eds. (Oxford: Clarendon Press, 1968 edition), 439, from the verb *yarash*: take possession of, inherit, dispossess. #2, inherit, be one's heir.

11. Louis Ginzberg, *The Legends of the Jews,* translated by Henrietta Szold. (Philadelphia: Jewish Publication Society of America, 1909), 237.

12. J. E. Manchip White, *Ancient Egypt: Its Culture and History* (New York: Dover, 1970), 15.

13. Jacob Neusner, trans., *Genesis Rabbah: The Judaic Commentary to the Book of Genesis. A New American Translation* (Atlanta: Scholars Press, 1985), 146.

14. *Jewish Encyclopedia,* Vol. 14, "The Torah: A Modern Commentary" (New York: Union of American Hebrew Congregations, 1981).

15. Rivkah Harris, "The Case of Three Babylonian Marriage Contracts," *Journal of Near Eastern Studies 33,* No. 4 (1974): 367.

16. See John Skinner, *A Critical and Exegetical Commentary on Genesis* (Edinburgh: T. & T. Clark, 1969), 343.

17. *Ibid.,* 333, and Claus Westermann, *Genesis 12–36, A Commentary,* translated by John J. Scullion, S.J. (Minneapolis: Augsburgh, 1985), 367.

18. Jack M. Sasson, "Circumcision in the Ancient Near East," *Journal of Biblical Literature 85,* (1966): 474. Although Sasson was referring to Egypt in particular, it was probably not practiced by the Patriarchs, since the earliest law codes of the Israelites do not enjoin the rite at any age.

19. I make this contention in Savina J.Teubal, *Sarah the Priestess: The First Matriarch of Genesis* (Athens, OH: Swallow Press, 1984), 130 f. Scholars (Skinner, *Commentary on Genesis,* 316) see Abimelech's designation as Philistine as an anachronism, because Philistines only subsequently occupied the territory. They think he was simply a Canaanite king (Westermann, *Genesis,* 321). However, I suggest the anachronism is used to describe an uncircumcised king, or Sarah would not have had a son by him.

20. I thank Dr. Miriyam Glazer for pointing this out to me.

21. Westermann, *Genesis,* 339.

22. Skinner, *Commentary on Genesis,* 322.

23. Westermann, *Genesis,* 344.

24. *Hebrew Lexicon,* 850.

25. *The Pentateuch and Rashi's Commentary, Exodus,* Vol. II (Brooklyn, NY: S. S. & R. Publishing Company, 1949) 403.

26. Teubal, *Sarah the Priestess,* 38–39. Scholars like Westermann suggest that "Such an interpretation is biased because it is looking for an explanation of Sarah's harshness (verse 10). Westermann bases this assumption on the supposition that, "It is a peaceful scene that meets Sarah's gaze" and "Sarah's reaction to the sight of her own son playing with the son of the maidservant is the harsh demand that Abraham expel the maid and her son." Westermann, *Genesis,* 339. Westermann, however, must restructure the Hebrew text to read, "But when Sarah saw the son of Hagar . . . playing *with her son Isaac."* The Bible records Sarah seeing Hagar's son "playing"; nothing is said about who he was playing *with.* It is easier to interpret *metzahek* as "playing," rather than having a sexual connotation, if it involves two boys. Furthermore, if it was a peaceful scene in which the boys were simply playing, Westermann is able to create an explanation for Sarah's behavior as "an uncompromising and relentless intervention on behalf of her son and his future that moves her." I prefer the interpretation given by Rabbi Aqiba, who bases his decision on a comparison with Genesis 39:17, stating, "The word 'making sport' [*metzahek*] bears only one meaning, namely, fornicating." Jacob Neusner, *Genesis Rabbah: The Judaic Commentary to the Book of Genesis, A New American Translation,* Vol. II (Atlanta: Scholars Press, 1985), 253.

27. David M. Schneider and Kathleen Gough, eds., *Matrilineal Kinship* (Berkeley: University of California Press, 1973), 13.

28. Rabbi Dr. H. Freedman and Maurice Simon, trans., *Midrash Rabbah, Genesis,* Vol. II (London: Soncino Press, 1951), 538–39.

29. Teubal, *Sarah the Priestess,* 60.

30. Abi-melech means "my father the king," which could have been the designation given to him by his son Isaak.

31. E. A. Wallis Budge, *The Gods of the Egyptians: Studies in Egyptian Mythology* (New York: Dover, 1969), 329–30.

8. The Desert Matriarch

1. P's connecting phrases are thought by Skinner to be the work of a Redactor, cf. "Introduction," John Skinner, *A Critical and Exegetical Commentary on Genesis* (Edinburgh: T. & T. Clark, 1969), 1vii.

2. *The Interpreter's Dictionary of the Bible,* Vol. 3 (Nashville: Abingdon, 1962), 1.

3. *Ibid.*

4. "Boy" is used in *The Torah: A New Translation According to the Masoretic Text* (Philadelphia: Jewish Publication Society of America, 1962), 34; "boy" and "child" alternate in A. E. Speiser, *Genesis: Introduction, Translation and Notes* (Garden City, NY: Doubleday), 154.

5. See, for example, Claus Westermann, *Genesis 12–36, A Commentary,* translated by John J. Scullion, S.J. (Minneapolis: Augsburgh, 1985), 342–43, for an in-depth analysis of the reworking of the text. Martin Noth, *A History of Pentateuchal Traditions,* translated by Bernhard W. Anderson (Englewood Cliffs, NJ: Prentice-Hall, 1972), 109, doubts that the narratives attached to the region of Hebron, and specifically to the famous sanctuary of the terebinths of Mamre, ever belonged to the original material of the Abraham tradition. Also Hermann Gunkel, *The Legends of Genesis: The Biblical Saga and History* (New York: Schocken, 1964), 98, re the establishment of the pedigree of the patriarchs by the joining together of diverse legends.

6. Jacob Neusner, trans., *Genesis Rabbah: The Judaic Commentary to the Book of Genesis. A New American Translation* (Atlanta: Scholars Press, 1985), 255.

7. W. B. Emery, *Archaic Egypt: Culture and Civilization in Egypt Five Thousand Years Ago* (Middlesex, England: Penguin, 1987), 113.

8. Westermann, *Genesis,* 343.

9. 2 Samuel:22; 22:35, from *II Samuel: A New Translation with Introduction and Commentary. The Anchor Bible* (Garden City, NY: Doubleday, 1984).

10. Cf. *Interpreter's Dictionary,* Vol. 3, 657.

11. John Van Seters, *Abraham in History and Tradition* (New Haven and London: Yale University Press, 1975), 194.

12. *Ibid.,* 37.

13. Gunkel, *Legends,* 92.

14. Van Seters, *Abraham,* 195, 199.

15. M. Th. Houtsma, J. Wensinck, E. Levi-Provencal, H. A. R. Gibb, and W. Heffening, eds., *Encyclopedia of Islam: Dictionary of the Geography, Ethnography and Biography of the Muhammadan Peoples* (Leiden: E. J. Brill, 1966), 193.

16. *Ibid.,* 543.

17. The Shekhina is the Divine Presence; the "feminine" aspect of Deity. For the reference to Gabriel, see T. K. Cheyne and J. Sutherland Black, *Encyclopedia Biblica: A Critical Dictionary of the Literary, Political and Religious History, The Archaeological Geography and Natural History of the Bible* (London: Adam and Charles Black, 1899), 543.

18. As translated by Charles D. Matthews, *Palestine—Mohammedan Holy Land* (New Haven: Yale University Press, 1949), 71.

19. Abdullah Yusuf Ali, *The Holy Qur-an: Text, Translation and Commentary* (Beirut, Lebanon: Khalil Al-Rawaf, 1965), 62.

20. Houtsma, *et al., Encyclopedia of Islam,* Vol. II, 537.

21. Budge, *Gods of Egypt,* Vol. I, 451.

22. *Ibid.*

23. "The fundamental design of the tombs of the archaic Egyptian remained the same throughout the period: a substructure built below ground level, covered by a brick superstructure in the form of an oblong rectangular platform built in imitation of the dwelling house or palace of the period." Emery, *Archaic Egypt,* 129. Budge., *Gods of Egypt,* Vol. II, 454, locates these in Saqqara.

24. Budge, *Gods of Egypt,* Vol. I, 30–31.

25. *Ibid.,* 462.

26. *Ibid.,* 92.

27. See Emery, *Archaic Egypt:* Neith-hotep with Narmer, 47; Her-Neith with Zer, 60; Meryet-Neith's consort is not identified, but Emery suggests her position was due to "matrimonial union," 69.

28. Budge, *Gods of Egypt,* Vol. I, 465.

29. *Ibid.,* 454; 451.

30. In one of her myths, known as the "Sorrows of Isis," this goddess saves her son from near death. Budge, *Gods of Egypt,* Vol. 2, 222–40.

31. *Ibid.,* 356.

32. *Ibid.,* 459.

33. J. E. Manchip White, *Ancient Egypt: Its Culture and History* (New York: Dover, 1970), 204.

34. Budge, *Gods of Egypt,* Vol. II, 290.

35. Van Seters, *Abraham,* 201.

36. Matthews, *Palestine,* 72–73.

9. Hagar the Egyptian: A Lost Tradition

1. Margaret Atwood, *The Handmaid's Tale* (Boston: Houghton Mifflin, 1986). I am using the title of Atwood's novel because the subject matter of her work is an excellent illustration of what the conventional message of Hagar's story could be, if taken to its extreme.
2. A. E. Speiser, *Genesis: Introduction, Translation and Notes* (Garden City, NY: Doubleday, 1964), 157.
3. John Skinner, *A Critical and Exegetical Commentary on Genesis* (Edinburgh: T. & T. Clark, 1969), 335.
4. *Ibid.*
5. This passage could also be acceptable as the explanation for the naming the son "Ishmael, El-Heard." However, Hagar's son is a young lad *(ha-na'ar)*, and presumably already had a name, given to him by his mother.
6. Claus Westermann, *Genesis 12–36: A Commentary,* translated by John J. Scullion, S.J. (Minneapolis: Augsburgh, 1985), 343.
7. The confusion between Hagar and the Desert Matriarch also confuses the issue of their descendants.
8. A nameless ancestor is inconsistent with biblical thought. In fact, the redundant verse 12 prophesying a son to Abraham may have belonged to the revelation to Hagar stating, "I will make him into a nation *because he is your offspring.*"
9. Skinner, *Commentary on Genesis,* 285.
10. *Ibid.*
11. Jacob M. Myers comments: The Hagarites, Naphash, and Nodab (Nadab) are found in Assyrian documents. *I Chronicles: Translated with Notes and Introduction* (Garden City, NY Doubleday, 1965), 38. (See W. F. Albright, "The Biblical Tribe of Massa . . . ," Studi orientalistici in onore di Giorgio Levi della Vita, I 1956, 1–14, especially 12–14.)
12. Translation by Myers, *I Chronicles,* 33. Meyers comments: The Hagarites were Arabs who appear in several points in the history of Israel. The conflict mentioned may refer to the Ammonite wars of Saul (I Sam. 11); the *exile,* after the conquest by Tilgath-pileser. Psalm 83:7 places the Hagarites in the vicinity of Moab.
13. Translation by Mitchell Dahood, *Psalms II:51–100, The Anchor Bible* (Garden City, NY: Doubleday, 1968), 274. Dahood simply comments, "the Hagarites: A semi-nomadic people of the desert regions east of Ammon and Moab."
14. T. K. Cheyne and J. Sutherland, eds., *Encyclopedia Biblica, A Critical Dictionary of Literary, Political and Religious History, The Archaeological Geography and Natural History of the Bible* (London: Adam and Charles Black, 1899), col.1934, n.1. The Temanites were a clan descended from Esau (Gen. 36:11, 15), that is: the Edomites.
15. John Van Seters, *Abraham in History and Tradition* (New Haven and London: Yale University Press, 1975), 62.
16. Patricia Crone and Michael Cook, *Hagarism: The Making of the Islamic World* (Cambridge: Cambridge University Press, 1977), 3; 8.
17. *Ibid.,* 9.
18. M. Th. Houtsma, J. Wensinck, E. Levi-Provencal, H. A. R. Gibb, W. Heffen-

ing, eds., *Encyclopedia of Islam: Dictionary of the Geography, Ethnography, and Biography of the Muhammadan Peoples,* Vol. III (Leiden: E. J. Brill, 1966), 1934.

20. See Skinner, *Genesis,* 352–53. This geographical location is too obscure to be of any use for our purposes.

21. Hermann Gunkel, *The Legends of Genesis: The Biblical Saga and History* (New York: Schocken, 1964), 138.

22. Rev. Charles Forster, B.D., *A Historical Geography of Arabia; or, The Patriarchal Evidences of Revealed Religion: A Memoir,* Vol. I (London: Duncan and Malcolm, 1844), 181 n.3. Forster dedicates a whole chapter to the regions and settlements of Hagarites and Ishmaelites (176–316), in which he makes the following surprising statement on the abode of Hagar's son, the wilderness of Paran: "we find Mount Sinai, in the heart of that wilderness, expressly entitled *Agar* in the New Testament, and popularly known by the name of *Hagar,* among the Arabs of the peninsula of Sinai at the present day. That it was originally so named after Hagar, the mother of Ishmael, appears incontrovertibly from the reasoning of Saint Paul; who introduces Sinai under its name of Agar, in argumentative connection with the opposition between the wife, and the concubine, of Abraham, and the son of the bond-maid, and the son of the free-woman: 'For it is written, that Abraham had two sons, the one by a bond-maid, the other by a free-woman. But he who was the son of the bond-woman, was born after the flesh; but he of the free-woman, was by promise. Which things are an allegory: for these are two covenants; the one from Mount Sinai, which gendereth to bondage, which is Agar. For this Agar, is Mount Sinai in Arabia,' " 181–82.

23. I have taken all the accounts of Hagar from Charles D. Matthews, *Palestine—Mohammedan Holy Land* (New Haven: Yale University Press, 1949). This quote, 65.

24. *Ibid.,* 68.

25. T. K. Cheyne and J. Sutherland Black, eds., *Encyclopedia Biblica: A Critical Dictionary of the Literary, Political and Religious History, the Archaeological Geography and Natural History of the Bible,* Vol. II (London: Adam and Charles Black, 1899), 543.

26. Matthews, *Palestine,* 68–69.

27. *Ibid.,* 71.

28. Cheyne and Black, *Encyclopedia Biblica,* 544.

PART III. CONCLUSIONS

10. The Meaning of the Life of Hagar

"Consciousness of a real and meaningful world is intimately connected with the discovery of the sacred," Mircea Eliade has written. "In short, the 'sacred' is an element in the structure of consciousness and not a stage in the history of consciousness."[1] It can also be maintained that the "sacred" is an element in the structure of religious history and not a stage in the history itself.

As I see it the voice of prophecy has been frozen in history: A male voice cried out in the wilderness and that voice was legitimated by making the sacred historical. Whether Hebrew prophet, Jesus, or Muḥammed, male vision has been affirmed—in linear progression—as the ultimate revelation. In this way female vision, present or ancient, has been undermined.

But visionary experience cannot be rooted to a stage in history—it is "an element in the structure of [human] consciousness." Whether ancient or contemporary, female or male, all visionary experience is valid. There is ample evidence, as shown in part in this study alone, that the ancient voice of the female prophet has been silenced. But the message in those silent texts is clamoring for recognition.

In the context of the story of Hagar, the power of the "sacred" in the text is a constant that requires renewal from generation to generation. The voice in the wilderness is female also—Hagar, the Desert Matriarch, Sarah, Rachel, Miriyam, and so on. Their stories have been left to us for a purpose: so that their traditions may serve future generations. The renewal of traditions is what my work is about: not to disavow tradition, but to allow it meaningful process. To have any significance for us, mythology and legend need to be focused on our own concerns and adapted to our own image.

This process of renewal is not new. "Even the earliest epic traditions of Israel did not reflect directly the religious milieu of the time of their origin."[2] As we have seen throughout this study they reflected the religious, cultural, and historical milieu of the time they were popularized.

The biblical stories are male centered because they were composed at a time when certain groups of men were attempting to take control of their society in order that it could expand and grow. The military elite were spreading out over rural lands. To reinforce their nationalistic project, they needed the image of the archetypal hero. Tragically, this archetype was created at the expense of women. Nevertheless, at that time, the image of the archetypal hero was felt to be a dire necessity because the survival of their group was at stake.

If, during the early monarchy's recompilation of the biblical material, the powerful tribe of the Hagarites was known to acknowledge the matriarch Hagar as their common ancestress, a problem would have been posed for the androcentric writers who were attempting to highlight the patriarch: Descent was to be changed to the male line. At that time the Ishmaelites also had close affiliation to the Israelites. The earliest reference to them is in the story of Joseph, who was sold to a caravan of Ishmaelites by his brothers (Gen. 37:25, 27–28; 39:1). The latest, for the chroniclers, was David's sister Abigail, who was married to "Jether the Ishmaelite" (1 Chron. 2:17). The Ishmaelites must also have acknowledged the story of their ancestry. The Desert Matriarch and the miraculous birth of her son must have been a familiar tale in the court of the king. But it too lacked the force of an absolute and exclusive patriarchal figure. By fusing the story of Hagar to that of the Desert Matriarch and the birth of the sons to the birth of Ishmael, Abraham would become the progenitor of the Hagarite, the Ishmaelite, and all of their descendants. Finally, under the influence of Babylonians and Assyrians, whose androcentric bias is all too well known, redactors would have been sufficiently prejudiced to relegate Hagar's role to that of concubine and slave.[3]

It is therefore essential that we attempt to envision the world of the matriarchs in early Israel as it may have been prior to the androcentric overlay. In the first place they lived in tribes gathered in small townships.[4] Their intent was the survival of the tribal unit, its religion, and its culture. Sarah's tribal unit was establishing itself on foreign soil. Nevertheless, their purpose was to obtain land rights for themselves and their livestock under the auspices of fostering deities—as opposed to conquering for possession of territory and booty in obedience to a father-god, as with the warrior elite of a monarchy. This is clearly illustrated in the peaceful separation of Abraham and Lot at a point where "the land could not support them staying together" (Gen. 13:6).[5] These two patriarchs neither bought nor conquered the land they chose; they simply set boundaries with grazing rights for their cattle. The land belongs to the deity who "gives" it (the rights) to Abraham and his descendants.

Despite the shared responsibilities of women and men in their means of survival and the transmittal of culture and religion, each functioned in distinct spheres. Women controlled every aspect of the propagation of their tribal unit, including the sexual activities of their men. A bonding between the women and their *sh'faḥoth*, their companions, facilitated this condition. I do not envision this situation as that of dominance of one gender over another, but as a condition that permitted women to regulate their pregnancies and sexual activity and avoid any sexual harassment directed at themselves, their daughters, or their companions.

The traditionally understood theme of Hagar's life has resonated deeply over the centuries, serving as a sanction to the enslavement of human beings in the Western world. Hagar's role has been that of the mistreated Egyptian slave, thrust empty-handed into the desert with her son, left to watch her child die of thirst under a bush where she had placed him, and being saved by the appearance of a miraculous well of water provided by the God of Abraham. According to the extant text the child's life is saved only because he is the seed of Abraham. This has been the basic text. As Phyllis Trible points out, Hagar moves "from bondage to flight to bondage" and then proceeds "from bondage to expulsion to homelessness."[6]

But this story elicits a troubling question: Why would any deity perpetrate such cruelty? Moreover, Sarah has been the major cause of Hagar's misfortune. She has been viewed as the haughty (white? Jewish?) slave-owner seemingly unconcerned with her role as victimizer.[7] On a more poetic level it is tempting to consider that the Hebrews were themselves enslaved by the Egyptians at a later date, as though some form of divine retribution was effected for the enslavement of Hagar.

But the archetypal image of Hagar as slave, concubine, and victim, and of Sarah as barren mistress, has denied women Eliade's "consciousness of a real and meaningful world, intimately connected with the discovery of the sacred." Furthermore, the focus on their role solely as procurers of male descendants has denied women the naming of female experience of empowerment.

In antiquity events in the lives of prophets, seers, and visionaries were not only narrated in oral tradition, they were also reenacted at seasonal festivals. As we have seen, however, the biblical texts recorded for the benefit of one generation have masked the spiritual experience of the matriarchs, which must have served to empower a previous generation of women. A reenactment of the *hieros gamos* of, say, Sarah/Nikkal and Abimelech/Yarih or the Desert Matriarch and El-ro'i and the birth of their semidivine offspring could not have failed to empower generations of women.

Furthermore, the main theme of the stories concerned neither sexual activity nor the birth of a son. The main theme established the core element that unified the tribal segment: the ancestor of a people. Androcentric obsession with sex and sons has only served to undermine the sacred roles of women.

Looked at anew Genesis 16 (verses 1–5) and 21 (verses 6–12, 14, 17, 18, 20a, 21) describe the matriarch Hagar and her association with Sarah, a priestess. Predicaments concerning the destinies of the matriarchs are the central theme throughout. Although the need of an heir/ess for Sarah is pivotal in the beginning, it also helps elucidate the origin of Hagar's pregnancy and the paternity of her future child. The main theme of the story, however, is derived from Hagar's theophany in the wilderness. There she is designated, by divine election, the ancestor of a people: the Hagarites. In this way Hagar's story is much like Sarah's.[8]

Indeed, Hagar's story parallels Sarah's to a surprising degree:

- Both Sarah and Hagar are exiles in a foreign land (Hebron). Sarah came from Ur, Mesopotamia, to the northeast; Hagar came from Egypt, to the southwest.
- Both women are isolated from their cultures and their kin.
- Both women spend many (presumably celibate) years in Canaan, before becoming pregnant.
- Both have the same husband.
- Each has only one pregnancy.
- Each woman is singled out by divinity to become the mother of a people.
- Each has a son.

In fact the texts give an insight into the nature of these women. Imagery in the stories describes their attributes as though emphasizing their distinct characteristics. Sarah's story, for instance, is associated with voice and hearing; Hagar and the Desert Matriarch's with vision. It is possible that the repetitious quality of the characterization was meant to infer oracular prophecy and visionary faculty, emphasizing the women's spiritual experience.

In Sarah's case we are told that

- Abram *heard* the *voice* of Sarah (Gen. 16:2)
- Sarah was *listening* at the tent entrance (Gen. 18:10)
- Sarah says: "Everyone who *hears* will laugh at/with me." (Gen. 21:6)
- And Elohim says to Abraham, "Whatever Sarah tells you *listen* to her *voice*." (Gen. 21:12)

Hagar, on the other hand,

- *Saw* that she was pregnant
- and (Sarah) was lowered in her *sight* (b'einecha), (Gen. 16:4)
- and Sarah says of Hagar, "I am lowered in her *sight*." (Gen. 16:5)

And it is the Desert Matriarch who is portrayed as visionary:

- YHWH said, *See,* you are pregnant. (Gen. 16:11)
- She said, "I cannot *look* on the death of the child." (Gen. 21:16)
- Elohim *opened* her *eyes* (Gen. 21:19)
- and she *saw* a well of water. (Gen. 21:19)
- She calls the deity "El-ro'i" *seeing* or visionary god. (Gen. 16:13), by which she meant "I *saw* after *seeing*." (Gen. 16:13)
- Therefore the well is called "Well of the living *vision*." (Gen. 16:14)

The Desert Matriarch, although nameless, distinguishes herself as *raiti ahrei ro'i* (I who saw [deity?] after my vision). Perhaps most impressive in the Desert Matriarch story is the fact that *she is the only person in the Bible to devise a name for the god* who rescued her and her son: El-ro'i, the visionary or seeing god.

Because of the identification of the Desert Matriarch as a separate character from Hagar, her story can be appreciated as a distinct unit. As became evident in chapter 7, this story contains elements of Egyptian mythology not apparent in the Hagar account. Features in the lives of the goddesses Neith and Isis permeate the Desert Matriarch text. Although stories of Egyptian goddesses include aspects of female empowerment lacking in their biblical counterparts, efforts were also made to limit their roles exclusively to that of motherhood. Isis, for example, was a childless goddess until, with modification and embellishment from generation to generation, she became the wife of Osiris.[9] And in the most well-known version of a myth, recorded by Plutarch in the first century of the Common Era, she conceived Horus from the body of her dead husband.[10] Isis became a devoted mother and remained the most popular and important of maternal goddesses as mother of Horus. According to Budge,

The pictures and sculptures wherein she is represented suckling her child Horus [Plate 16] formed the foundation for the Christian figures and paintings of Madonna and Child . . . many of the attributes of Isis, the God-mother, the mother of Horus, and of Neith, the goddess of Sais, are identical to those of Mary the Mother of Christ.[11]

It is nevertheless intriguing that ancient Near Eastern goddesses, like the biblical matriarchs, are never portrayed in a relationship with a daughter comparable to that of Demeter and Persephone, although vestiges of these may remain. Isis, who was identified with Persephone, was the dark-skinned daughter of Nut, the sky goddess.[12] She was born at Dendara, where a birth-chamber, the *mammisi,* was constructed for a ritual performance of her birth.[13] It is possible, if not probable, that stories of relationships between goddesses and their daughters became the "silent texts" of the Egyptians after the appearance of the "Followers of Horus," founders of the dynastic monarchy of Egypt. Likewise there are no biblical stories of mother-daughter relationships. Dinah is the only daughter mentioned in the Genesis narratives whose mother is named. But despite her tragic story there is no account of her mother Leah's reaction to her daughter's experience. Did the court of

PLATE 16. "Isis suckling her child Horus formed the foundation for Christian figures and paintings of Madonna and Child."
Isis suckling Horus. Egyptian Museum, Cairo.

David silence those texts? The closest approximation to a mother-daughter bonding is in the story of Ruth and Naomi, a mother/daughter-in-law story. But even that beautiful tale was coopted to serve the monarchy. The last line awkwardly gives Ruth's child a name: "Obed; he was the father of Jesse, father of David"![14]

We must also be careful not to overlook the importance of the goddess in Jewish heritage. Even a cursory reading of Raphael Patai's extraordinary book *The Hebrew Goddess,* which traces goddess veneration from early Israel to the kabbalistic era of the sixteenth century, is testimony enough to the reality of a nonmonotheistic Judaism in which goddess worship played a prominent part in religion.[15] But even here there is no bonding between the great goddess Asherah and her daughter Anat.

The biblical stories, then, are not about banal wives or concubines. They are, in part, stories of oracular priestesses and visionaries, who acknowledged the female deities of the land and were empowered to prophesy and envision the future through divine inspiration. Furthermore, these matriarchs were empowered—or empowered themselves—to change the social order.

The story of Hagar and Sarah, like that of Abraham and Lot, is also a story of separation. This new order stresses individualism as opposed to cooperation. What began as a cooperative effort between Hagar, Abraham, and Sarah, for the benefit of community, ended with each party concerned solely with his or her own future. Sarah reorders her life around her one descendant, Isaak; Hagar, the companion of Sarah, is directed to find companionship in her only son; and Abraham renegotiates life with a new wife, Keturah.

A step is also taken toward individual theology, separation in the religious sphere. The god/dess who approved of cooperation is exchanged, in each case, for the guidance of an individual regional deity. Thus Sarah's god admonishes Abraham to "do as Sarah says"; Hagar's god leads her away to establish her own community; Abraham accepts membership into an order that requires circumcision and obedience to a sole deity. Even the Desert Matriarch envisions her own personal divinity.

Thus Hagar's story is not just the record of change in a social system, it is a reevaluation of social values, a reordering of a philosophy of life. The significance of her life is that Hagar was able to attain both social and spiritual freedom. The biblical account is not explicit as to what extent Hagar was instrumental in severing her career as *shifḥah,* whose main responsibility was to care for the needs of the priestess Sarah and provide her with offspring. Her first step to autonomy was in claiming her own child; whether her comportment with Sarah had any influence on the outcome is not clear. But if separation was an element in the new order, responsibility of a mother for her own child was axiomatic. Furthermore, potential freedom of choice for her own sexual relationships is now viable to her.

It is in times of crisis that religious traditions are able to renew themselves. The monarchy is no more, its heritage is being challenged, and a new age is at hand. As Adrienne Rich has wisely noted, "Women [were] made taboo to women— not just sexually, but as comrades, cocreators, conspirators. In breaking this taboo, we are reuniting with our mothers, we are breaking this taboo."[16] In breaking this taboo we redeem our ancient foremothers as well.

There is no question that Hagar must be redeemed for Muslim as well as Jewish and Christian women. Her courage in the face of adversity, her faith in herself and in her destiny, guided by her own spiritual power, must be a revelation to all women. Above all, her close relationship with divinity and her inspiration to forge her own community must not be forgotten.

The matriarchs' return to cosmic consciousness offers spiritual guidance that has been denied women for millennia: Reject victimization, seek empowerment in community.

NOTES

10. The Meaning of the Life of Hagar

1. Mircea Eliade, *A History of Religious Ideas: From the Stone Age of the Eleusinian Mysteries,* translated by W. R. Trask, Vol. I (Chicago: University of Chicago Press, 1978), xiii.

2. Frank Moore Cross, *Canaanite Myth and Hebrew Epic: Essays in the History of the Religion of Israel* (Cambridge: Harvard University Press, 1973), 3.

3. Savina J. Teubal, "Women, the Law, and the Ancient Near East," in *Fields of Offerings: Studies in Honor of Raphael Patai,* edited by Victor D. Sanua, (London and Toronto: Associated University Presses, A Herzl Press Publication, 1983), 305 ff.

4. Without hard evidence of their existence it is futile to attempt to date the period in which the matriarchs lived. However, as I have stated elsewhere, the physical nature of their settlements seems similar to that found at the archaeological site of Jemdet Nasr, in Mesopotamia. Whether this type of settlement existed parallel to that of the warrior elite is of no consequence, provided the latter's influence was not in evidence in the stories.

5. The peaceful element is often attributed to the magnanimous nature of Abraham (see A. E. Speiser, *Genesis: Introduction, Translation and Notes* (Garden City, NY: Doubleday, 1964), 98, for instance), but I contend that Abraham's choice had to include consideration of a sacred site for Sarah, and because of this he chose to encamp close to the sacred terebinth grove of Mamre. (See Savina J. Teubal, *Sarah the Priestess: The First Matriarch of Genesis* (Athens, OH: Swallow Press, 1984), 28.)

6. Phyllis Trible, *Texts of Terror: Literary-Feminist Readings of Biblical Narratives* (Philadelphia: Fortress Press), 1984, 10.

7. As described by Dolores Williams, Claremont Colleges, Claremont, CA, February 1989.

8. David Bakan accurately suggests: "Not all the offspring of Abraham are Israelites: the Israelites stem only from Sarah. Sarah is more definitely the ancestor of the Israelites than Abraham." David Bakan, *And They Took Themselves Wives* (San Francisco: Harper & Row, 1979), 37.

9. E. A. Wallis Budge, *The Gods of the Egyptians: Studies in Egyptian Mythology,* Vol. 2 (New York: Dover, 1969), 204.

10. Jill Kamil, *Sakkara and Memphis: A Guide to the Necropolis and the Ancient Capital,* 2d. ed. (London: Longman, 1985), 18–20.

11. Budge, *Gods of the Egyptians,* 220.

12. *Ibid.,* 217.

13. *Ibid.,* 108.

14. Edward F. Campbell, Jr., *Ruth: A New Translation with Introduction and Commentary. The Anchor Bible* (Garden City, NY: Doubleday, 1975), 169.

15. Raphael Patai, *The Hebrew Goddess* (New York: KTAV, 1967).

16. Adrienne Rich, *Of Woman Born: Motherhood as Experience and Institution* (Toronto: Bantam Books, 1977), 259.

Appendix A
The New Genesis Text

Sequence of events:

1. Genesis 16: The Question of Motherhood
   Conception and birth of Hagar's son.
2. Genesis 22: The Birth of Rebekah
3. Genesis 18: The Feast Before the Ceremony
4. Genesis 20: Sarah's *Hieros Gamos* with Abimelech
5. Genesis 18: The Oracle
6. Genesis 21: Sarah Gives Birth
7. Genesis 23: The Testament and Death of Sarah
8. Genesis 21: The Theophany of Hagar
9. Genesis 16 and 21: The Desert Matriarch

1. THE QUESTION OF MOTHERHOOD

16 2 She [Sarai] had an Egyptian *shifḥah* and her name was Hagar; so Sarai said to Abram, "See how it is, I cannot bear children; pray go into my *shifḥah* perhaps I may be built up by her.

4 And Abram heard the voice of Sarai and he went into Hagar and she conceived.

And when she saw that she was pregnant she claimed equality with her mistress.

5 So Sarai said to Abram, "The wrong done me is on you! I myself put my *shifḥah* into your arms; now that she sees she is pregnant, she takes what I say lightly.

And she said to Hagar: "May the deity judge between me and between you!"

Hagar gives Birth to Her Son

2. THE BIRTH OF REBEKAH

22 20 Sometime later, Sarah was told, "Milcah [your brother's daughter] too has borne children: 21 Uz, the firstborn, and

Buz his brother, and Kemuel the father of Amram; and 22 Chesed, Hazo, Pildash, Jidlaph and Bethuel—23 Bethuel being the mother of Rebekah. These eight Milkah bore. And her *shifḥah,* whose name was Reumah, also bore children: Tebah, Gaham, Tahash, and a daughter, Maacah.

3. THE FEAST BEFORE THE CEREMONY

18 2 Looking up he [Abram] saw three men *(anashim)* standing near him. As soon as he saw them he ran from the entrance of the tent to greet them and, bowing to the ground, 3 he said, 4 let a little water be brought; bathe your feet and recline under the tree, 5 and let me fetch a morsel of bread that you may refresh yourselves; then go on, seeing that you have come your servant's way. They replied, "Do as you have said" 6 Abraham hastened into the tent to Sarah and said, "Quick, three seahs of fine flour. Knead and make cakes *(ugot)*! 7 Then Abraham ran to the herd, took a calf and he gave it to the servant-boy *(hana'ar),* who hurried to prepare it; 8 He took curds and milk and the calf that had been prepared, and set these before them; and he waited on them under the tree while they ate. 9 They said to him, "Where is your wife Sarah?" And he replied, "There, in the tent."

4. SARAH'S HIEROS GAMOS WITH ABIMELECH

20 1 So Abimelech king of Gerar had Sarah brought to him. 14 Abimelech took sheep and oxen, and male and female slaves, and gave them to Abraham; 15 And Abimelech said, "Here, my land is before you; settle wherever you please."

5. THE ORACLE

18 1 He appeared to him near the oaks of Mamre, he was sitting at the entrance to the tent as the day grew hot. 3 He said, "My Lord *('dny)* if it please you, do not go on past your servant, 10 and He said, "I will return to you when life is due, Sarah has a son." Sarah was listening at the entrance of the tent, "he will be His heir," she thought. 11 Sarah had stopped menstruating. 12 And Sarah laughed to herself saying, "Shall I in truth bear a child?" 13 Then He said to her "Why did you laugh saying 'Shall I in truth bear a child?' 14 And he said, "Is anything too difficult for Me? I will return to you, when life is due Sarah, you have a son." 15 Sarah concealed what she had thought, saying, "I did not laugh," for she was frightened. He replied "But you did laugh." 20:16 And Abimelech said to Sarah, "I herewith give your brother a thousand pieces of silver; this will serve you as a covering of the eyes before all who are with you, and you are cleared before everyone."

6. SARAH GIVES BIRTH

21 1 He (Abimelech) *(p-q-d)* impregnated Sarah as he had said and He did for Sarah as he had promised.

2 Sarah conceived and bore a son . . . Isaak.

6 Sarah said, "Elohim has brought me laughter; everyone who hears will laugh for me. 7 And she added, "Who would have said to Abraham that Sarah would suckle children! Yet I have borne a son in his old age."

8 The child grew up and was weaned, and Abraham held a great feast on the day that Isaak was weaned.

7. THE TESTAMENT AND DEATH OF SARAH

9 Sarah saw the son, whom Hagar the Egyptian had borne to Abraham showing sexual maturity. 10 She said to Abraham, "Dismiss Hagar and her son [after my death], for her son will not share in the inheritance with my son." 11 The matter distressed Abraham greatly, for it concerned a son of his. 12 But Elohim said to Abraham, "Do not be distressed over the boy or Hagar; whatever Sarah tells you, do as she says for it is through Isaak that offspring shall be continued."

23 1 Sarah's lifetime—the span of Sarah's life—came to one hundred and twenty-seven years. Sarah died in Kiriath-arba—now Hebron—in the land of Canaan; and Abraham proceeded to mourn for Sarah and bewail her. 19 And then Abraham buried Sarah his wife in the cave of the field of Machpelah, facing Mamre—now Hebron—in the land of Canaan.

8. THE THEOPHANY OF HAGAR

21 14a Early next morning Abraham ... sent Hagar away 14c And she wandered in the Desert of Beer-sheva. 17 Elohim heard the voice of the *lad* (hə-na'ar) and Elohim called Hagar and said to her, "What troubles you Hagar? Fear not, for Elohim has heard the voice of the *lad* where he is. 18 Rise, lift up the *lad* and hold your hand on him, for I will make a great nation of him." 20a Elohim was with the *lad* and he grew up; 21 They lived in the wilderness of Paran; and Hagar got a wife for him from the land of Egypt.

9. THE DESERT MATRIARCH TEXT

16 7 He found her by a spring of water in the desert, the spring on the road to Shur and said,
11b "See, you are now pregnant
and you will have a son.
12 and he will be a wild ass of a man
his hand against all
and everyone's hand against him
and against the face of all his brothers will he rule.

21 14b And He [the deity] gave her bread and a skin of water setting them on her shoulder with the child. 15 When the waters were gone from the water-skin she left the child under one of the bushes 16 and she went and she sat herself across [from him], like [the distance of] the shooting of a bow, because, she said, "I cannot look on the death of the child," and she sat across [from him] and she cried out loudly. 19 Then He opened her eyes and she saw a well of waters so she went and filled the water-skin and she gave the child to drink. 11a and He told her further, "you shall call his name Ishmael for I heard your suffering."

16 13 And she called the name of the one speaking to her, "You are El-ro'i," because, she said, "Now here I saw Him after my vision." Therefore He called the well Beer lahai-ro'i. (Well of the visionary who gave life.) It is between Kadesh and Bered.

20 19 Ishmael dwelt in the desert and became a bowman.

25 17 These were the years of the life of Ishmael: one hundred and thirty-seven years; then he breathed his last and died, and was gathered to his kin.

Appendix B

Traditional Genealogical Table of the Patriarchs

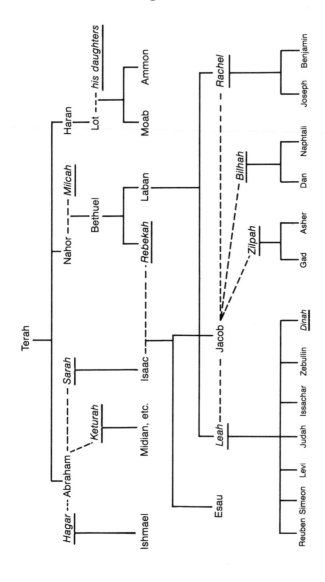

Appendix C

Names of Goddesses and Gods

Canaanite/Ugaritic/ Hebrew	Egyptian		Mesopotamian
GODDESSES			
Asherah	Neith		Ashratum
	Isis		Inanna/Ishtar
Anat daughter of Asherah			
Astarte			Ashtar
Nikkal			Ningal mother of Inanna
Shehinah	Sakina		
GODS			
El husband of Asherah			
Elohim			
El elyon			
El olam			
El ro'i			
El shaddai			
	Heru-ur	son of Hat-Hor	
Baal son of Asherah	Horus	son of Isis	
	Osiris	husband of Isis	Dumuzi
	Sebek	son of Neith	Sin
	Ptah		Marduk
YHWH			

Appendix D

Chronology

Date	Mesopotamia	Egypt	Canaan
Before the Common Era			
3200			
3100		(First Dynasty) Neith-Hotep/	
3000	Jemdet Nasr	Narmer Hor-Aha	
2370	Sargon I	Meryet-Neith Eleventh Dynasty Amenemhet II	Sarah? Hagar? Abram?
2200			
2113	Ur-Nammu		
1930	Lipit-Ishtar		
1792	Hammurapi		
1500			
		Nineteenth Dynasty	Moses
		Ramses II	(Exodus?)
1200			
1100			Saul/Michal David
1000			Solomon
640			Josiah
587			
	Babylonian Exile		
430?			Ezra? Nehemiah?

Glossary

HEBREW

'am	nation
akedah	binding (of Isaak)
almah	young woman
amaḥot	female slaves
anashim	men
avriyah	female slave
batzek	unleavened dough
beini u-benḥa	(masc) between me and between you
beini u-beineḥ	(fem) between me and between you
ḥamasi aleḥa	my fury is upon you/curse
hoveket ben	you shall have a son
ibane	build up
kaet haya	as presently
kavanim	sacred cakes
kesef	silver
l'ishah	to wife
leḥem	bread
letzaḥek	to laugh
metzaḥek/et	to laugh to him/herself
midbar	desert
mikvah	purifying pool
mishpaḥah	family, household, clan

na'ar	lad
pilegesh	concubine
quemah	special flour
rehem	womb
shad/shaddayim	breast/breasts
shevet	tribe
shifhah/sh'fahot	handmaid/s
tehom	abyss
teraphim	sacred images
toledot	genealogy
tyirash	to inherit
tz'hok asah	played a joke/will laugh with me
ugot	cakes, round bread
vatzitzhak	laughed
ve-hine ben	and you have a son
ve-hu aharav	after him/behind him
ve-yoledet ben	you will give birth to a child
yeled	child
yetzahek	will laugh
yitzhak	Isaak
zahav	gold

AKKADIAN

entu/en	High Priestess/High Priest
naditu	Priestess
qadistu	Holy Woman
kulmasitu	Votaress
sugetu	lay-sister/priestess
bitum epsum	a house within a cloister

gipar	sacred grove
ŝeriktu	dowry
nudunnu	large dowry
terḫatu	dowry (sum of money)
ina-semiris	ring-money
maru	acquired in sonship, adoption

ARABIC

Ehgar	to become a Muslim
Ethhaggar	
Hadjar	Hagar
Hidjir	burial place
Ibrahim	Abraham
Isma'il	Ishmael
Ka'ba	ancient sanctuary
Mahgraye	Muslim
Sa'y	Hagar's course between the mountains
Surah	chapter in the Qur'an
Qur'an	Holy Book of Islam

Bibliography

Ali, Abdullah Yusuf, trans. *The Holy Qur-an: Text, Translation and Commentary.* Beirut, Lebanon: Khalil Al-Rawaf, 1965.

Astour, Michael C. "Tamar The Hierodule: An Essay in the Methods of Vestigal Motifs." *Journal of Biblical Literature #85* (1966).

Atwood, Margaret. *The Handmaid's Tale.* Boston: Houghton Mifflin, 1986.

Bakan, David. *And They Took Themselves Wives.* San Francisco: Harper & Row, 1979.

Ben Yehudah Dictionary and Thesaurus of the Hebrew Language, Complete International Centennial Edition. New York: Thomas Yoseloff, 1959.

Bible. Authorized King James Version. Chicago: Consolidated Book Publishers, 1950.

Boling, Robert G. *Judges: A New Translation with Introduction and Commentary. The Anchor Bible.* Garden City, NY: Doubleday, 1975.

Briffault, Robert. *The Mothers.* New York: Atheneum, 1977.

Bright, John, trans. *Jeremiah: Introduction, Translation, and Notes. The Anchor Bible, Vol. 21.* Garden City, NY: Doubleday, 1965.

Brown, F., S. R. Driver, and C. A. Briggs. *Hebrew Lexicon of the Old Testament.* Oxford: Clarendon Press, 1951.

Budge, E. A. Wallis. *The Gods of the Egyptians: Studies in Egyptian Mythology.* Volume I. New York: Dover, 1969.

Campbell, Jr., Edward F., ed. *Ruth: A New Translation with Introduction and Commentary. The Anchor Bible.* Garden City, NY: Doubleday, 1975.

Chavel, Rabbi Dr. Charles B., trans. *Ramban, (Nachmanides): Commentary on the Torah. Genesis. Translated and Annotated with Index.* New York: Shilo, 1971.

Cheyne, T. K. and J. Sutherland, eds. *Encyclopedia Biblica: A Critical Dictionary of Literary, Political and Religious History. The Archaeological Geography and Natural History of the Bible.* London: Adam and Charles Black, 1899.

Christ, Carol P. *Laughter of Aphrodite: Reflections on a Journey to the Goddess.* San Francisco: Harper & Row, 1987.

Coogan, Michel David. *Stories from Ancient Canaan.* Philadelphia: Westminster Press, 1978.

Cornfeld, Gaalya and David Noel Freedman. *Archaeology of the Bible: Book by Book.* San Francisco: Harper & Row, 1976.

Crone, Patricia and Michael Cook. *Hagarism: The Making of the Islamic World.* Cambridge: Cambridge University Press, 1977.

Cutler Torrey, Charles. *The Jewish Foundation of Islam.* New York: Bloch, 1933.

Dahood, Mitchell, trans. *Psalms I and II: Translated and with an Introduction and Notes. The Anchor Bible.* Garden City, NY: Doubleday, 1968.

Davies, Steve. "The Canaanite-Hebrew Goddess." In *The Book of the Goddess Past and Present: An Introduction to Her Religion.* New York: Crossroad, 1985.

Day, John. "Asherah in the Hebrew Bible and the Northwestern Semitic Literature." *Journal of Biblical Literature 105,* No. 3 (1986).

De Vries, Simon J. "Moses and David as Cult Founders." *Journal of Biblical Literature 107,* No. 4 (1988).

Eliade, Mircea. *A History of Religious Ideas: From the Stone Age of the Eleusian Mysteries.* Translated by W. R. Trask. Chicago: University of Chicago Press, 1978.

Emery, W. B. *Archaic Egypt: Culture and Civilization in Egypt Five Thousand Years Ago.* Middlesex, England: Penguin Books, 1987.

Forster, Rev. Charles D. *A Historical Geography of Arabia; or, The Patriarchal Evidences of Revealed Religion: A Memoir.* Volume I. London: Duncan and Malcolm, 1844.

Fox, M. V. *The Song of Songs and Ancient Near Eastern Love Songs.* Madison: University of Wisconsin, 1985.

Fox, R. *Kinship and Marriage: An Anthropological Perspective.* Garden City, NY: Penguin Books, 1967.

Freedman, Rabbi Dr. H and Maurice Simon, trans. *Midrash Rabbah. "Genesis."* London: Soncino Press, 1951.

Friedman, Richard Elliott. *Who Wrote the Bible?* New York: Summit Books, 1987.

Fripp, Edgar Innes. *The Composition of the Book of Genesis, with English Text and Analysis.* London: David Nutt, 1892.

Fuchs, Esther. "Structure and Patriarchal Functions in the Biblical Betrothal Type-Scene: Some Preliminary Notes." In *Journal of Feminist Studies in Religion 3,* No. 1 (Spring, 1987).

Gardiner, Sir Alan. *Egypt of the Pharaohs.* London: Oxford University Press, 1961.

Ginzberg, Louis. *The Legends of the Jews.* Translated by Henrietta Szold. Philadelphia: Jewish Publication Society of America, 1909.

Gordon, Cyrus H. *Ugaritic Literature: A Comprehensive Translation of the Poetic and Prose Texts.* Rome: Pontificum Institutum Biblicum, 1949.

_____. *The Common Backgrounds of Greek and Hebrew Civilizations.* New York: W. W. Norton, 1965.

Graves, Robert and Raphael Patai. *Hebrew Myths: The Book of Genesis.* New York: McGraw-Hill, 1963.

Gunkel, Hermann. *The Legends of Genesis: The Biblical Saga and History.* New York: Schocken, 1964.

Habel, Norman C. *Literary Criticism of the Old Testament.* Philadelphia: Fortress Press, 1973.

Hackett, Jo Ann. "Sadday in its Ancient Near Eastern Context." Unpublished.

Hallo, William W. and J. J. A. van Dijk. *The Exaltation of Inanna.* New Haven and London: Yale University Press, 1968.

Harris, Rivkah. "The Female 'Sage' in Ancient Near Eastern Literature." Unpublished.

———. "The Case of Three Babylonian Marriage Contracts." *Journal of Near Eastern Studies 33,* No. 4 (1974).

The Holy Bible, Revised Standard Version, New York: NAL Penguin Inc., 1974.

Houtsma, M. T., A. J. Wensinck, E. Levi-Provencal, H. A. R. Gibb, and W. Heffening, eds. *Encyclopaedia of Islam: A Dictionary of the Geography, Ethnography and Biography of the Muhammadan Peoples.* Leiden: E. J. Brill, 1936.

The Interpreter's Dictionary of the Bible. Nashville: Abingdon, 1962.

Jewish Encyclopedia, Vol. 14. "The Torah: A Modern Commentary." New York: Union of American Hebrew Congregations, 1981.

Kamil, Jill. *Sakkara and Memphis: A Guide to the Necropolis and the Ancient Capital.* 2d ed. London: Longman, 1985.

Keller, Mara Lynn. "The Eleusinian Mysteries of Demeter and Persephone: Fertility, Sexuality, and Rebirth." *Journal of Feminist Studies in Religion 4,* No. 1 (1988).

Kenyon, Kathleen. *The Bible and Recent Archaeology.* Rev. ed. Atlanta: John Knox Press, 1987.

Knight, Douglas A. "The Pentateuch." In *The Hebrew Bible and Its Modern Interpreters.* Edited by Douglas A. Knight and Gene M. Tucker. Philadelphia: Fortress Press, 1985.

Manchip White, J. E. *Ancient Egypt: Its Culture and History.* New York: Dover, 1970.

Mattews, Charles D. *Palestine—Mohammedan Holy Land.* New Haven: Yale University Press, 1949.

McCarter, Jr., P. Kyle, ed. *I Samuel: A New Translation with Introduction and Commentary. The Anchor Bible.* Vol. 8. Garden City, NY: Doubleday, 1980.

———. *II Samuel: A New Translation with Introduction and Commentary. The Anchor Bible.* Vol. 9. Garden City, NY: Doubleday, 1984.

Mendenhall, George E. *The Tenth Generation: The Origins of Biblical Tradition.* Baltimore and London: The Johns Hopkins University Press, 1973.

Meyers, Carol. *Discovering Eve: Ancient Israelite Women in Context.* Oxford: Oxford University Press, 1988.

Meyers, Jacob, translator. *I and II Chronicles: Translated with Notes and Introduction.* Garden City, NY: Doubleday, 1965.

Miller, William T. *Mysterious Encounters at Mamre and Jabbok.* Brown Judaic Studies 50. Chico, CA: Scholars Press, 1984.

Moore Cross, Frank. *Canaanite Myth and Hebrew Epic: Essays in the History of the Religion of Israel.* Cambridge: Harvard University Press, 1973.

Negev, Avraham, ed. *The Archaeological Encyclopedia of the Holy Land.* Nashville: Thomas Nelson Publishers, 1986.

Neumann, Erich. *The Great Mother: An Analysis of the Archetype.* Translated by Ralph Manheim. Princeton: Princeton University Press, 1972.

Neusner, Jacob, trans. *Genesis Rabbah: The Judaic Commentary to the Book of Genesis. A New American Translation.* Atlanta: Scholars Press, 1985.

Newmann, M. "Hagar." In *The Interpreter's Dictionary of the Bible.* Vol. 2. Nashville: Abingdon, 1962.

Rabbis Nosson Scherman and Meir Zlotowitz, eds. Bereshis: *A New Translation with Commentary Anthologized from Talmudic, Midrashic and Rabbinic Sources.* Brooklyn, NY: Mesorah Publications, 1978.

Noth, Martin. *A History of Pentateuchal Traditions.* Translated by Bernhard W. Anderson. Englewood Cliffs, NJ: Prentice-Hall, 1972.

Oden, Jr., Robert A. "Jacob as Father, Husband and Nephew: Kinship Studies and the Patriarchal Narratives. *Journal of Biblical Studies 102,* No. 2 (June 1983).

Olyan, Saul M. *Asherah and the Cult of Yahweh in Israel.* Society of Biblical Literature Monograph Series, # 34. Atlanta: Scholars Press, 1988.

Patai, Raphael. *The Seed of Abraham: Jews and Arabs in Contact and Conflict.* Salt Lake City: University of Utah Press, 1986.

———. *The Hebrew Goddess.* New York: KTAV, 1967.

The Pentateuch and Rashi's Commentary, Genesis, Vol. I & Exodus, Vol. II. Brooklyn, NY: S. S. & R. Publishing Company, 1949.

Portman, Ian. *The Temple of Dendara.* Cairo, Egypt: The Palm Press, 1984.

Pritchard, James B., ed. *The Ancient Near East: A New Anthology of Texts and Pictures.* 2 Vols. Princeton: Princeton University Press, 1975.

Reeves Sanday, Peggie. *Female Power and Male Dominance: On the Origins of Sexual Inequality.* Cambridge: Cambridge University Press, 1981.

Rich, Adrienne. *Of Woman Born: Motherhood as Experience and Institution.* Toronto: Bantam Books, 1977.

———. *On Lies, Secrets, and Silence: Selected Prose 1966–1978.* NY: W. W. Norton, 1979.

Saggs, H. W. F. *The Greatness That Was Babylon: A Sketch of the Ancient Civilization of the Tigris-Euphrates Valley.* New York and Toronto: New American Library, 1962.

Sarna, Nahum N. *Understanding Genesis: The Heritage of Biblical Israel.* New York: Schocken, 1970.

Sasson, Jack M. "Circumcision in the Ancient Near East." *Journal of Biblical Literature 85* (1966), 473–76.

Schneider, David M. and Kathleen Gough, eds. *Matrilineal Kinship.* Berkeley: University of California Press, 1973.

Scott, R. B. Y. *Proverbs-Ecclesiastes.* Garden City, NY: Doubleday, 1965.

Setel, Drorah. "The Significance of Female Figurines in Relation to Popular Yahwistic Tradition and Practice." 1982. Unpublished.

Skinner, John. *A Critical and Exegetical Commentary on Genesis.* Edinburgh: T. & T. Clark, 1969.

Speiser, A. E. *Genesis: Introduction, Translation and Notes.* Garden City, NY: Doubleday, 1964.

Teubal, Savina J. "Women, the Law, and the Ancient Near East." In *Fields of Offerings: Studies in Honor of Raphael Patai.* Edited by Victor D. Sanua. London and Toronto: Associated University Presses, A Herzl Press Publication, 1983.

————. *Sarah the Priestess: The First Matriarch of Genesis.* Athens, OH: Swallow Press, 1984.

Thomas, D. Winton, ed. *Documents from Old Testament Times.* Translated with Introductions and Notes by Members of the Old Society for Old Testament Study. New York: Harper & Row, 1961.

Thompson, Thomas L. *The Origin Tradition of Ancient Israel.* Sheffield: JSOT Press, #55, 1987.

————. *The Historicity of the Patriarchal Narratives: A Quest for the Historical Abraham.* Berlin and New York: Walter de Gruyter, 1974.

The Torah: A New Translation According to the Masoretic Text. Philadelphia: Jewish Publication Society of America, 1962.

Treasures of the Holy Land: Ancient Art from the Israel Museum. New York: Metropolitan Museum of Art, 1986.

Trible, Phyllis. *Texts of Terror: Literary-Feminist Readings of Biblical Narratives.* Philadelphia: Fortress Press, 1984.

Tucker, Gene M. *Form Criticism of the Old Testament.* Philadelphia: Fortress Press, 1971.

Van Seters, John. *Abraham in History and Tradition.* New Haven and London: Yale University Press, 1975.

Von Rad, Gerhard. *Genesis: A Commentary.* Translated by John H. Marks. Philadelphia: Westminster Press, 1972.

Walker, Barbara. *The Woman's Encyclopedia of Myths and Symbols.* San Francisco: Harper & Row, 1983.

Ward, William A. *Essays on Feminine Titles in the Middle Kingdom and Related Subjects.* Beirut, Lebanon: American University of Beirut, 1986.

Westermann, Claus. *Genesis 12–36, A Commentary.* Translated by John J. Scullion, S.J. Minneapolis: Augsburgh, 1985.

Wilson, Robert R. *Genealogy and History in the Biblical World.* New Haven and London: Yale University Press, 1977.

Wolf, C. Umhad. "The Terminology of Israel's Tribal Organization." *Journal of Biblical Literature* 65 (1946): 45–49.

Index